MUSIC IN THE KITCHEN

Number Twenty-four
Jack and Doris Smothers Series in Texas History, Life, and Culture

MUSIC IN THE KITCHEN

Favorite Recipes from *Austin City Limits* Performers

COMPILED BY Glenda Pierce Facemire
WITH Leigh Anne Jasheway-Bryant
PRINCIPAL PHOTOGRAPHY BY Scott Newton

University of Texas Press Austin

Publication of this work was made possible in part by support from the J. E. Smothers, Sr., Memorial Foundation and the National Endowment for the Humanities.

Additional support was provided by W Austin Hotel and Residences.

Printed in China
First edition, 2009

♾ The paper used in this book meets the minimum requirements of ANSI/NISO Z39.48-1992 (R1997) (Permanence of Paper).

LIBRARY OF CONGRESS CATALOGING-IN-PUBLICATION DATA

Facemire, Glenda Pierce.
Music in the kitchen : favorite recipes from Austin city limits performers / edited by Glenda P. Facemire, with Leigh Anne Jasheway-Bryant.
p. cm. — (Jack and Doris Smothers series in Texas history, life, and culture ; series number 24)
ISBN 978-0-292-71815-9 (alk. paper)
1. Cookery, American. 2. Musicians—United States. 3. Austin city limits (Television program).
I. Jasheway-Bryant, Leigh Anne. II. Title.
TX715.F1645 2009
641.5973—dc22

2009011110

Dedicated to the fans

Table of Contents

Foreword

Terry Lickona

In my 30-plus years as producer of *Austin City Limits*, I've often referred to the show as a "musical stew" or "gumbo" of many different voices, styles, and genres. Little did I realize that my loose metaphors might some day take on an entirely different meaning, or that the hundreds of singers, songwriters, and musicians appearing on *ACL* might have other hidden talents besides those on display on stage in front of our cameras and millions of fans around the globe.

I've always said that my primary criterion for choosing performers for *Austin City Limits* is originality—artists who have unique ways of expressing themselves through their singing, writing, or playing. And thanks to this book, now they have a new way of expressing themselves!

Through her passion and tireless efforts, Glenda Facemire, our long-time makeup artist and stylist, has unearthed a bounty of unique and original recipes that are as creative, eclectic, and adventurous as the artists who have shaped the *ACL* legacy and made it the longest-running popular music series in American television history. You may not be able to play an instrument, write a hit song, or bring an audience to its feet, but there's a good chance you'll be able to recreate one of these treats in your own kitchen. Be brave, be bold, and let's eat!

Acknowledgments

Music in the Kitchen was prepared with lots of love and with the support of many people. First, my deepest appreciation goes to *Austin City Limits*, which in 2009 celebrates its thirty-fifth year on PBS. How delicious is that! Congratulations! This cookbook sends immeasurable thanks and personal toasts to this amazing success story that will continue for many more years!

To KLRU-PBS, Austin, Texas, where this amazing music show is produced and taped, thank you for your continued support since the show's conception in 1975. My thanks to Bill Stotesbery, CEO, president, and general manager of KLRU-PBS. Thank you for making everything possible for *Austin City Limits* and KLRU. Your help made it easier to move forward with the project. Thank you for the opportunity. You're the best!

A big "Hook 'em Horns" thank-you to the University of Texas Press. They are an awesome and talented group of people. My personal and very special thanks to Bill Bishel, my sponsoring editor, for believing in me and the project. Thank you for all your help and support and for taking all my calls when you were so very busy.

I would have loved to have contacted each and every artist who has ever performed on the show. Regrettably I only had one year to reach as many contacts as time would allow, but every artist who contributed a recipe to the cookbook is representative of all the artists who have performed on the legendary *Austin City Limits* stage. My personal thanks to everyone who has played a part in *Music in the Kitchen*. Many, many genuine thanks. You gave me, kindly, so much of your time, support and generosity. And, I love you for it. Avoiding all genres here, you rock also!

Special thanks to Terry Lickona, producer of *Austin City Limits*, who has kept hiring me every year since 1989—wow! What an amazing twenty years it has been. Thank you for continuing to believe in me. You are an amazing producer and one of the very best in the music industry. Thank you for all your support with this project. Thank you Dick Peterson, executive producer, for always being there. You were so instrumental! And you kept my vision clear. Thanks to Jeff Peterson and Leslie Nichols, our associate producers! You guys are amazing. Thank you Leslie for all your extra time, support, and help with the cookbook. You helped so much.

Thanks to our very talented and devoted television crew (I love you all) and KLRU staff (you know who you are). Thanks to all the volunteers I have had the pleasure to know over the years. Lots of thanks also to my four security volunteers on the fifth floor, especially to Lonnie and Linda.

My deepest and most sincere thanks to all the artists, musicians, managers, personal assistants, publicists, agents, photographers, and public relations firms. Thank you for believing in this project because you all made it possible. There were lots of emails, and I feel we all know each other very well. What a year! But it was such fun to work with so many thoughtful and dedicated people. Every time a recipe came in I felt like celebrating. Thank you! We have a musicians' cookbook because of you!

To Leigh Anne Jasheway-Bryant—friend, writer, author, comedienne: What a talent you truly are, and what a devoted friend, not to mention how much you love *Austin City Limits* and the fact that you are a University of Texas graduate. It took a professional like you to support this project from the beginning and stay with it. You are incredible.

Thanks and extra thanks to a longtime friend Gretchen Raatz. What a wonderful, and considerate person you truly are. You have always kept me under your wings, protecting me, and still do. I have always appreciated your kindness.

This book was on a tight deadline, and the following sweet ladies met the deadlines with their help and dedication. My favorite seven are all University of Texas students or graduates who gave a lot of their precious time to complete this book. They were my rock! In order of appearance, my deepest thanks to Allison Ullrich, Mashaal Ahmed, Sandy Linczer, Tiffany Ducummon, Kaitlin Einkauf, Varsha Naik, and Jennifer Whitcomb, who, with dedication and determination, helped bring in the manuscript on time. What an awesome crew of seven young, beautiful ladies. I love you all. And thank you from the bottom of my heart.

Finally, lots of love and appreciation goes to friends and colleagues who have supported me over the years. Each and every one of them knew I needed bits of encouragement to keep my dream going. They all believed in me, and many thanks again and again to them. Thank you dear friends Richard Hall, Georgeanna Fischer, Debrah Dubay, Bodie Lyman, Stephanie Lain, Steve Maedl, Mary Alice Valentine, and Lisa Morgan. Thanks also to my working buddies, especially David Grimes (Photographer) and The Texas Crew.

Thanks to Scott Newton, *Austin City Limits* staff photographer, for helping with so many memorable and beautiful photos for the cookbook. A big thank-you to Richard Kemp for all his help and support.

I want to thank all the producers, directors, production managers, production companies, and photographers who supported me over the many years. Please know I am eternally grateful. Thank you!

Now, let's cook with *Music in the Kitchen*!

Introduction *Face to Face*

Never before has there been a cookbook that will make you want to whip up something in the kitchen and boogie down to the music at the same time!

If you enjoy cooking, eating, listening to music, or are simply a fan of *Austin City Limits*, you will love this one-of-a-kind cookbook. Dip into the musicians' recipes, experiment with flavors—both musical and culinary—and stir up a little music history. We can't all be talented musicians, but we certainly can enjoy cooking like them.

On one of my very first shows in 1989 as key makeup artist for *Austin City Limits*, I had the chance to meet and work with the great Stevie Ray Vaughan. And what an incredible show that was! Twenty years later I look back and I'm awestruck by so many of these incredible artists and their original musical styles. How fortunate to be in *ACL*'s Studio A with a studio audience and to listen to so much wonderful live music. It takes my breath away just thinking about it! It has been an exciting and unbelievable journey thus far.

Working with *ACL* gave me the up-close and personal opportunity to meet many more gifted musicians. On occasion, if time allowed before the show, the artists and I would share a tête-à-tête. Yes, there have been several great stories, some legendary tales, countless jokes, and even showbiz gossip. I wish I could share, but *what happens in the makeup chair stays in the makeup chair*!

When it comes to cooking, I'm looking for the next great recipe. And when you can talk about cooking and sharing some recipes with some of the most amazing performing artists in music history, it doesn't get any better than that. After many years of talking appetizers and barbecue and main dishes with the artists, I thought, "Wouldn't it be great to share all this with the treasured fans of *ACL*?" So I decided to pitch the idea for this cookbook to the show and they loved it! They wanted to help as much as they could despite already having a lot on their plate, especially considering the show's other venue, the *Austin City Limits* Music Festival, held annually in October.

So off I went, writing, calling, chatting with artists and musicians or their managers and publicists, and asking them if they'd be willing to contribute a favorite recipe to this book. They were all very positive, generous, and enormously supportive. I also thought it was important that this cookbook support charity for awareness only, and decided to ask the artists to let people know about the important community, national, and international organizations they support with their time and money, so that if you were so inspired, you too could lend a helping hand. After all, when it comes to cooking up a better world, there can't be too many cooks.

So when you entertain your guests with any of these yummy dishes, you will most definitely take pleasure in saying "Oh, it's a recipe from B. B. King, Willie Nelson, Dolly Parton, Loretta Lynn, Femi Kuti, Bruce Hornsby, Alan Jackson, Vince Gill, David Gray, Joan Baez, or Joss Stone," just to name a few. That's sure to make your guests sit up and applaud!

So, fire up the grill, light up the stove, and if you want something real tasty, turn on *Austin City Limits*! Because everything tastes better with a little *Music in the Kitchen*!

Bon appetit! Cheers! And enjoy the music!

Glenda

MUSIC IN THE KITCHEN

Samplers

APPETIZERS

Willie Nelson

SHOW DATES:

1975
1977
1980
1981
1982
1984
1991
1994
1996
1997
1998
2000

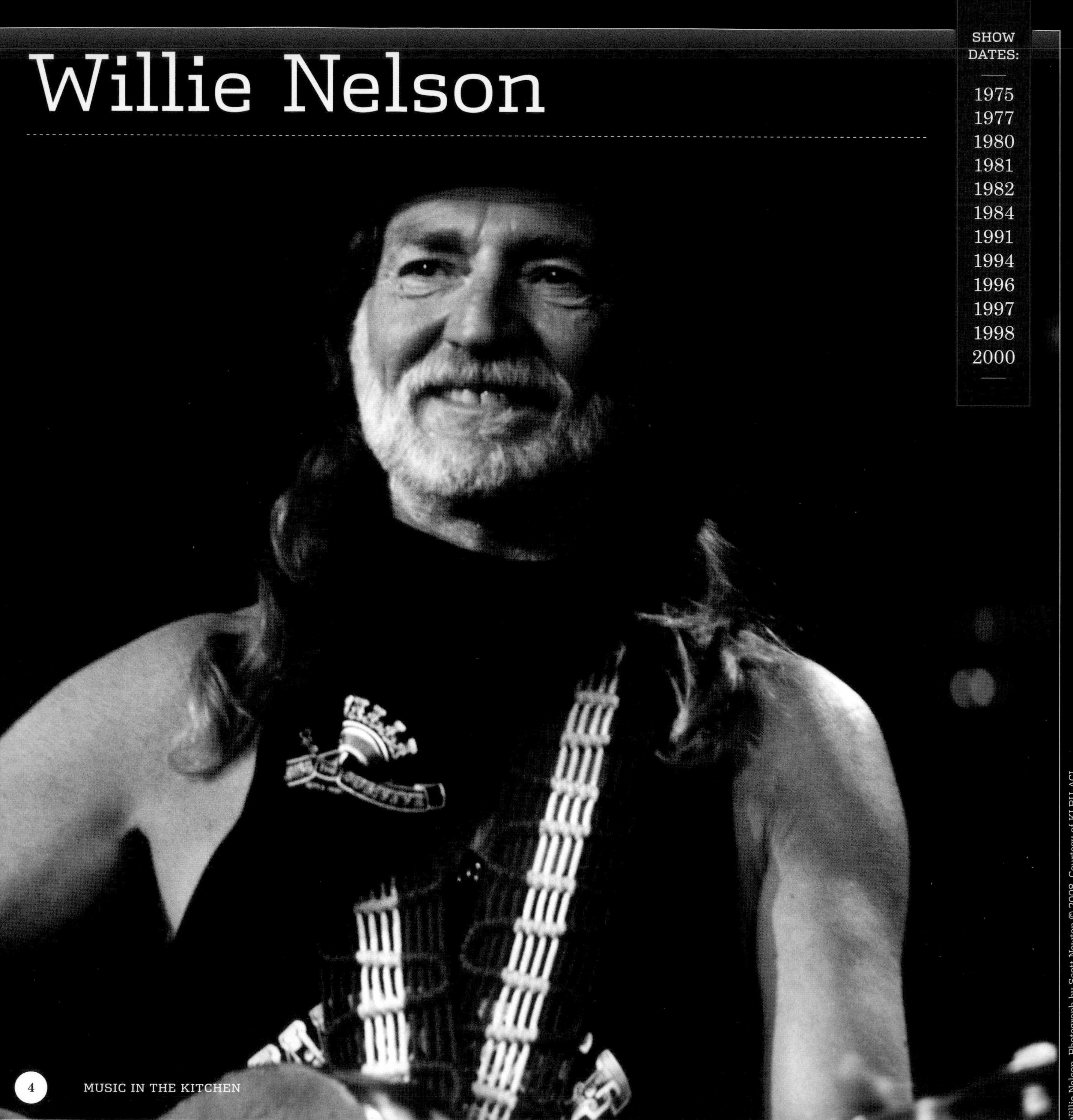

Willie Nelson. Photograph by Scott Newton © 2008. Courtesy of KLRU-ACL.

Willie's Tequila-Mango Salsa

⅓ c. Austin Slow Burn Spiced Peach Jam with Habanero
3 T. red onion, diced
¼ c. cilantro, chopped
2 c. mango, coarsely chopped
1 large avocado, chopped
1 c. strawberries, chopped (optional)
½ c. jalapeños, diced (optional)
Jose Cuervo Especial to taste (set to the side with a shot glass and drink at your own risk)

Mix all ingredients and serve with chips. Great on chicken or fish.

SERVING UP: Country, country rock, outlaw country

A FEW INGREDIENTS: Nothing says Texas like a heaping helping of the music of Willie Nelson. His career began as a teenager, singing in a Baptist church and playing guitar in polka bands. After moving to Austin, Willie quickly became an enormously successful performer, recording jazz standards, country-rock, and gospel in his distinctive singing style. He has become an international icon, winning countless American Music Awards, Country Music Association Awards, Academy of Country Music Awards, and Grammy Awards (including a Lifetime Achievement Award in 2000), and appearing in hundreds of benefit concerts. He is most proud of his work with charities such as Farm Aid, which he co-founded in 1985 with Neil Young and John Mellencamp, and the Spears Foundation for Hepatitis C Awareness.

Willie has also had a successful acting career, appearing in almost two dozen movies.

MORE TASTY MORSELS: willienelson.com WILLIE'S CHARITY: Farm Aid, farmaid.org

Joan Baez

SHOW DATE:
1994

Joan Baez. Photograph by Scott Newton © 2008. Courtesy of KLRU-ACL.

Sweet Potato Dip

3 c. sweet potato (about 1 lb.), chopped, peeled
2½ c. onion, chopped
1½ c. carrot, chopped
1 T. olive oil
¼ c. tahini
¼ tsp. salt
⅛ tsp. pepper

Combine first 4 ingredients in a large bowl. Transfer to baking sheet and cook for 1 hour at 350°. Remove from oven. Combine with remaining ingredients in a food processor.

Serve with crackers and raw vegetables. Yield: 3 cups.

SERVING UP: Folk, roots, Americana, pop, rock, gospel, country

A FEW INGREDIENTS: For decades Joan's music has been a tasty dish served up with heaping helpings of human rights, justice, and peace. She stood in the fields alongside César Chávez and migrant farmworkers striking for fair wages, sang on the steps of the Lincoln Memorial at Dr. Martin Luther King's March on Washington, and opposed capital punishment at San Quentin State Prison during a Christmas vigil. In the 1970s she helped establish Amnesty International on the West Coast. In 2008 she stood behind Nelson Mandela at a ninetieth birthday celebration in his honor in London's Hyde Park.

Eight of Joan's albums have been certified gold, and in 2007 she was awarded the Grammy for Lifetime Achievement. Joan's appreciation of distinctive songwriting has been heightened over the past decade as a result of collaborative mentoring with an impressive roster of younger artists and songwriters; Joan's album *Play Me Backwards* featured songs by Mary Chapin Carpenter, John Hiatt, John Stewart, and others.

MORE TASTY MORSELS: joanbaez.com JOAN'S CHARITY: Bread & Roses, breadandroses.org

Guster

SHOW DATE:

2004

Guster. Photograph by C. Taylor Crothers © 2006. Courtesy of Nettwerk Management.

Artichoke and Spinach Dip

Submitted by Ryan Miller

2 T. butter
2 T. flour
1 c. milk
Louisiana hot sauce
1 (10-oz.) pkg. of frozen spinach, thawed and drained
1 large can of artichoke hearts
1 c. Monterey Jack cheese
1 c. grated Parmesan cheese

SERVING UP: Alternative rock, jangle pop

A FEW INGREDIENTS: Guster's unique sound is served with memorable live performances, dashes of humor, and an ever-present environmental consciousness. Before their first two albums, 1994's *Parachute* and 1998's *Goldfly*, they had only a strong cult following. Today they can sell out New York City's fabled Radio City Music Hall and perform with the Boston Pops at Symphony Hall.

The ecofriendly Campus Consciousness Tour, founded by the band, uses buses powered by biodiesel and performances powered by wind power. In 1997 Guster received the Best Live Act Award at the Boston Music Awards. Their music been featured on many movies and television shows, such as *Wedding Crashers*, *Life as a House*, and *The OC*.

MORE TASTY MORSELS: guster.com
GUSTER'S CHARITY: ALS Therapy Development Institute, als.net

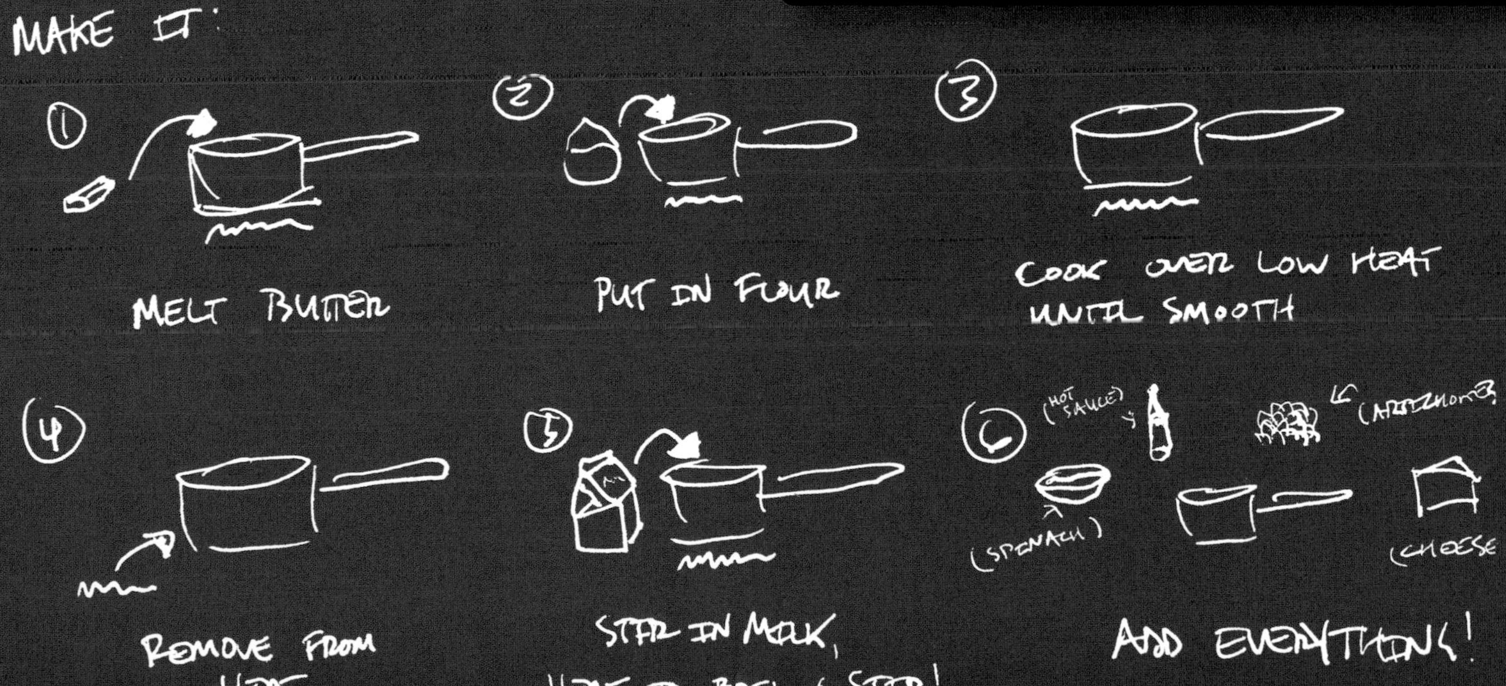

Lorrie Morgan

SHOW DATE:

1990

Lorrie Morgan. Photograph by Chuck Jones. Courtesy of Chuck Jones.

Spinach Dip

1 (10-oz.) pkg. frozen spinach, thawed and drained
1 c. sour cream
1 c. mayonnaise
½ c. parsley, chopped
½ c. green onion, chopped
½ tsp. dill weed
juice of ½ lemon
seasoning salt to taste

Combine all ingredients and mix well. Serve with raw veggies or crackers.

SERVING UP: Country

A FEW INGREDIENTS: Lorrie Morgan started stirring up music as early as thirteen, when she made her debut appearance at the Grand Ole Opry with her father, the late George Morgan. Her career really heated up when she released "Dear Me" in 1989 and it became a top-ten hit. She's gone on to have over a dozen top-ten hits, and three of her songs went to number one: "Five Minutes," "What Part of No," and "Didn't Know My Own Strength." She's had three platinum-selling albums: *Leave the Light On* (1989), *Something in Red* (1991), and *Watch Me* (1992). Eight of her videos made it to number one at CMT.

Lorrie has earned nine TNN Music City News awards for Female Vocalist of the Year. She has also appeared on many major network television shows including the *Late Show with David Letterman*, the *Tonight Show with Jay Leno, and Good Morning America.*

MORE TASTY MORSELS: lorrie.com
LORRIE'S CHARITY: The Humane Society of Sumner County, Tennessee, sumnerhumane.org

Chuck Prophet

SHOW DATE: 2003

SERVING UP: Soul, folk, indie

A FEW INGREDIENTS: RollingStone.com once called Chuck Prophet's music "the kind of fat, greasy blues you can make a meal on." By age fifteen Chuck was a superlative guitarist, and before he turned twenty he had already played on eight albums and toured the U.S. and Europe with the cosmic country rock band Green on Red. Artists such as Solomon Burke, Kim Richey, Jim Dickinson, and Heart have recorded his songs, and he has participated in studio recordings with Warren Zevon, Bob Neuwirth, Jonathan Richman, Penelope Houston, Cake, Kelly Willis, and many others.

MORE TASTY MORSELS: chuckprophet.com
CHUCK'S CHARITY: Loaves and Fishes, loavesandfishesmn.org

Chuck Prophet. Photograph by Scott Newton © 2008. Courtesy of KLRU-ACL.

Guacamole

I grew up in a town called La Habra, California, in the foothills along the avocado belt. The avocado orchards up above my house in La Habra Heights were endless. That's where the Hass originated, so I remain true to my school. The Hass avocados are dark green, almost black. They are easy to spot as they've become obscenely expensive. On occasion I've tried to save a few pennies by buying those odd, thin-skinned, green avocados, but they never fail to bum me out.

Back in my back-in-the-day days, when me and my friends needed to raise some cash, we would ride our ten-speed Schwinns up into "the Heights," jump the fences, and help ourselves to avocados by the score, ignoring the guard-dog signs. I had a paper route and my canvas carrier bag came in handy. We'd set our makeshift stand up on Whittier Boulevard with a sign: "Avocados: five for a dollar." People would slam on their brakes and line up.

Be true to your school, Chuck Prophet

Hass avocados
salt and pepper
lemon juice
Tabasco sauce or other hot sauce

Mash some ripe Hass avocados in a bowl with a fork. (Tip: avocados won't really ripen on the tree—if your avocados aren't ripe, put them in a brown paper bag under the sink. That'll do the trick.)

Add fresh squeezed lemon juice, salt, pepper, and some Tabasco (or hot sauce of your choice). Enjoy with a bag of chips.

Lisa Loeb

SHOW DATE:

1996

SERVING UP: Contemporary folk, rock, indie

A FEW INGREDIENTS: The breakout song of native Texan Lisa Loeb, "Stay (I Missed You)," landed at number one on the charts in 1994, a remarkable feat for an unsigned artist. Not long after her friend and New York neighbor, Ethan Hawke, got a lead role in *Reality Bites* and he helped put "Stay" on the movie's soundtrack and into the record books. Lisa took her early success and cooked it into a multilayered career that includes music, film, television, voice-over work, and recordings for children. Her five acclaimed studio albums include the Grammy-nominated *Firecracker*. In 2004 she starred in *Dweezil and Lisa*, a weekly culinary adventure on Food Network. Lisa has an award-winning children's CD and companion book with Elizabeth Mitchell called *Catch the Moon*, and a second collection of children's music, *Camp Songs*, the proceeds of which benefit the Camp Lisa Foundation.

MORE TASTY MORSELS: lisaloeb.com

LISA'S CHARITY: The Camp Lisa Foundation, lisaloeb.com

Seven-Layer Dip

When I think about my home state, Texas, and food, I think about fun and this recipe. When you serve it in a clear glass casserole dish, the colorful celebration begins. It displays layer after layer of sour cream, yellow cheddar cheese, beans, guacamole, tomatoes, salsa, and the most important ingredient: shredded iceberg lettuce, a vegetable whose cool, crisp crunch has the powers of a time machine to bring you back to swimming parties, homecoming dances in backyards, and slumber parties, even if you never had them.

olive oil
½ c. white onion, chopped
1 (16-oz.) can refried pinto or black beans, strained
1 T. taco seasoning mix
¾ tsp. table salt, divided
¾ tsp. white pepper, divided
½ c. cheddar cheese, shredded and divided
2 large avocados
½ tsp. garlic salt
2 tsp. Cholula Hot Sauce
½ tsp. lemon juice
1 c. low-fat sour cream
½ c. fresh spinach
½ c. iceberg lettuce
¾ c. (6-oz.) fresh salsa (either red tomato or green tomatillo salsa can be used)
1 fresh medium tomato

Sauté the chopped onions in the olive oil for about five minutes or until they are translucent. In a small saucepan combine the cooked onions with the beans, taco seasoning, salt, and pepper, and heat over medium heat. (To achieve a smoother texture, if desired, whole beans can be mashed with a potato masher before heating.) Taste and adjust seasonings to your liking. Transfer to 9 × 9 × 2–inch clear glass dish and spread evenly. Top with ¼ c. grated cheddar cheese.

Peel and mash avocados in medium-size bowl. Mix in ⅓ c. of diced onions, salt, pepper, garlic salt, Cholula Hot Sauce, and lemon juice. Carefully spread over the bean layer.

Spread sour cream evenly over the guacamole.

Wash and thoroughly dry greens. Remove stems from spinach. Cut spinach and iceberg into fine shreds. Layer on top of sour cream.

Evenly spread fresh salsa on top of the greens. Remove the core of a medium sized tomato. Cut in half lengthwise and spoon out the seeds and soft pulpy part. Cut into a medium dice and sprinkle over the salsa.

Sprinkle remaining shredded cheddar cheese over the tomatoes.

Serve immediately or cover and refrigerate until ready to eat. Don't forget to serve with your favorite chips! (Also a good idea to serve with a spoon and let people scoop it on to their individual plates, as some of the ingredients are heavy and don't stand up to a chip.) Yield: 4–6 servings.

Alan Jackson

SHOW DATES:

1991
1995

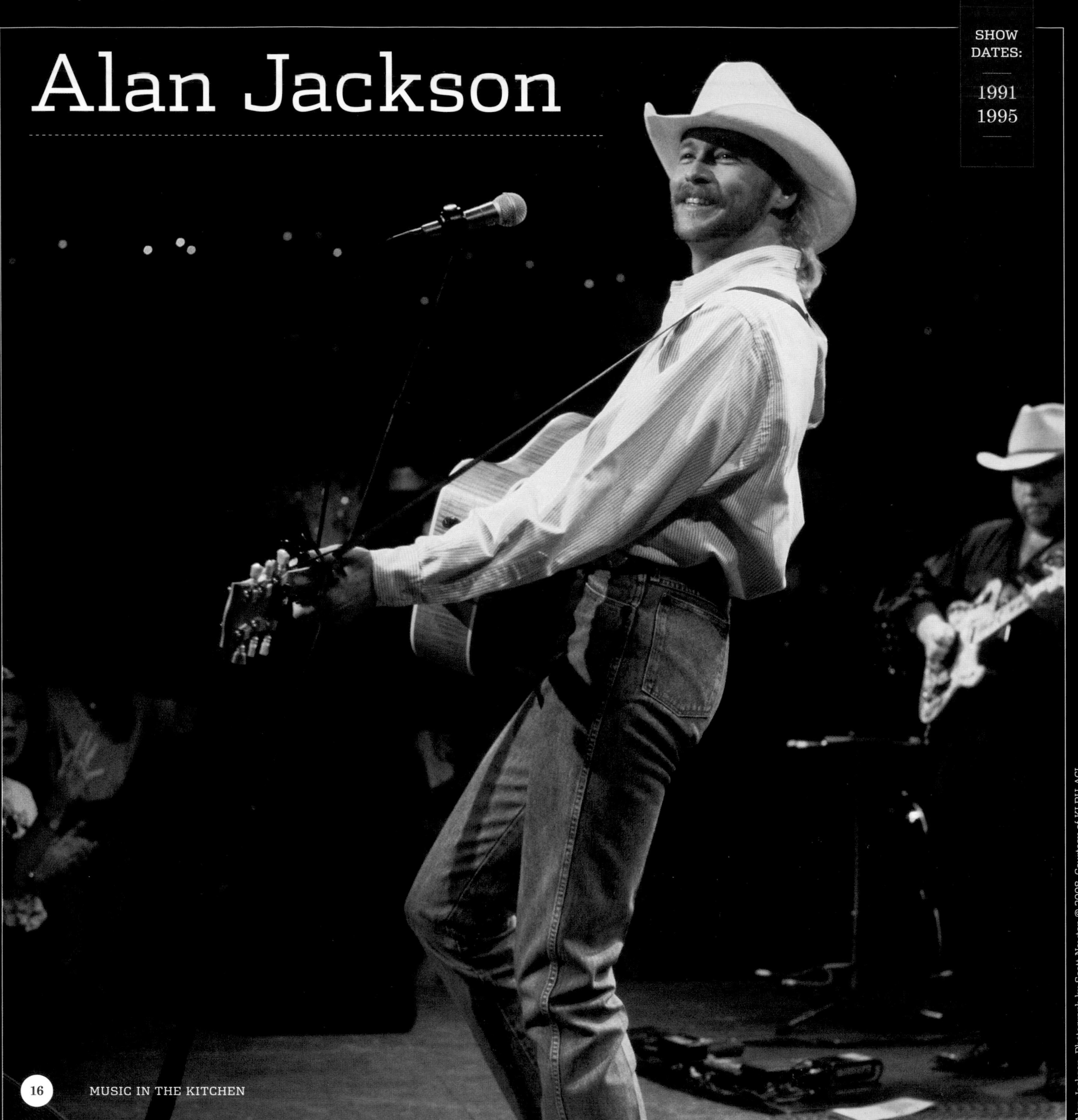

Alan Jackson. Photograph by Scott Newton © 2008. Courtesy of KLRU-ACL.

Sausage-Cheese Balls

The Jackson family eats these on Christmas morning. This recipe is from *Who Says You Can't Cook It All* by Alan Jackson with contributions from Denise Jackson and Ruth Jackson, © Real World Tours, Inc.

1 lb. hot sausage
2 c. extra sharp cheddar cheese, grated
3 c. Bisquick baking mix

Mix all ingredients well by hand. Roll into balls. Bake on an ungreased baking sheet at 350° until golden brown. Yield: 4 to 5 dozen balls.

SERVING UP: Country

A FEW INGREDIENTS: Over the course of his career, with sixteen gold, platinum, and multiplatinum albums. Alan Jackson has become one of country music's most respected and honored artists. He has sold more than fifty million albums and has more than one hundred major industry awards to his credit. Jackson is a three-time Country Music Association Entertainer of the Year and the most nominated artist in CMA history. A prolific songwriter, Alan penned twenty-three of his thirty-three number one singles, including the Grammy-winning, "Where Were You (When the World Stopped Turning)."

Alan, a native of the small town of Newnan, Georgia, was the first artist signed to the fledgling Arista Nashville record label in 1989, and with the release the following year of his debut album, *Here in the Real World*, his songs immediately connected with fans leading to four number one singles from that record alone.

Alan's *Good Time* collection became the fourth album of his career to debut at number one simultaneously on *Billboard*'s Top Country Albums and the all-genre *Billboard* 200 album sales charts. The seventeen-song release also marked a career first for Jackson, as the only time he has been the sole writer of every song on the album.

MORE TASTY MORSELS: alanjackson.com

ALAN'S CHARITY: Angel's House: Newnan Coweta Children's Shelter, Newnan, Georgia, theangelshouse.org

Cindy Cashdollar

SHOW DATES:

1992
1993
1996
1998
2006

SERVING UP: Western swing, bluegrass, gutbucket blues, honky-tonk, swampy R&B

A FEW INGREDIENTS: Cindy is one of the premier steel guitarists and dobro players in the world, and was named Instrumentalist of the Year by the Academy of Western Artists Awards in 2003. She puts on a show that sizzles and whets audiences' appetites for more. Her 2004 debut album, *Slide Show*, displayed her range, from Hawaiian-style pieces to hardcore western swing to airy pop numbers. She spent eight years touring with Asleep at the Wheel, which brought her five Grammy Awards and opportunities to work with musicians such as Willie Nelson, Van Morrison, Merle Haggard, Dolly Parton, and the Dixie Chicks.

And, in answer to her most frequently asked question, yes, Cashdollar is her real name.

MORE TASTY MORSELS: cindycashdollar.com CINDY'S CHARITY: Austin Animal Trustees, animaltrustees.org

Cindy Cashdollar. Photograph by Rob Buck © 2007. Courtesy of Cindy Cashdollar.

Roasted Red Pepper and Goat Cheese Baguette

1 fresh baguette
¼ c. olive oil
2 cloves garlic, peeled
1 c. goat cheese crumbles or spread
black pepper to taste
2 large red bell peppers, roasted (from a jar or prepare ahead; recipe follows)
3 T. fresh basil leaves, chopped
10 Kalamata olives, pitted
1 pkg. mozzarella cheese, grated

Preheat oven to 350°. Slice baguette lengthwise. Lightly drizzle and spread olive oil on bread and rub with garlic half (or, if you're a garlic lover, sprinkle with finely chopped garlic). Place baguette on baking sheet in preheated oven and toast very lightly.

Remove from oven. Spread goat cheese on baguette and grind some fresh black pepper over it to taste. Place roasted red pepper slices over this, and top with chopped basil leaves. Place back onto baking sheet and give it about 5 more minutes in the oven, until cheese and peppers feel warm to touch.

ROASTED RED PEPPER

2 red bell peppers
olive oil
lemon juice
sea salt
1 clove fresh garlic (optional)

Preheat oven to broil. Wash peppers, cut in half, and place on aluminum foil in oven. Broil each side until black, turning with tongs for even roasting. Place peppers in brown paper bag to cool—this makes it easier to slip off the skins. Remove skin and seeds, and slice into long pieces. These will keep in a jar with some olive oil and a little lemon juice and sea salt. Add fresh clove garlic if you want.

Glenda is Superwoman: applying makeup backstage to everyone waiting in line, soothing nerves, supplying gum, water, encouragement, jokes . . . whatever you want, she's there, and she makes you look real good, too.

—*Cindy Cashdollar*

Mary Chapin Carpenter

SHOW DATES:

1990
1992
1993
1994
1997
2000
2001

Mary Chapin Carpenter. Photograph by Scott Newton © 2008. Courtesy of KLRU-ACL.

Real Margaritas

This recipe is adapted from the *Barefoot Contessa's Parties* book.

½ c. freshly squeezed lime juice (5 limes)
2 T. freshly squeezed lemon juice (1 lemon)
1 c. Triple Sec
3 c. ice
1 c. white tequila
Kosher salt (optional)

Put lime juice, lemon juice, Triple Sec, and ice in blender and blend well.

Add tequila and purée a few seconds more.

Rim glasses with salt, add ice cubes, and pour. Yield: About 6 margaritas.

SERVING UP: Country, folk

A FEW INGREDIENTS: Mary Chapin Carpenter is a five-time Grammy Award-winning singer-songwriter who has sold over thirteen million records over her twenty-year career. One of her albums, the critically acclaimed *The Calling*, features songs both political and personal, and transcends musical boundaries and radio-station categorizations. She has performed all over the world and has advocated on behalf of causes and campaigns addressing literacy, the environment, health issues, and the arts.

MORE TASTY MORSELS: marychapincarpenter.com

Carolyn Wonderland

SHOW DATE: 2008

SERVING UP: Blues, rock, country, soul

A FEW INGREDIENTS: Carolyn Wonderland likes to mix up all types of music—rock, blues, country, swing, zydeco, surf, gospel, soul, cumbia—to create a musical dish that is uniquely her own. In addition to her trusty guitars, "Tele" and "Leslie Pauline," and her lapsteel, "Goldie," Carolyn has been regularly playing her trumpet and mandolin and she's threatening to take up nose flute if someone doesn't stop her!

Carolyn's songs have been featured on TV shows like *Homicide* and *Time of Your Life*, on the soundtrack for the feature film *Harold*, and her song "Annie's Scarlet Letter" was featured in a video public service announcement for the Houston chapter of NORML.

She has toured with Buddy Guy and Johnny Winter, sat in with the String Cheese Incident, Robert Earl Keen, and Los Lobos, recorded with Asleep at the Wheel, Jerry Lightfoot, and Vince Welnick, and jammed with Bob Dylan! Before she moved to Austin she virtually swept the Houston Press Music Awards for several years running, winning trophies for Best Guitarist, Vocalist, Songwriter, Release of the Year, and Musician of the Year.

MORE TASTY MORSELS: carolynwonderland.com
CAROLYN'S CHARITY: The Uncle John Turner Foundation, ujtfoundation.org

Carolyn Wonderland. Photograph by Scott Newton © 2008. Courtesy of KLRU-ACL.

Road Salsa

I like listening to bands play live partially due to the improvisations on stage that keep songs fresh and vital. I treat this recipe in much the same manner. Once you are comfy with the measurements, try jamming with some mangoes in place of the tomatoes for a groovin' breakfast salsa, add avocado to the mix, play with different herbs, have fun, and make messes! Remember this: if it's too watery, it's spicy Tex-Mex gazpacho, and if it's too chunky, it's pico de gallo.

peppers (for mild salsa: 1–2 jalapeños; for medium salsa: 1–2 jalapeños and 1 serrano; for *Whoa-Hey!* salsa: 1–2 jalapeños or serranos and 1 habanero)
juice of one lime
1 tsp. powdered cumin
dash of sea salt
⅓ white 1015 onion, diced
2–4 cloves garlic
1–2 green onions, chopped
handful of cilantro
3–5 vine-ripe tomatoes
1 bag tortilla chips

Wash peppers, remove tops, and slice lengthwise into quarters. Remove the seeds.

Liquefy chopped peppers in blender with the juice of one lime. Add cumin and dash of salt. Add white onion and garlic. Cut tomatoes in eighths. Put the blender on a low setting and add half of the chopped tomato. Blend for a few seconds. Toss in green onions, one big handful of cilantro tops, and stir.

Check your consistency and taste. To thicken, fold in the remainder of tomatoes minus the inner juices (perhaps chopping them more finely) and don't lay heavy on the blender cycle. You can also add an avocado. To thin, add the remainder of the tomatoes and blend on medium setting for a few seconds.

Dig in with those chips, but bear in mind: the longer it sets, the hotter and more melded the flavors become. Always refrigerate. If you added avocado, store your salsa in the fridge with the avocado seed in the bowl and add a squeeze of lemon juice.

Beto and the Fairlanes

SHOW DATE: 1980

SERVING UP: Latin jazz, swing, and world beat

A FEW INGREDIENTS: Sometimes you just gotta boogie, and Beto and the Fairlanes is just the band to get your toes tapping. With musical "head chef" and band founder, Robert Skiles, Beto has been cooking up danceable rhythms peppered with large amounts of humor since the late 1970s. With six critically acclaimed albums—*Mongoose Island*, *Beto Vivo*, *Midnight Lunch*, *Salsafied*, *Eye of the Hurricane*, and *Congo Salsa*—concert tours, music festivals, and children's shows, the band has become a favorite of fans everywhere.

Robert has collaborated with major U.S. symphony orchestras as a composer and conductor, and has worked with acclaimed Austin singer-songwriter Tish Hinojosa. He currently teaches in the Commercial Music Management Department of Austin Community College and is the music director at Unity Church of the Hills in Austin.

MORE TASTY MORSELS: betoandthefairlanes.com   BETO AND THE FAIRLANES' CHARITY: The Seton Fund, setonfund.org

Beto and the Fairlanes. Photograph by Scott Newton © 2008. Courtesy of KLRU-ACL.

Chappy's Green Salsa

This famous Texas recipe has been handed down through generations of the venerable Bozarth family to the ever vigilant Bozarth twins, Evan and Dustin, whose Web site, tacotown.org, is known for its recipes and taco reviews. After sampling many recipes nationwide, this one has been chosen by Mr. Beto himself as the official hot sauce of Beto and the Fairlanes. The beauty of Chappy's is its simplicity. It contains only three main ingredients, yet it's packed with rich flavors. The twins make huge batches of this stuff about 3–4 times a year, then give it away to friends and family. People love it so much they've started offering money for it, and admittedly it's not very cost effective to make, so it's very much a labor of love.

5 lb. fresh tomatillos
¼ lb. fresh serrano peppers
1 fresh poblano pepper
1 can pickled serrano peppers

FIRE UP THE GRILL! Roast those tomatillos, fresh serranos, and the fresh poblano on an open flame until the skins are black and charred—that's the *sabor*! The char will give our salsa that smoky flavor and dark color.

CHOPPIN' PEPPERS. Wearing gloves, cut and deseed the canned serranos. Be sure to save the vinegar juice from each can—we'll use it later.

KEEP 'EM SEPARATED. Now back to the grilled items. Deseed the roasted poblanos and blend them in a food processor with the charred tomatillos. Set aside the charred serranos—we'll use them to control the heat factor at the end. Add blended peppers, deseeded canned serranos, and vinegar from the cans to a large pot.

BRING THE HEAT. Now cut and deseed those grilled serranos. Blend them in the food processor, then add to your big pot, making sure to taste as you go. Remember, the spiciness will mellow out after about 24 hours, so don't be afraid to kick it up a notch. Give the pot about 2 hours to simmer on low heat.

CANNED HEAT. Carefully pour finished salsa straight from the pot into the clean Mason jars. Screw those lids on tight. Now set the finished product in a cool, dry place. The jars should keep for a year or more. (Refrigerate after opening.)

GET SALSAFIED! Get out those tortilla chips and beer, turn on the salsa music, and proceed to enjoy Chappy's Green Salsa. It's also excellent on tacos, eggs, and poultry, but try it on anything!

Vince Gill

SHOW DATES:

1985
1992
1995
1999
2003

SERVING UP: Country, bluegrass, blue-eyed soul

A FEW INGREDIENTS: Some recipes become favorites right from the start. That is certainly true for Vince Gill, the unofficial ambassador of country music, who, since 1984, has sold more than twenty-six million albums. He has earned eighteen CMA Awards, including Entertainer of the Year in 1993 and 1994. He is tied with George Strait for winning the most CMA Male Vocalist of the Year Awards (five), and is currently second only to Brooks and Dunn for accumulating the most CMA Awards in history. Vince is a member of the Grand Ole Opry, and has received nineteen Grammy Awards to date, the most of any male country artist. In 2007 the Country Music Association inducted Gill to the revered Country Music Hall of Fame.

Besides being known for his talent as a performer, musician, and songwriter, Gill is regarded as one of country music's best-known humanitarians, participating in hundreds of charitable events throughout his career. Gill established "The Vinny" in 1993, a celebrity pro golf tournament that raises money for the Junior Golf program. The TNN & CMT Country Weekly Music Awards honored Gill with its Career Achievement Award in 2001, for both his music and his many good works.

MORE TASTY MORSELS: vincegill.com
VINCE'S CHARITY: Project See Inc., Nashville, Tennessee

Vince Gill. Photograph by Scott Newton © 2008. Courtesy of KLRU-ACL.

Black Bean–Corn Salsa

Submitted by Vince Gill and Amy Grant

I always double this recipe when I'm having a large party.

- 3 c. tomato, diced
- 3 cloves garlic, chopped
- ½ c. green onions, chopped
- 1–2 jalapeños, seeded and chopped
- 1 c. shoe-peg corn, fresh or frozen
- 1 (14-oz.) can Goya black beans, drained and rinsed
- ½ c. cilantro, chopped
- 1 tsp. balsamic vinegar
- 1 T. olive oil
- 3 T. lime juice
- kosher salt and black pepper to taste

In a large bowl, combine all the ingredients and stir well. Be careful not to add too much lime juice because you do not want the flavor to take over. This is great as an appetizer with tortilla chips, or as a side with your favorite grilled fish.

Rick Trevino

SHOW DATE: 1995

SERVING UP: Country

A FEW INGREDIENTS: Austinite Rick Trevino is a singer-songwriter who really lights a fire under his fans. His early number-one singles included "She Can't Say I Didn't Cry," "Running Out of Reasons to Run," and "Learning As You Go." He has recorded albums in both English and Spanish—one, his self-titled debut, was certified gold.

In the late 1990s he became part of an all-star group of Mexican-American singers—including Freddy Fender, Ruben Ramos, Flaco Jimenez, and members of Los Lobos—and they called themselves Los Super Seven. The group won the Grammy for Best Mexican-American Music Performance in 1999 for their self-titled debut album.

MORE TASTY MORSELS: ricktrevino.com

Rick Trevino. Photograph by Scott Newton © 2008. Courtesy of KLRU-ACL.

Sausage and Cheese-Stuffed, Bacon-Wrapped Jalapeños

A long time ago, a close friend of mine gave me this recipe and it has been a hit with my family and friends for many years. I thought I would share this with you because it makes an excellent appetizer.

Warning: This is not a low-fat appetizer. Also, how meticulous you are when you gut the jalapeño seeds will determine the intensity of the spiciness. Ninety percent of the time these stuffed jalapeños are extremely spicy. Be careful not to burn them because the grease drips could cause quite a fire. This is also is a very time-consuming appetizer, especially if you are making a bunch of 'em. And I recommend wearing dishwashing gloves because handling all those jalapeños can sting your fingers—and the sting doesn't go away for at least twenty-four hours. So besides the big fire that the grease might cause, and the half a day it takes to make everything, and possibly getting injured during the preparation of these wonderful appetizers, I think you will enjoy them.

venison pan sausage
cheese
bacon
30–60 jalapeños

Go hunting and harvest a deer. Or borrow some deer pan-sausage from your neighbor. (You might be a redneck if you can borrow some deer pan sausage from you neighbor or neighbors easily. I do it quite often.)

Slice the stems off of 30–60 big jalapeños and gut 'em. You're looking at 2–3 jalapeños per person. I usually cook 60.

Cook the deer pan sausage on a gas grill until fully cooked, then add the shredded cheese to the pan.

Stuff sausage and cheese into jalapeños. Wrap each jalapeño with bacon and stick toothpicks through each.

Throw the jalapeños on grill. Cook until bacon is completely cooked, take off of the grill and serve. Yield: 60 pieces.

Groovin' with Soups, Stews, Salads, and Breads

Asleep at the Wheel

SHOW DATES:

1976
1978
1981
1986
1988
1993
1996
1998
2002

Ray Benson. Photograph by Wyatt McSpadden.

Ray Benson's Corn Soup

2 T. cornstarch
6–8 c. whole milk, divided
1 medium onion, peeled and chopped
1 clove garlic, minced
1½ sticks unsalted butter (do not use margarine)
2 tsp. chili powder
2 tsp. ground cumin
1 tsp. garlic powder
½ tsp. black pepper
1–1½ tsp. salt, or to taste
4 c. fresh or frozen corn
½ c. masa harina
3–4 green chilies, chopped
cheddar or Monterey Jack cheese, shredded for garnish
picante or pico de gallo (optional)

Dissolve cornstarch in 1 c. of milk and set aside.

In a large saucepan or soup pot, sauté the onion and garlic in butter until soft and translucent, about 8–10 minutes. Add spices and stir to dissolve them. Add corn and then transfer to a blender or food processor. With the processor running, add the reserved 1 c. of dissolved cornstarch and milk.

Return contents of processor to medium heat and add masa harina and the remaining milk, stirring occasionally. Add the green chilies and cook for 10–15 minutes. Salt to taste.

To serve, pour hot soup into oven-proof serving bowls. Top with grated cheese and heat in the oven just long enough to melt the cheese. Do not brown. Top with picante or pico de gallo, and serve with chips. Yield: 6 servings.

SERVING UP: Country, western swing

A FEW INGREDIENTS: Ray Benson is a founding member, lead singer, and guitar player for the nine-time Grammy award-winning band Asleep at the Wheel. Asleep at the Wheel is a full meal that is never served the same way twice. In their thirty-six years as a band, there have been over eighty members, all of whom support Ray's efforts to keep big band western swing music alive and well into the twenty-first century and beyond. In 2003 Ray released his first solo album, *Beyond Time*, which earned two Grammy nominations.

If Ray were a food, he'd be macaroni and cheese or banana pudding—the kind of dish that always brings a smile to your face.

MORE TASTY MORSELS: raybenson.com and asleepatthewheel.com

RAY'S CHARITY: Health Alliance for Austin Musicians (HAAM), healthallianceforaustinmusicians.org

Allison Moorer

SHOW DATES:

1997
2001

SERVING UP: Country

A FEW INGREDIENTS: In 1998 Allison Moorer's song "A Soft Place to Fall" was included on the soundtrack of the movie *The Horse Whisperer*. It garnered rave reviews and resulted in an Academy Award nomination and a performance on the award telecast.

Since then Allison has released four critically acclaimed records, including *Mockingbird*, which features covers of songs by Nina Simone, Patti Smith, Cat Power, and her sister Shelby Lynne. In early 2008 Moorer performed in Howard Zinn and Anthony Arnove's *Rebel Voices*, the theatrical production based on their best-selling book *Voices of a People's History of the United States*. She has also toured with her husband, songwriter Steve Earle.

MORE TASTY MORSELS: allisonmoorer.com

ALLISON'S CHARITY: Women In Need, Inc., women-in-need.org

Allison Moorer. Photograph by Scott Newton © 2008. Courtesy of KLRU-ACL.

Italian Meatball Soup

I got this recipe from epicurious.com, and it was originally called Italian Meatball Soup *Rapido*. But I replaced the canned beans with dry ones and the frozen meatballs with fresh ones, so it's not so *rapido* anymore. And it's better! Of course, *rapido* is always good, but if you have time to do it the long way, it's worth it.

I make this as a vegetarian soup because I don't eat meat, but I suggest making the meatballs on the side for those that do (like my husband Steve), and they can add them if they like.

¼ c. olive oil
1 c. frozen chopped onions (about 6 oz.)
4 cloves garlic, chopped
1 celery stalk, halved lengthwise and thinly sliced crosswise
2 carrots, halved lengthwise and thinly sliced crosswise
5¼ c. vegetable stock
2½ c. water
1 lb. lean ground beef or turkey (optional)
1 lb. dry white beans (navy beans or Great Northerns will do as well)
1 (5- to 6-oz.) bag baby spinach, coarsely chopped
½ c. finely grated Parmigiano-Reggiano (optional)
¾ tsp. salt, or to taste
¼ tsp. black pepper

Soak beans overnight or do the "quick soak" method.

Heat 2 T. oil in a 5- to 6-qt. pot over high heat until hot but not smoking, then cook onions, garlic, celery, and carrots, stirring occasionally, until onions are pale golden, about 4 minutes. Stir in stock and water and bring to a boil, covered.

Meanwhile, heat remaining 2 T. oil in a 12-inch heavy skillet over high heat until hot but not smoking, and then cook meatballs, turning occasionally, until browned. Set aside on paper towels to soak up excess oil.

Add beans to soup and briskly simmer, covered, stirring occasionally, until vegetables are tender and beans are heated through, about 15 minutes.

Stir in spinach, cheese (optional: you can also add the cheese as a topping), salt, and pepper and simmer, uncovered, until spinach is wilted, about 1 minute. For meat eaters, serve over meatballs.

Sara Hickman

SHOW DATE: 1991

Sara Hickman. Photograph by Scott Newton © 2008. Courtesy of KLRU-ACL.

Lemongrass Soup

6 stalks of lemongrass
8 c. chicken stock
16 large shrimp, peeled and deveined
½–1 tsp. crushed red pepper
1 bunch cilantro
1 medium can straw mushrooms
1 c. snow peas
⅓ c. carrots, shredded
juice of 1 lime
1 chili pepper, cut into rings
4 T. nam plah (you can find at specialty food stores)

Gently hammer along the lemongrass stalks with the blunt side of a knife to break the "cells" and release more flavor.

Bring broth to a simmer. Add crushed red pepper and shrimp.

Simmer for 5 minutes. Add lemongrass and simmer for another 4 minutes.

Add the rest of the ingredients and simmer a few minutes more.

Be careful not to overcook or the vegetables will lose their color and get limp. Yield: 4 servings.

SERVING UP: Rock, folk, pop, children's music

A FEW INGREDIENTS: If Sara Hickman were a dessert, she'd be angel food cake. Her heavenly voice and joyous energy are rivaled only by her devotion to making a difference in the world.

After she wrote and performed her first song at age eight and won an award for it, she was hooked. Since 1989 Sara has been recording and touring with both major and indie labels. In the mid-nineties, she moved to Austin, Texas, and had the opportunity to tour with Nanci Griffith and Dan Fogelberg. *Two Kinds of Laughter* came to light in 1998, produced by esteemed guitarist Adrian Belew, with King Crimson, David Bowie, and Frank Zappa all on board. A later recording, *Motherlode*, released in 2006, offers a unique platter for the listener; the double album included one disc of upbeat music, the other full of woe. Her series of releases for children (and their parents)—fourteen albums in all—are wildly popular and have won many awards.

MORE TASTY MORSELS: sarahickman.com SARA'S CHARITY: The Miracle Foundation, miraclefoundation.org

Kevin Welch

SHOW DATE: 1992

SERVING UP: Country

A FEW INGREDIENTS: Although he has enjoyed the success of his solo outings, Kevin Welch prefers being part of a musical casserole that brings together the tastes and talents of those he is closest to. Kevin and friends—Kieran Kane, Harry Stinson, Mike Henderson, and Tammy Rogers—started their own label, Dead Reckoning Records, in the early 1990s and released twenty-one records over the next several years, both as solo artists and as a collective called A Night Of Reckoning (with Fats Kaplin and Allison Prestwood).

In 2000 Kevin and Kieran released a live record titled *11/12/13: Live from Melbourne, Australia*. They later formed a trio with Fats, and were nominated for American Music Awards in the category of Duo/Group of the Year in 2007 and again in 2008.

MORE TASTY MORSELS: kevinwelch.com
KEVIN'S CHARITY: St. Jude Children's Research Hospital, stjude.org

Kevin Welch. Photograph by Scott Newton © 2008. Courtesy of KLRU-ACL.

Resurrection Chicken Soup

the leftovers from a big roasted chicken
1 small yellow onion, diced
6–8 cloves fresh garlic, minced
2 T. olive oil
1 large carrot, chopped
1 celery stalk, chopped
1 c. fresh or frozen corn
1 medium can Ro-Tel Tomatoes and Green Chilies
other veggies to taste (a handful of fresh green beans, a head of broccoli, etc., but no potato)
soy sauce to taste
salt and fine ground pepper to taste
red wine to taste (can be over the hill; it's best to use leftovers from the last bottle you opened)

DAY ONE: Roast a nice big chicken, eat a nice dinner. Save at least half the bird, and later in the evening put it in a big pot and boil it down for about an hour. If you have the energy to do it before you go to bed, take the chicken out of the pot. Put the bird on a large platter and start cutting off all the good meat, piling it on another platter or just dropping it back in the pot. Be careful and make sure that all the nasty bits and funky bizness gets tossed. Put the lid on the pot and store it overnight in the refrigerator.

DAY TWO: Pop in a Hoagy Carmichael CD. Skim most of the congealed fat off the top. Start warming the pot and make sure the chunks of meat are bite-size. Now, you don't have to do this, but if you feel like it, take a cast-iron skillet and heat some olive oil. Olive oil has a low smoking point so be careful. Sauté the diced onion. When the onion is clear, toss in the minced garlic. It's OK to burn the onion a little, but not the garlic. Add the contents of the skillet to the pot, the oil, too. If you don't want to do all that, you can skip the skillet part, but if you do, you're not my buddy. Add chopped veggies, as discussed in the ingredients. Start tasting the broth. Add Ro-Tel, taste some more. If it wants salt, try soy sauce first. Add plenty of pepper, it's hard to use too much. If the broth doesn't taste full enough, add a little red wine and some bouillon. Once you get it like you like it, put the lid on the pot and put it back in the fridge. By now, you'll be pretty sick of chicken so you'll be fine with this. Make something else for dinner.

DAY THREE: Heat, tweak, and eat. Ladle over rice, or better, have some good bread, some strong cheese, and a new bottle of wine. Amen.

Carrie Rodriguez

SHOW DATE:

2008

SERVING UP: Alternative, folk, country

A FEW INGREDIENTS: Many fans of Carrie Rodriguez got their first taste of her music at the South by Southwest music festival in Austin in 2001. After years of classical training and inspiration from Andrea Zonn, Lyle Lovett's fiddle player, she can play a mean fiddle.

Chip Taylor was among those who loved what he heard at SXSW, and he invited her to perform with him in Europe. They teamed up to record 2002's *Let's Leave this Town*, followed by *The Trouble with Humans* in 2003 and the critically acclaimed *Red Dog Tracks* in 2005. Carrie loves collaboration, which shows in the numerous duets she's performed and the songs she has co-written with musicians such as Gary Louris (the Jayhawks), Dan Wilson (Semisonic), Jim Boquist (Son Volt) and Mary Gauthier. She has also toured and recorded with Lucinda Williams.

Her debut solo album, *Seven Angels on a Bicycle*, was released in 2006.

MORE TASTY MORSELS: carrierodriguez.com

CARRIE'S CHARITY: World Hunger Year, whyhunger.org

Carrie Rodriguez. Photograph by Scott Newton © 2008. Courtesy of KLRU-ACL.

Roasted Tomato and Bean Soup with Quesadilla Dumplings

3 tomatoes
2 cloves garlic
½ small onion
4 c. pinto or Anasazi beans
3 T. canola or avocado oil
sea salt
3 c. chicken stock
cilantro
sour cream
Quesadilla Dumplings (prepare ahead; recipe follows)

Broil tomatoes and leave skin on.

Add broiled tomatoes, garlic, and onion to blender, and purée. Remove this mixture from blender and set aside.

Boil beans. Pour beans and small amount of bean broth into blender and purée.

Cook tomato purée in hot oil in large pot over medium heat for 8 minutes. Add bean purée and cook another 8 minutes, stirring occasionally. Add chicken broth and cook 8 more minutes over low heat, adding sea salt to taste.

Ladle soup into bowls and garnish with cilantro, sour cream, and Quesadilla Dumplings. Yield: 6 servings.

QUESADILLA DUMPLINGS

2 T. canola or avocado oil
1 doz. corn tortillas
1½ c. shredded white cheese

Heat oil in frying pan. Place tortilla in hot oil and sprinkle with cheese. Cover with a second tortilla. Flip in pan until quesadilla is crisp on both sides. Cut into quarters. Yield: 24 dumplings.

Cowboy Junkies

SHOW DATE:

1991

Cowboy Junkies. Photograph by Chris Buck.

Chicken Gnocchi Stew

Submitted by Peter Timmins

4 chicken breasts, bone and skin on
olive oil
salt and pepper
2 sweet onions, chopped
4 c. chicken stock
1 T. hot paprika
1 (1-lb.) pkg. fresh gnocchi

Heat oven to 400°.

Wash chicken and pat dry. Season breasts with salt and pepper. Heat oil on stovetop in oven-proof pan. Cook chicken in pan, skin-side down. Cook until skin is crispy, about 5 minutes.

Sauté onions in same pan. Add stock to chicken and onions. Add paprika. Transfer to oven and cook uncovered for 30 minutes. Add gnocchi to pan and continue cooking in oven until gnocchi is done, around 10 to 15 minutes.

SERVING UP: Rock and alternative rock

A FEW INGREDIENTS: The spare and quiet songs of Cowboy Junkies, with their languid guitars and ethereal vocals, provide the perfect soundtrack for a peaceful evening of dining and relaxing. The band—Michael, Margo, and Peter Timmins, and Alan Anton—debuted in 1986 with the release of their album, *Whites Off Earth Now!!* Their first wide release was 1988's *The Trinity Session*, which was recorded in one night inside Toronto's Church of the Holy Trinity. Cowboy Junkies was also featured on the Beatles tribute album *This Bird Has Flown*. They were nominated for Group of the Year at the Juno Awards in 1990 and 1991.

MORE TASTY MORSELS: cowboyjunkies.com
COWBOY JUNKIES' CHARITY: Brady Center to Prevent Gun Violence, bradycenter.org

Double Trouble

SHOW DATES:

1984
1990
2000
2003

SERVING UP: Blues, rock

A FEW INGREDIENTS: Tommy Shannon and Chris Layton have been heating up the stage for a long time. They are both members of the band Double Trouble, which featured Stevie Ray Vaughan. They racked up four Grammys including Best Contemporary Blues Album, and Best Rock Instrumental recording in 1999. Following Stevie Ray Vaughan's death, Tommy and Chris have toured, recorded, and played with many artists including the Arc Angels, Storyville, Susan Tedeschi, Kenny Wayne Shepherd, Eric Clapton, the Rolling Stones, Little Richard, and Jeff Beck to name a few.

Double Trouble reformed in 2001 and released *Been a Long Time,* their only album without Stevie Ray. This album featured many guest performers taking Stevie Ray's place in the front man role.

MORE TASTY MORSELS: tommyshannon.com

DOUBLE TROUBLE'S CHARITY: Austin Humane Society, austinhumanesociety.org

Double Trouble. Photograph by Scott Newton © 2008. Courtesy of KLRU-ACL.

Bev's Lazy Tommy-tillo Stew and Burrito Filling

Submitted by Beverly Howell

I love this recipe, submitted by my loving friend, tireless publicist, and Web wench extraordinaire, Beverly Howell. She's the cherry on top of our recipe for life!

—Tommy Shannon

2½–3 lb. ground pork or beef
1 can V8 Vegetable Juice
2 bottles Herdez Salsa Verde
1 can Herdez Salsa Casera
1 can water
2–3 medium potatoes, peeled (if desired) and cubed
1 large onion
salt, pepper, and granulated or fresh garlic to taste (I'm a garlic fanatic so I pour it on!)
½ c. grated cheese, room temperature
fresh flour tortillas
fresh cilantro (optional)

DAY ONE: Brown the meat, if desired, or the lazy route (my preference) is to just dump it right from the package into a crockpot. Pour in V8, salsa verde, and salsa casera. Refill one of the cans with water and add it to the crockpot. Add potatoes and onion.

I set my old crockpot on high for 4–5 hours, then on low for an additional 3–4 hours or until the house smells so good I can no longer resist, then the stew is ready to serve.

DAY TWO: Toss 2–3 ladles of leftover stew into a frying pan, and heat on medium, until most liquid is absorbed. Mash some of the potatoes while it's warming to help it thicken. Spoon into warm flour tortillas, sprinkle with grated cheese and fresh cilantro, and enjoy!

Austin City Limits is the tastiest dish in town! We can never get enough!

—Tommy Shannon

B. J. Thomas

SHOW DATE: 1983

SERVING UP: Rock, pop, gospel

A FEW INGREDIENTS: It's a good thing B. J. Thomas doesn't keep his musical trophies in the kitchen because there'd be no room for food. After more than four decades of performing, his many honors include: two platinum records, eleven gold records, five Grammy Awards, and two Dove Awards for gospel recordings. B. J. is the only artist ever to have a song simultaneously on the pop, country, and gospel charts.

In the course of his career he has sold more than seventy million records and had fifteen hits crack pop charts, including "Raindrops Keep Fallin' on My Head" (the theme song for *Butch Cassidy and the Sundance Kid*), "Eyes of a New York Woman," "Hooked on Feeling," "Rock and Roll Lullaby," and "I Just Can't Help Believing." B. J. has also had ten hits on the country chart including "(Hey Won't You Play) Another Somebody Done Somebody Wrong Song," "Whatever Happened to Old Fashioned Love," and "Two Car Garage."

MORE TASTY MORSELS: bjthomas.net

B. J.'S CHARITY: Pathways to Spirit, pathwaystospirit.org

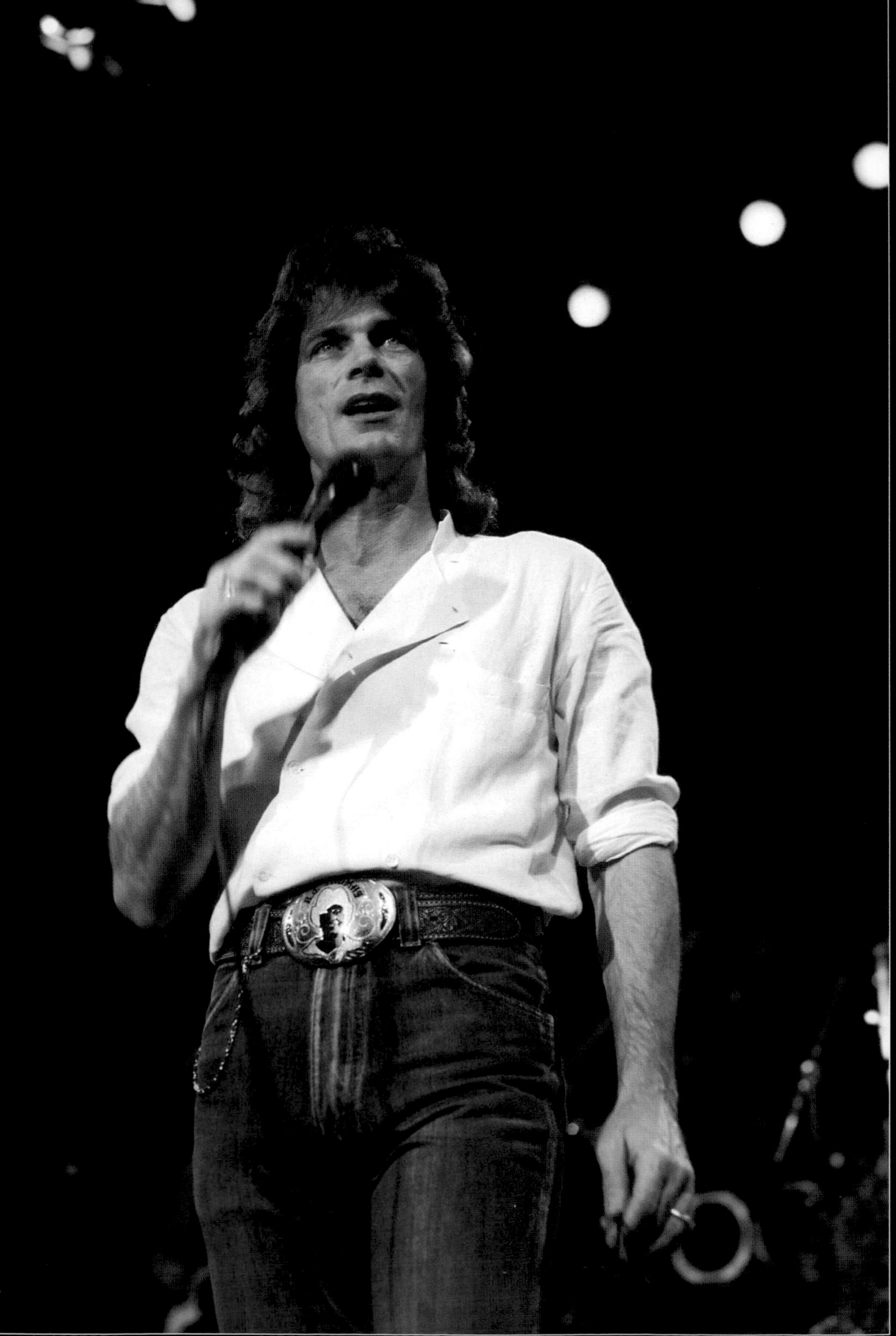

B. J. Thomas. Photograph by Scott Newton © 2008. Courtesy of KLRU-ACL.

Watermelon and Feta Cheese Salad

Submitted by Nora Thomas Cloud, B.J.'s daughter

2 c. seedless watermelon, diced into ½ inch cubes
1 c. fresh parsley, chopped
¼ small purple onion, sliced thin
2 T. pine nuts, toasted
½ c. feta cheese, crumbled
¼ c. green olives, sliced or quartered
Dressing (recipe follows)
salad greens

In a large bowl, combine 2 c. watermelon cubes (it's best to use room temperature watermelon, which is sweeter and crisper), parsley, onion, pine nuts, olives, and feta cheese. Toss with dressing. Season with salt and pepper. Serve over salad greens. Yield: 6 side salads.

DRESSING

1 c. seedless watermelon, diced into ½ inch cubes
½–¼ c. fresh lemon juice
½ c. extra virgin olive oil

In a blender, purée the remaining 1 c. watermelon. Strain and discard pulp. Combine watermelon juice and lemon juice in a medium bowl. Slowly whisk in olive oil.

Carlene Carter

SHOW DATE: 1994

Carlene Carter. Photograph by Robert Matteau. Courtesy of Carlene Carter.

C. C.'s Summer Salad

I jam in the kitchen! These amounts listed in the ingredients list aren't exact. You can leave something out, and this salad will still taste great. Have fun with it!

6 c. spring mix lettuce
1 apple, cored and diced
¾ c. blueberries
1 carrot, shredded
2 avocados, cubed
20 red seedless grapes, halved
1 beefy red tomato, chopped
2 small yellow tomatoes, chopped
1 handful of raisins
1 handful of sunflower seeds
½–1 c. blue cheese crumbles (if you like it)

Toss all ingredients in your favorite dressing and serve. (I recommend Marie's Creamy Italian Garlic Dressing.) It also works on it's own, without any help. Yield: 6 servings.

SERVING UP: Country

A FEW INGREDIENTS: As the daughter of June Carter and stepdaughter of Johnny Cash, Carlene Carter grew up with the sounds of country music bubbling all around her, and it's no surprise that she has cooked up a tasty musical career herself. She's recorded twelve albums, which included three tunes that became top-ten hits on the *Billboard* Hot Country Songs chart. Her 1990 album, *I Fell in Love*, was named one of the year's ten best in any genre by *Time*, *People*, and *Stereo Review* magazines. She was nominated for a Top New Female Vocalist Award in the 1990 Academy of Country Music Awards, and for Best Female Country Vocal Performance in the 1991 Grammys. Carlene was the first country-music video jockey on VH1 with *The Carlene Carter Show*. She also had a cameo role in the 1994 film, *Maverick*, and in 2005 she was played by Victoria Hester in *Walk the Line*.

MORE TASTY MORSELS: myspace.com/carlenecartermusic

CARLENE'S CHARITY: Santa Fe Animal Shelter and Humane Society, sfhumanesociety.org

Eric Johnson

SHOW DATES:

1985
1989
1997
2000
2001

SERVING UP: Instrumental rock, acid rock

A FEW INGREDIENTS: Austin native Eric Johnson is a perennial favorite at the Austin Music Awards, having won Musician of the Year, Best Electric Guitar, and Best Acoustic Guitar. The Grammys have taken notice, too: several of his songs ("Zap" in 1987, "Pavilion" in 1997, and "S.R.V." in 1998) have been nominated for the awards, the platinum-selling album *Ah Via Musicom* was nominated for Best Rock Instrumental in 1991, and he won Best Rock Instrumental in 1992 for the single "Cliffs of Dover." Eric is also a member of Alien Love Child, a trio of talented Austin musicians, whose single "Rain" from their 2000 album *Live and Beyond* was nominated for a Best Pop Instrumental Performance Grammy.

Eric has also been honored with his own signature Martin acoustic guitar and a Fender Signature Series Stratocaster electric guitar.

MORE TASTY MORSELS: ericjohnson.com

Eric Johnson. Photograph by Scott Newton © 2008. Courtesy of KLRU-ACL.

E. J.'s Supersalad

1 head butter lettuce, shredded
1 head romaine lettuce, shredded
2 tomatoes, chopped
1 yellow bell pepper, diced
1 large cucumber, diced
2 avocados, diced
roasted and salted cashews
pumpkin seeds
sesame seeds
toasted hemp seeds
grated Asiago cheese (optional)
sun-dried tomatoes (optional)
black olives (optional)
salt and pepper to taste
olive oil

Combine first 6 ingredients in large bowl and toss. Sprinkle generously with any or all of these: cashews, pumpkin seeds, sesame seeds, or toasted hemp seeds. Add grated Asiago cheese, sun-dried tomatoes, and a few black olives, if desired.

Add sea salt and fresh ground pepper to taste, and a generous amount of extra virgin olive oil. Toss and voilà!

Tift Merritt

SHOW DATE:

2006

Tift Merritt. Photograph by Scott Newton © 2008. Courtesy of KLRU-ACL.

My Mother's World's Greatest Salad Dressing

one part olive oil
one part apple cider vinegar
salt and pepper to taste
1 clove garlic
juice of ½ lemon
1 tsp. Dijon mustard
2 generous pinches of sugar

Stir all ingredients and let steep overnight. Don't leave out the sugar, or the recipe will not work. You can double and triple the recipe for big batches that will only get better over time. Add fresh herbs from the garden in summer to taste.

SERVING UP: Rock, country, alt-country

A FEW INGREDIENTS: What do you get when you mix alt-country, rock, and soul, and serve it up with something sweet and delicate on the side? The musical recipes of Tift Merritt.

When Tift released her debut album, *Bramble Rose*, in 2002, *Time* magazine called it one of the ten best CDs of the year and British newspaper the *Times* said it was "the best release by a new artist, in any genre." She was nominated for a Grammy in 2004 for Best Country Album for *Tambourine* and received three nominations from the Americana Music Association—Album of the Year, Artist of the Year, and Song of the Year—for her work on *Good Hearted Man*.

Tift also hosts an artist-to-artist radio interview program called "The Spark with Tift Merrit," which airs on Marfa Public Radio, and is available as a podcast.

MORE TASTY MORSELS: tiftmerritt.com
TIFT'S CHARITY: Neuse River Foundation, neuseriver.org

Delbert McClinton

SHOW DATES:

1977
1979
1983
1989
1993
1996
1997
2001
2002

COOKING UP: Blues, rock, country

A FEW INGREDIENTS: Delbert McClinton started stirring together the ingredients for his musical career long ago, backing blues giants like Howlin' Wolf, Sonny Williamson, Lightnin' Hopkins, and Jimmy Reed. Legend has it that on a tour of the UK with Bruce Channel, Delbert met a young John Lennon and advised him on his harmonica technique, resulting in the distinct sound heard on the Beatles hit "Love Me Do." He's an accomplished songwriter, too: Emmylou Harris had a number one hit in 1978 with Delbert's composition "Two More Bottles of Wine," and his "B Movie Boxcar Blues" was used in the 1980 movie *The Blues Brothers*. Delbert's 1980 single "Givin' It Up for Your Love," from *The Jealous Kind*, made the top ten of the *Billboard* Hot 100.

In 1991 a duet with Bonnie Raitt, "Good Man, Good Woman," earned him a Grammy, and another duet of his, "Tell Me About It," sung with Tanya Tucker, reached the top of the country charts.

After he cut two studio albums in the early 2000s, a career retrospective was released in 2003 under the title *Delbert McClinton Live*. In 2006 he won another Grammy, this time for Best Contemporary Blues Album for *The Cost of Living*.

MORE TASTY MORSELS: delbert.com

DELBERT'S CHARITY: Attachment Parenting International, attachmentparenting.com

Delbert McClinton. Photograph by Scott Newton © 2008. Courtesy of KLRU-ACL.

Crunchy Asian Slaw

2 (3-oz.) pkg. ramen noodles, crushed
2 T. sesame seeds
1 c. blanched, slivered almonds
½ c. melted butter or margarine
1 large head Napa cabbage, chopped or shredded
2 bunches scallions, chopped
Dressing (recipe follows)

In a medium skillet, brown the ramen noodles, sesame seeds, and almonds with the melted butter or margarine. Remove from heat once everything is browned, and allow to cool.

In a large bowl, combine the chopped cabbage and chopped green onions, and add the ramen noodle mixture. Add the dressing and toss. Serve.

DRESSING

¾ c. vegetable oil
½ c. white sugar or Splenda
¼ c. distilled white vinegar
2 T. soy sauce

In a saucepan bring the vegetable oil, sugar or Splenda, and vinegar to boil for 1 minute. Allow to cool, and add soy sauce.

Austin City Limits is different than any other show an artist can do. I would always look forward to playing there because ACL would let me rock straight through without technical interruptions. It was always such an honor to be asked on the show.

—Delbert McClinton

Jimmie Vaughan

SHOW DATES:

1990
1995
1999
2001
2007

Jimmie Vaughan. Photograph by Scott Newton © 2008. Courtesy of KLRU-ACL.

"Come and Take It" Coleslaw

1 head cabbage
½ c. sunflower seeds
½ c. slivered almonds
½ c. green onion, chopped
1 jalapeño, chopped (optional)
Dressing (recipe follows)

Combine all ingredients in large bowl. Pour dressing over coleslaw. Toss and refrigerate. Let sit one hour, toss again, and serve.

DRESSING

¾ c. oil
6 T. cider or red wine vinegar
4 T. sugar
salt and pepper to taste

Combine all ingredients.

SERVING UP: Blues, Texas blues, jazz

A FEW INGREDIENTS: Jimmie Vaughan is a legend. Like a great meal, he is at once hot and cool, simple and complex, raw and elegant. Once you've had a taste, you can't help but want more.

At sixteen he joined the Chessman, who would eventually open concerts in Dallas for Jimi Hendrix. In the mid-1970s, Jimmie founded the Fabulous Thunderbirds with Kim Wilson. He recorded eight albums with the Thunderbirds including *Tuff Enuff*, which was certified platinum and was nominated for a Grammy.

In 1990 he and his brother Stevie Ray toured and recorded as the Vaughan Brothers and received two Grammy awards that year—one for Best Rock Instrumental Performance and one for Best Contemporary Blues Recording. His tribute to Stevie Ray, *SRV Shuffle*, which also featured Art Neville, B.B. King, Bonnie Raitt, Buddy Guy, Dr. John, Eric Clapton, and Robert Cray, won the Best Rock Instrumental Performance Grammy in 1996.

Jimmie's solo album, *Do You Get the Blues?*, won a Grammy for Best Traditional Blues Album and received much critical acclaim. He has made guest appearances on albums with B.B. King, Eric Clapton, Bob Dylan, Willie Nelson, Carlos Santana, and Don Henley.

MORE TASTY MORSELS: jimmievaughan.com

JIMMIE'S CHARITY: Children International, children.org

Darden Smith

SHOW DATES:

1988
1994

SERVING UP: Folk, country, pop

A FEW INGREDIENTS: In the more than twenty years since Darden Smith's career began, he has released twelve albums and toured tirelessly, hitting every state except for Hawaii and South Dakota.

His musical accomplishments are diverse; he has composed music for dance, theater, radio, and television, and he is active in the local arts scene. The Austin Symphony commissioned "Grand Motion" from him in 1999, and "Marathon," a theatrical work co-written with fellow Austinite Jesse Sublett, was produced by the University of Texas Performing Arts Center in 2008. Darden's Be An Artist program—begun in 2003—encourages children to pursue their artistic dreams.

MORE TASTY MORSELS: dardensmith.com

DARDEN'S CHARITY: Armstrong Community Music School, Austin, Texas, austinlyricopera.org

Darden Smith. Photograph by Michael O'Brien © 2004. Courtesy of Michael O'Brien

Basic Bread

I grew up with white bread, and I thought that's all there was out there in the world in the way of things that hold jelly, fried bologna, and such.

Touring in Europe changed this. This recipe is adapted from *The Bread Book*, which I bought at Books for Cooks off Portobello Road in London. When I returned home from tour and started baking, around 1989, I realized it was hard to find a good loaf of bread in Austin. So my motivation was born from necessity. Now, it's a must around my house. I hate most store-bought bread, and my kids are absolute snobs about it.

Though this recipe lives in my brain, I still use the book for other loaves, particularly the Pugliese.

2 packets active yeast
1 tsp. sugar
4½ c. lukewarm water, divided
6 c. white flour (King Arthur if you can get it), sifted
4 c. stone ground flour, sifted
3 tsp. salt
flour and lukewarm water for kneading
warm salt water or egg yolk (optional)
soaked oat groats or buckwheat groats (optional)

Dissolve yeast and sugar in ½ c. lukewarm water; let rise.

Combine both flours and salt in large bowl and make a well in the middle. When the yeast foams (about 10 minutes) pour it in the well. Add 4 c. lukewarm water to the well. Put a bit of flour into the liquid in the well and mix by hand, until the clumps of flour are dissolved.

Cover liquid with a layer of flour and let stand for 20 minutes; check periodically and cover any liquid that rises with more flour. Blend liquid and flour together by hand until it forms into a sticky mass. Place dough onto a floured work surface and knead for 10 minutes. If dough is too wet, add flour 1 T. at a time; if too dry, add more water. This is a feel thing and you'll only know when it's perfect from experience.

Pull dough into a ball and lightly dust with flour. Place in cleaned and well-oiled bowl, and cover with damp towel. Let stand for two hours or until it has doubled in size. After dough has risen, turn it onto work surface and divide dough into 3 equal parts. Shape dough and place it into well-oiled loaf pans; cover with damp towel and let stand for one hour.

Preheat oven to 450°. Place small oven-proof container filled with water in oven to start steaming. Place loaf pans in oven, spaced an inch or so apart. Let stand in oven for 15 minutes. After 7–10 minutes, rotate pans to ensure even baking.

Reduce oven temp to 375°. Bake for 10–15 more minutes, or until loaves sound hollow when tapped on bottom.

Let cool on rack 10–15 minutes before devouring. Once the loaves cool, place them in plastic or paper bags; loaves will last a couple of days without refrigeration. Toasting is recommended. It brings out the flavor of the flour. Yield: 3 loaves.

OPTIONS

Sometimes I add soaked oat groats or buckwheat groats to the dough. And depending on how much time I have, sometimes I repeat the yeast rising one or two times; I find that it doesn't hurt the dough and actually makes a better texture—the exact timing on this phase isn't critical. I've let it go for three hours before with no negative effect.

Another option: after placing them in the pans, deeply score the loaves with a sharp knife and let rise.

For a different texture, brush the loaves with warm salt water (for a dull sheen) or egg yolk (which makes it dark brown and glossy) just before placing them in the oven.

You can also remove the loaves from the pans once they are solid and place them directly on the oven rack, to get more even color on the sides and bottom.

Eric Taylor

SHOW DATES:
2001
2002

Eric Taylor. Photograph by Scott Newton © 2008. Courtesy of KLRU-ACL.

Blue Ruby Cornbread

Double all ingredients if using a large cast-iron skillet.

1 egg
½ c. sour cream
1 (8-oz.) can of creamed corn
¼ c. vegetable oil
¾ c. cornmeal
½ c. flour
1 tsp. salt
½ c. green bell pepper, chopped
½ c. yellow onion, chopped
½ c. green onions, chopped
jalapeños, sliced, to taste (I use pickled and fresh)
1 c. shredded mozzarella
1 c. shredded cheddar

Preheat oven to 400°.

In a large mixing bowl, beat 1 egg. Then add sour cream, creamed corn, oil, cornmeal, flour, salt, green pepper, onions, jalapeños, and cheeses.

Grease a cast-iron skillet, and heat in oven for at least 5 minutes. Pour cornbread mixture into heated skillet.

Bake at 400° for 75 minutes. Check with a knife to see if the middle is done. Cook longer, if need be. Then you eat it.

SERVING UP: Americana, country, folk

A FEW INGREDIENTS: Eric Taylor started cooking at the 1977 Kerrville Folk Festival, where he won the prestigious New Folk Competition and began building his reputation as a highly literate and sought-after songwriter.

His talents have been noted by the likes of Nanci Griffith and Lyle Lovett, who have both recorded songs that he penned. He has eight studio albums so far including 1999's *Resurrect*, which was named an "essential record" by *Buddy* magazine. Eric has headlined the prestigious Newport Folk Festival, and toured extensively. He also enjoys teaching, and has mentored musicians and conducted songwriting workshops around the world.

MORE TASTY MORSELS: bluerubymusic.com
ERIC'S CHARITY: SafePlace, Austin, Texas, safeplace.org

We taped my show on *Austin City Limits* on September 25, 2001—the first taping of ACL after 9/11. Fourteen days after the attack, the world was still reeling. Originally we were to tape with John Hammond, Jr., but John still couldn't get out of Newark. We taped that day with Charlie Robison. We all got through it.

—Eric Taylor

Lloyd Maines

SHOW DATES:

numerous times as a musician backing up other artists

Lloyd Maines. Photograph by Scott Newton © 2008, Courtesy of KLRU-ACL

Bubba Toast

First, let me say, I've never liked the name or term "Bubba." It falls into the same category as "Good Buddy" and "Hoss," but as it turns out, my grandkids call me "Bubba" so it's OK. And it is the name of this simple breakfast recipe that is a favorite at my house.

whole grain bread
natural peanut butter
Cheerios or another whole-grain cereal
pure maple syrup or honey

Take some good whole grain bread and toast it to your liking. Then spread peanut butter evenly on the toast. (If you have peanut allergy, then use almond or cashew butter.)

Take Cheerios or some other whole-grain cereal and sprinkle it on the peanut butter.

Top it off with a bit of pure maple syrup or honey. It's a good, quick, easy, and wholesome way to start the day. I like mine with a glass of nonfat milk, then black coffee.

SERVING UP: Country

A FEW INGREDIENTS: If he were any more Texan, Lloyd Maines would have barbecue sauce coursing through his veins. A multi-instrumental country music performer known for his pedal steel playing, he was born and raised in Texas. He plays nearly every instrument associated with country music, but is most renowned for pedal steel guitar. Lloyd has toured and recorded as a member of the Joe Ely Band, and has also played with Guy Clark, Butch Hancock, Terry Allen, Jimmie Dale Gilmore, and other Texas musicians.

As a record producer, he has worked with many well known musicians, including Jerry Jeff Walker, the Lost Gonzo Band, Robert Earl Keen, Pat Green, and the Waybacks. In 2003 the Dixie Chicks won the Grammy Award for Best Country Album for *Home*, an album produced by Lloyd and featuring his daughter, Natalie Maines.

MORE TASTY MORSELS: takecountryback.com/features/lloydmaines.html
LLOYD'S CHARITY: Health Alliance for Austin Musicians (HAAM), healthallianceforaustinmusicians.org

Susan Tedeschi

SHOW DATES:

1999
2003

Tedeschi: Photograph by Scott Newton © 2008. Courtesy of KLRU-ACL

Banana Bread

1 c. sugar
⅓ c. butter, softened
2 eggs
3 to 4 medium ripe bananas, mashed
⅓ c. water
1⅔ c. all-purpose flour
1 tsp. baking soda
½ tsp. salt
¼ tsp. baking powder
½ c. chopped nuts (optional)

Heat oven to 350°. Grease and flour 9 × 5 × 3–inch loaf pan.

Mix sugar and butter in bowl. Stir in eggs until blended. Add bananas and water and beat for 30 seconds. Stir in remaining ingredients (except nuts) until moist, then add nuts and pour into pan. Bake 55 to 60 minutes, or until a wooden toothpick comes out clean.

Allow to cool at least 5 minutes Then remove from pan. Cool completely before cutting. Yield: 1 loaf.

SERVING UP: Soul, blues

A FEW INGREDIENTS: In the years since she captured the public's musical imagination with her 1998 breakthrough album *Just Won't Burn*, Susan has become well known and loved for her ability to mix up ingredients from blues, rock, soul, R&B, folk, and gospel into a dish with her own distinctly individual flavor. She is also widely respected for her fiery guitar work.

She has toured all over the United States, opening for illustrious musicians like John Mellencamp, B.B. King, and Bob Dylan. Her CD *Just Won't Burn* earned a gold record, a rare feat for a blues album.

MORE TASTY MORSELS: susantedeschi.com
SUSAN'S CHARITY: St. Johns Riverkeeper, stjohnsriverkeeper.org

Toni Price

SHOW DATE: 2000

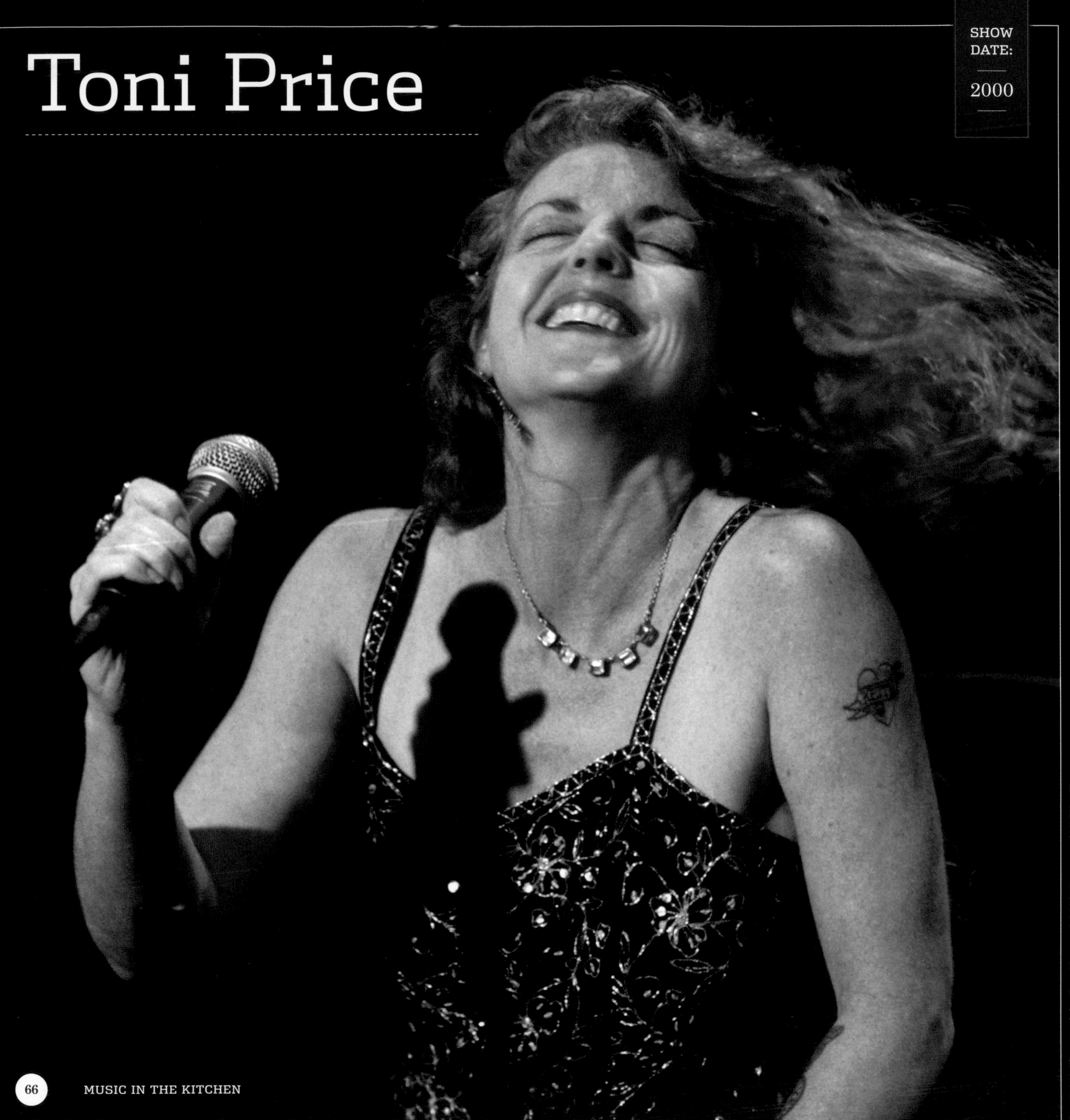

Toni Price. Photograph by Scott Newton © 2008. Courtesy of KLRU-ACL.

Barn Dance Buttercream Biscuits

This is the best biscuit recipe ever! Warm and buttery!

2 c. unbleached flour
1 tsp. salt
1 T. baking powder
2 tsp. sugar
1½ c. heavy cream
⅓ c. (5⅓ T.) butter

Combine flour, salt, baking powder, and sugar in mixing bowl. Stir with fork. Slowly add cream, stirring constantly.

Gather dough, place it on a floured board, and knead, folding over and pressing down repeatedly for 1 whole minute. Pat the dough into a square ½ inch thick. Cut with knife into 12 squares and dip each into the melted butter so all sides are coated.

Place biscuits 2 inches apart on baking sheet. Bake at 425° for about 15 minutes or until lightly brown. Serve hot at breakfast or dinner or a barn dance. Yummy! Yield: 12 biscuits.

SERVING UP: Country, blues

A FEW INGREDIENTS: One of Austin's most beloved musicians, Toni Price, at times sounding like Patsy Cline and Bonnie Raitt, serves up a dish that is uniquely her own. Her debut album from 1993 was *Swim Away*, and her most recent, released in 2007, was *Talk Memphis*. Toni has won numerous awards, including Musician of the Year and two Best Album Awards at the Austin Music Awards. She has been featured on NPR's *Morning Edition*, and sang at the wedding of Julia Roberts and Daniel Moder.

MORE TASTY MORSELS: toniprice.com

TONI'S CHARITY: The American Humane Association, americanhumane.org

Dan Hicks and the Hot Licks

SHOW DATE: 1992

Dan Hicks and the Hot Licks. Photograph by Scott Newton © 2008. Courtesy of KLRU-ACL

SERVING UP: American roots music, folk

A FEW INGREDIENTS: Dan Hicks is a defining figure in American roots music with a sound all his own, borrowing ingredients from genres as varied as psychedelia and blues.

The original Dan Hicks and the Hot Licks, started performing in 1968, and recorded critically acclaimed and commercially successful albums *Where's the Money?*, *Striking It Rich*, and *Last Train to Hicksville*. *Rolling Stone* put Dan on the cover three times.

The most recent incarnation of the band released *Beatin' the Heat* in 2000, chosen by Time.com as one of the ten best albums of the year. It featured collaborations with artists as talented and varied as Bette Midler, Elvis Costello, Tom Waits, Rickie Lee Jones, and Brian Setzer. In 2004 *Selected Shorts* was released, featuring, among others, Willie Nelson and Jimmy Buffett.

MORE TASTY MORSELS: danhicks.net

DAN'S CHARITY: Bread & Roses, breadandroses.org

Dan Hicks' "Treat" Sandwich

D.H. '07

(NOT FOR THE FAINT OF HEART, OR THE AUTOMATICALLY-GUILTY PERSON)

BEST TIME: about 4 in the afternoon

BEST INGREDIENTS:

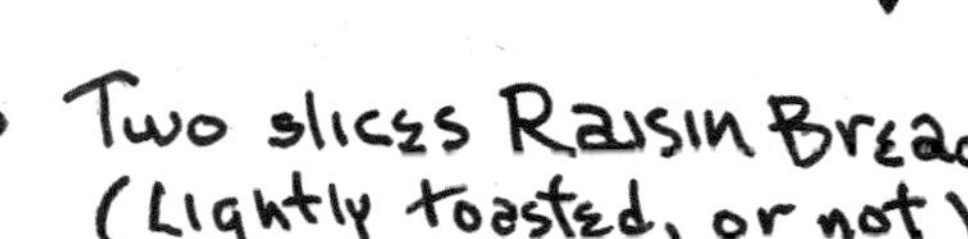

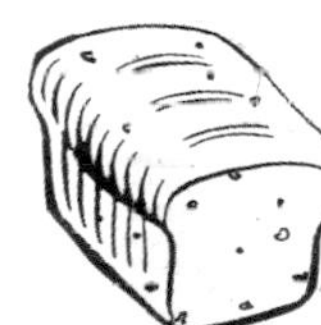

- Two slices Raisin Bread (Lightly toasted, or not)
- Ample Peanut Butter (crunchy, or not)
- Discreet amount of mayonnaise

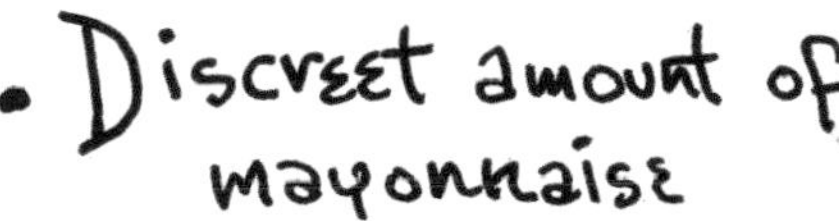

OPTIONAL:

- Thin layer of butter
- Slice o' American cheese

WHAT YOU DO

APPLY INGREDIENTS INSIDE SLICES OF BREAD, CUT SANWICH IN HALF. TAKE BITE, CHEW, AND SWALLOW. REPEAT UNTIL FOOD IS GONE AND EUPHORIA HAS SET IN!

IF NOT YET EUPHORIC, DRINK GLASS OF MILK AND EAT CAN OF PURPLE PLUMS.

BR549

SHOW DATE: 1997

SERVING UP: Alt-country

A FEW INGREDIENTS: BR549 never uses a cookbook, preferring instead to create their own recipe for musical success. And after multiple Grammy nominations, a heavy international touring schedule, and appearances with fellow musicians like Faith Hill, Tim McGraw, Ani DiFranco, and the Black Crowes, they've proven that mixing things up their way works just fine.

The band's self-titled debut album rose to number thirty-three on the U.S. country charts and number eleven on the Canadian country charts. BR549's 2006 outing, *Dog Days* continues to heat things up. Their tasty mix of country, western swing, honky-tonk, and rockabilly keeps things fresh more than a decade later.

MORE TASTY MORSELS: br549.com BR549'S CHARITY: Horses for Healing, horsesforhealing.org

Lentil and Apricot Soup

Submitted by Chuck Mead

This is a recipe from Armenia that I got from a cookbook some time ago.

3 T. olive oil
1 onion, finely chopped
2 cloves garlic, finely chopped
⅓ c. dried apricots
1½ c. red lentils, rinsed and dried
5 c. chicken stock
½ tsp. ground cumin
½ dried thyme
3 ripe plum tomatoes, peeled, seeded, and chopped
2 T. lemon juice
salt and pepper to taste

Heat the oil over medium heat. Add the onion, garlic, and apricots. Sauté about 12 minutes, or until onions are soft. Add lentils and stock, reduce heat to a simmer, and cover. Cook for 30 minutes until lentils are tender. Then stir in spices and tomatoes and cover the pot. Cook for another 10 minutes this way. Remove half the soup and purée it in a food processor. Return the purée back to the pot, then add the lemon juice and salt and pepper. Simmer for 2–3 minutes longer and then serve. Yield: 6 servings.

BR549 always dreamed of playing *Austin City Limits* and it was everything that we could have hoped for. My parents knew we had really made it then!

—Chuck Mead

Accompaniments

SIDES, SAUCES, SPREADS, AND JAMS

Old Crow Medicine Show

SHOW DATE:

2007

Corse Country Cottage Fries

Submitted by Sketch Secor

Cottage fries. Pan fries. Home fries. Whatever you call them they're just plain good. Here's a recipe I learned from my friend Vernon Corse, a long-time naval cook and resident of Beech Mountain, North Carolina.

5–7 large Kennebec or Yukon Gold potatoes
6 T. oil or bacon drippings
1 c. Vidalia onions, diced
1 tsp. curry powder
salt and pepper to taste
fresh parsley

The secret to great home fries is parboiling the potatoes the day before and refrigerating them overnight.

The next day, start with a well-oiled griddle or deep cast-iron frying pan. Add the whole potatoes to the pan, chunking them into cubes with a cookie cutter. (Vernon always cuts his with the lid of his Armour Corned Beef Hash can.)

Let cook 25 minutes, turning often. Add onions and spices and cook another 15 minutes until potatoes are golden and crispy.

Remove from heat and finish with dash of parsley.

SERVING UP: Folk, country, Americana, bluegrass

A FEW INGREDIENTS: Mix a little New York City attitude, some North Carolina down-home southern style, and the flavor of Nashville, and you have the music of Old Crow Medicine Show (OCMS).

Soon after moving to Nashville, OCMS opened for Dolly Parton at the Grand Old Opry. They also make frequent guest appearances on NPR's *A Prairie Home Companion* and have toured with Merle Haggard. Their 2004 self-titled album was selected by Country Music Television as one of the top ten bluegrass albums of that year. Their next album, *Big Iron World*, featured a cover of "Down Home Girl" by the Rolling Stones, and it became the second most added song to Triple A Radio. In 2007 the band played to sold-out crowds across the U.S. and in Europe.

MORE TASTY MORSELS: crowmedicine.com

OLD CROW MEDICINE SHOW'S CHARITY: Common Ground Relief, commongroundrelief.org

Eliza Gilkyson

SHOW DATES:

1984
2001

Eliza's Heart-Healthy Butter Spread

Here is my butter replacement and secret sauce that goes on everything and is vaguely good for you. Make lots and store in the fridge.

2 heaping T. almond butter (or tahini)
1 heaping T. fresh ginger, chopped
1 tsp. umeboshi plum paste (or more, depending on your taste)
1 c. olive oil
1 T. Gomasio Seaweed Sesame Shake seasoning salt

Combine all ingredients.

SERVING UP: Folk

A FEW INGREDIENTS: Eliza is a third-generation musician who, as a teenager recorded demos for her dad Terry, a successful songwriter who wrote hits like "Memories Are Made of This," which Dean Martin took to number one on the charts, and "Bare Necessities" from Disney's *The Jungle Book*. After a period in Europe working with Swiss composer and harpist Andreas Vollenweider, Eliza returned to the United States, moved to Austin, and released *Through the Looking Glass* in 1996 and *Redemption Road* in 1997 (which has recently been reissued). Her career began to simmer with the 2000 release of *Hard Times in Babylon*, followed by *Lost and Found* (2002), and *Land of Milk and Honey* (2004). Eliza has also been on several compilations, including a Bob Dylan tribute album, *Nod to Bob*, and a Greg Brown tribute called *Going Driftless*, which benefited a breast cancer research group. In 2003 she was inducted into the Austin Music Hall of Fame.

MORE TASTY MORSELS: elizagilkyson.com
ELIZA'S CHARITY: The Land Institute, thelandinstitute.org

Maura O'Connell

SHOW DATE:

1992

Maura O'Connell. Photograph by Scott Newton © 2008. Courtesy of KLRU-ACL.

Mama Gail's Catsup

Thanks to Ellen Robins, granddaughter of Gail Meyers McHaney, of Piggot, Arkansas. This Victorian-era recipe comes from Mama Gail's mother, or perhaps further back. It has a chutneylike quality, and can be used on vegetables and meats. Mama Gail always served it on black-eyed peas at New Years. (It's an American thing!)

1 qt. tomatoes, sliced
2 large onions, sliced
1 pt. of vinegar
3 T. salt
½ tsp. dry mustard
¾ lb. brown sugar
½ tsp. cayenne pepper
1 tsp. cinnamon
1 tsp. allspice
1 tsp. ground cloves
1 tsp. mace

Combine all ingredients in a pot. Let simmer 4 hours.

Put through a food mill to remove tomato seeds and skins.

Bottle when cool. Keeps indefinitely without refrigeration.

SERVING UP: Celtic, jazz, pop

A FEW INGREDIENTS: From her appearance as a lead vocalist with the celebrated traditional Celtic group De Danaan in 1981, to her latest solo CD, *Don't I Know*, Maura O'Connell has whisked together her rich, deep voice and her talent for performing music that pulls fans into the heart of a song. Although she had success as a folk artist originally, Maura was attracted to the experimental roots music of American band New Grass Revival. She liked their instrumental focus and their unbridled creativity so much that she followed their sound to Nashville and the rest is history. Her CD, *Helpless Heart*, was nominated for a Grammy, and Martin Scorsese cast Maura as an Irish migrant street singer in the movie, *The Gangs of New York*.

MORE TASTY MORSELS: mauraoconnell.com

The Oak Ridge Boys

SHOW DATE: 1985

The Oak Ridge Boys. Photograph by Jarrett Gaza. Courtesy of Jarrett Gaza.

SERVING UP: Country, gospel, pop

A FEW INGREDIENTS: This band has been cooking on all burners since its founding in 1945. Originally called the Oak Ridge Quartet, they changed their name to the Oak Ridge Boys in the 1950s and soon after they were featured in *Time* magazine as one of the top-drawing gospel groups in the nation. In the 1970s they changed their focus from gospel to country music. Their string of hits includes the pop chart-topper "Elvira," as well as "Bobbie Sue," "Dream On," "American Made," "Fancy Free," "Gonna Take A Lot Of River" and many others. They've had ten gold, three platinum, and one double-platinum album, one double-platinum single, and more than a dozen number one singles. They are also heavily involved in charitable and civic causes, serving as spokesmen and/or board members of fund-raisers for the Boy Scouts of America, the National Committee for Prevention of Child Abuse, Feed the Children, and many more.

MORE TASTY MORSELS: oakridgeboys.com
DUANE'S CHARITIES: Feed the Children, feedthechildren.org, Salvation Army, salvationarmyusa.org, Red Cross, redcross.org, and United Way, unitedwayint.org
JOE'S CHARITY: Feed the Children
RICHARD'S CHARITIES: Feed the Children, Joe Niekro Foundation, joeniekrofoundation.com, and Epidermolysis Bullosa (EB) Foundation, ebkids.org
WILLIAM'S CHARITY: Feed the Children

Uncle Luther's Stuffin'

Submitted by Joe Bonsall

This recipe is named for my old friend Luther, who made the best stuffin' I've ever eaten. I even wrote a song about it. The Oak Ridge Boys recorded "Uncle Luther Made The Stuffin'" for our *Christmas Cookies* CD.

1 stick of margarine
1 large onion, chopped
3 c. celery, chopped
3 (6-oz.) pkg. of season crouton mix
3 eggs, lightly beaten
hot broth from the cooked turkey

About ten minutes prior to the turkey coming out of the oven, place the margarine in a large cast-iron skillet and melt it over low heat. Add the chopped onion and celery; turn the heat up to medium, and sauté the vegetables until they are soft but not browned.

In the meantime place the crouton mix in a large mixing bowl. Add the eggs and the sautéed vegetables. Take the turkey out of the oven when done, and carefully pour the broth out of the turkey pan into the mixing bowl. Mix well. Use enough broth to moisten the mixture, but it should not be soggy. If you don't have enough broth from the turkey, you may substitute chicken broth, as needed.

Pour the mixture into the cast-iron skillet. Adjust the oven to 350° and bake uncovered until browned, about 30 minutes. While stuffin' is baking, turkey will cool enough to be carved.

Michelle Shocked

SHOW DATES: 1990 2000

SERVING UP: Folk, rock, blues

A FEW INGREDIENTS: Michelle's musical career started cooking when a bootleg recording of an evening of music around a campfire at the Kerrville Folk Festival was released in England under the title *The Texas Campfire Tapes*. Since that unexpected introduction to the world Michelle has grown as a singer-songwriter whose political activism and self-assured style shine on stage and on CD.

Her songs "Anchorage," "Come a Long Way," and "On the Greener Side" were all successful among fans. In 2001 Michelle started her own record label, Mighty Sound, and released two albums and a trilogy—*Don't Ask, Don't Tell*, *Got No Strings*, and *Mexican Standoff*. And in 2003 her album, *To Heaven U Ride*, featuring gospel songs recorded live at the Telluride Bluegrass Festival, was released.

MORE TASTY MORSELS: michellshocked.com

MICHELLE'S CHARITY: Save Africa's Children, saveafricaschildren.com

Grandma's Honey-Lavender Strawberry Jam

If you want the best, you've got to make your own. This jam is a simple delight and a wonderful use of fresh summertime strawberries. The mild scent of lavender adds a unique twist.

2 c. sugar
1 c. honey
7 sprigs fresh lavender
1 qt. fully ripe strawberries, washed and stemmed
2 T. fresh lemon juice
½ (1½-oz.) pouch liquid fruit pectin

Place the sugar and honey in a nonreactive 4-qt. saucepot and stir with a wooden spoon over medium heat until the sugar is dissolved. Add the lavender and allow mixture to come to a boil. Remove saucepot from heat and allow to sit for 45 minutes.

Remove and discard the lavender. Add the strawberries and lemon juice to the saucepot. Over high heat bring mixture to a boil, stirring constantly. Boil rapidly for 1 minute and add the pectin. Continue cooking until mixture reaches a rolling boil for another minute. Remove from heat and spoon off any foam.

Ladle hot jam into prepared jam jars. Or, for refrigerator storage, pour mixture into clean jars or containers and allow to cool. When mixture reaches room temperature, seal containers with lids and store in the refrigerator for up to 2 weeks. Yield: 4 8-ounce jars.

If you really want to get ambitious, here is a recipe for homemade pectin.

HOMEMADE PECTIN

2 lb. underripe Granny Smith apples, washed and cut into eighths (not peeled or cored)
4 c. water

In a large saucepan over high heat, bring the apples and water to a boil. Reduce the heat to medium and simmer for 20 minutes or until apples are tender. Remove from the heat and cool.

Line a large bowl with dampened cheesecloth. Pour the pulp and juice through the cheesecloth. Gather the corners of the cheesecloth, and tie in a knot. Suspend from a cabinet knob or handle and allow to drip into a bowl overnight. The next day, measure the apple juice and pour into a large pot. Bring the liquid to a boil over high heat and cook until reduced by half.

Refrigerate and use within 4 days or pour into containers and freeze for up to 6 months. Yield: 1½ cups.

It's great to be a part of the ACL family history. —Michelle Shocked

David Gray

SHOW DATE: 2001

Bramble Jelly

10 lb. fresh blackberries
3⅓ pt. of water
1 lb. of sugar (for every 1 pt. of juice after sieving)
juice of 1 lemon

Pick 10 lb. blackberries. Allow ⅓ pt. of water for every lb. of fruit. Boil it down. Put mixture through a sieve and get the juice. Add 1 lb. of sugar for every 1 pt. of juice. Add the juice of 1 lemon. Stir until the setting point. Jar up.

SERVING UP: Rock, alternative, folk rock

A FEW INGREDIENTS: After three albums and eight years of touring, David Gray released *White Ladder* in 1998, taking his career from the slow-cooker to the front burner. With six million copies sold, David quickly became one of Britain's leading musicians. In fact, *White Ladder* remains Ireland's best-selling album of all time.

In addition to his commercial success, David has won two Ivor Novello Awards for songwriting, a Q Award for Best Single, a GQ Award for Best Solo Artist, two Brit nominations for Best Male, and a Grammy nomination for Best New Artist.

MORE TASTY MORSELS: davidgray.com

Ozomatli

SHOW DATE:

2004

Roasted-Habanero Chili

Submitted by Justin Poree

3 Roma tomatoes
3 tomatillos
3 habanero chiles (4 if you dare)
3 cloves garlic
salt to taste
gas mask (optional)
fan (optional)

Put all ingredients except salt in a pan and roast slowly. Remember, I said slowly, so that means a low flame. If the fumes cause you to tear up and cough too much, throw on your gas mask and turn on the fan.

Keep turning ingredients so they become charred evenly. Don't let garlic get too charred. When the tomatoes and tomatillos become soft and juicy and the skins are splitting, put the lid on the pan and turn the flame up all the way for about 5 seconds. Turn off the flame, and shake the pan with the lid still on.

Let the ingredients sit for a couple hours or even overnight. Go play a round of golf if you get impatient. Put the contents of the pan, including the juices from the tomatoes and tomatillos in the blender. Blend to consistency of your preference—some like it chunky and some like no chunks. If it is unbearably thick, add a little water until you get it just right. Whatever floats your boat.

Salt to taste, and let it sit in the fridge a couple hours before eating. Trust me, if you eat it right away, your stomach is not gonna like you very much.

SERVING UP: Latin, funk, jazz, hip-hop, salsa, reggae

A FEW INGREDIENTS: Ozomatli is a multiethnic band with as many styles as members. The band met through the Peace and Justice Center of Los Angeles, and their first performance was for picketers during a strike. Carlos Santana offered the band one of their early breaks as his opening act during his 1998 tour to promote *Supernatural*. The group received Grammys for Best Latin Rock/Alternative Album in 2002 and 2005.

Ozomatli appeared in the movie *Never Been Kissed*, which featured their song "Cumbia de los muertos," in an episode of HBO's *Sex and the City*.

MORE TASTY MORSELS: ozomatli.com
OZOMATLI'S CHARITY: Critical Resistance, criticalresistance.org

Thievery Corporation

SHOW DATE:
2008

Live Forever Shake

Submitted by Eric Hilton

2 heaping T. raw cocoa powder
1 handful organic baby spinach
½ c. frozen wild blueberries
10 oz. organic hemp milk
1 T. organic agave nectar

Blend all the ingredients and drink.

The cacao gives a huge boost in endorphins and antioxidants. The spinach provides mega green nutrients with little taste. The blueberries also provide antioxidants. The hemp milk is rich in omega-3. The agave will sweeten the whole concoction without jolting your glycemic index. After you drink it, you feel like superman.

SERVING UP: Lounge, dub, trip-hop, downtempo

A FEW INGREDIENTS: Rob Garza and Eric Hilton concocted the musical recipe that became Thievery Corporation in 1997 and have been heating things up ever since. The group's debut album, *Sounds from the Thievery Hi-Fi*, defined a new genre of electronic music for an international audience. Over the years, Rob and Eric have seasoned the pot with a growing cast of collaborators—musicians and vocalists who contribute to a dynamic fifteen-member live band.

With the help of their long-time partners the United Nations World Food Programme, Thievery Corporation also tries to open the ears, eyes, and minds of listeners. Their live shows mix music and culture with band members from all corners of the earth singing in Spanish, Portuguese, French, and other languages.

MORE TASTY MORSELS: thieverycorporation.com

THIEVERY CORPORATION'S CHARITY: United Nations World Food Programme, wfp.org

Main Attractions

POULTRY, MEATS, SEAFOOD, AND GAME

Chicken

Beef

Pork and Lamb

Seafood

Game

Bettye LaVette

SHOW DATE: 2008

SERVING UP: Soul, country, rock, gospel, funk

A FEW INGREDIENTS: When you want to both heat things up and cool them down, Bettye LaVette serves up just the right dish. Among her more notable recordings from her decades-long career are the sultry "He Made a Woman Out of Me" (later covered by Bobbie Gentry), the disco club hit "Doin' the Best That I Can," and "Hey Love," written for her by Stevie Wonder. Bettye also spent several years on Broadway and touring with the musical "Bubbling Brown Sugar" opposite Cab Calloway.

Bettye's 1972 album, *Child of the Seventies*, was re-titled and re-released as *Souvenirs* in 2000, and again reissued as *Child of the Seventies* in 2006. This led to a career revival that has so far included a live album and two new albums, including 2005's *I've Got My Own Hell to Raise*. Bettye won the Contemporary Blues Female Artist of the Year at the Blues Music Awards in 2008.

MORE TASTY MORSELS: bettyelavette.com

BETTYE'S CHARITY: The United Negro College Fund, uncf.org

Chicken Curry LaVette

2 boneless chicken breasts
1 can of creamed chicken soup
1 bunch of blanched broccoli florets
1 c. of grated cheddar cheese
1 c. of mayonnaise
½ tsp. of lemon juice
1 T. of curry powder
bread crumbs (seasoned or unseasoned)
butter
chicken broth

Poach 2 chicken breasts in a bit of chicken broth, until just done. Set aside.

In a bowl, mix the broccoli florets, can of soup, cheese, mayonnaise, lemon juice, and curry powder. Cube the chicken breasts and add that to the mixture. Blend together with a spoon.

Pour evenly into a buttered 9 × 13–inch 3-qt. baking dish. Sprinkle the top with bread crumbs. Drizzle the top lightly with butter.

Bake in preheated oven at 375° for 30 minutes, or until top is crispy brown and casserole is bubbly.

Christine Albert

SHOW DATE:
1994

Lily's Olive and White Wine Chicken

When Glenda invited me to contribute a recipe to *Music in the Kitchen*, I remembered a dish that my Parisian grandmother, Lily, used to prepare whenever she came to visit. I hadn't tasted it since my childhood but I always intended to revive the recipe. One evening in 1985, while visiting Lily in Paris, I even tape-recorded our dinner conversation and asked her to share with me how she made her Olive and White Wine Chicken. With this book, I finally found the motivation to dig out the cassette tape and transcribe the recipe. Twenty-two years later, and ten years after Lily's death, it was a gift to hear her voice and relive that special dinner. I hope that this easy, delicious French dish will bring *joie de vivre* to your table.

1 whole chicken
salt and pepper to taste
flour
2 T. olive oil
2 T. butter
1½ c. white wine
¼ c. chicken broth
10 pitted green olives
1½ tsp. tomato paste
1 c. mushrooms
1 T. heavy cream

Cut a small, whole chicken into parts. Cover liberally with salt and pepper, dredge in flour, and brown in olive oil and butter for 20–25 minutes (preferably in a cast-iron Dutch oven), turning halfway. When chicken is golden brown, add white wine, chicken broth, pitted olives, tomato paste, and salt and pepper to taste. Cover and let simmer for one hour, very slowly. Just before serving add one T. heavy cream. Serve over rice. Yield: 4 servings.

SERVING UP: Folk, rock, country, blues, bluegrass, and French music

A FEW INGREDIENTS: Like an expensive champagne served with the finest barbecue, Christine Albert blends two distinct cultures—French and Texan—in her music and her life. Christine, the "Texas Chanteuse," as she has been called, has performed and recorded both as part of Albert and Gage with her partner Chris Gage, and as a solo artist.

In 1992 she released *Texasfrance*, a bilingual album, followed that up with *Texasfrance Encore!* in 2003, and in 2008 she released *Paris, Texasfrance*. All three albums were critically acclaimed. *3rd Coast Magazine* said Christine has "one of the best and purest voices in Austin, Texas." When not on the road, Christine and Chris stay busy helping produce other artists, such as fellow Austinites Cowboy Johnson and Michael Austin, on their label MoonHouse Records.

MORE TASTY MORSELS: christinealbert.com
CHRISTINE'S CHARITY: Swan Songs, swansongs.org

Clay Walker

SHOW DATE: 1998

SERVING UP: Country

A FEW INGREDIENTS: Clay Walker started off playing Texas honky-tonks in the early 1990s, but has really turned up the heat and now has a career that really sizzles. To date, he has had a remarkable thirty-one songs on the *Billboard* Country Singles chart, and has earned four platinum and two gold records.

Clay never strays far from his Texas roots or the Lone Star lifestyle, despite being one of the busiest performers on the road. One of the accomplishments Walker is most proud of is having placed seventh in the cutting horse competition at the Houston Livestock Show and Rodeo, the largest rodeo in the United States.

MORE TASTY MORSELS: claywalker.com

CLAY'S CHARITY: Band Against MS, bandagainstms.org

Clay's "To Die For" Chicken

4 skinless, boneless chicken breasts
salt and pepper to taste
1 c. flour
2 T. vegetable oil
Amazing Sauce (recipe follows)

Place each piece of chicken in a Ziploc bag to avoid spatter and pound the larger side of the breast to even the thickness to about ¾ inch. Salt and pepper to taste. Dredge chicken through flour until evenly coated. Heat oil on medium-high heat. Place chicken in pan. (Do not use a nonstick pan because you will be using the drippings for my famous sauce.) Cook on each side until just golden brown. (Use a spatter screen, if you have one, to avoid hot oil spatter and mess.) Remove with tongs and leave any flakes in the pan that may fall off (to add flavor in the sauce). Avoid puncturing the breasts, which can dry out the meat. Remove skillet from heat. Place chicken in foil to keep warm and juicy until we have prepared the Amazing Sauce.

AMAZING SAUCE

2 T. oil
1 shallot or ½ bunch of scallions, finely chopped
1 c. chicken broth
½ c. dry vermouth or dry white wine (Vermouth is better. Trust me, it's worth a trip to the store.)
1 tsp. salt
½ c. heavy whipping cream

Heat oil over medium-high heat in the same skillet used for the chicken, which should have some bits of cooked flour stuck to it. Sauté the shallot until translucent, about 2–3 minutes. Pour in the chicken broth and vermouth and use a wooden spoon to scrape bits from bottom of pan over medium-high heat. Bring to a rolling boil. Add salt. Reduce until it just covers the bottom of pan at a depth of about ⅛ of an inch, about 15 minutes. Be patient, it's worth the wait. Add heavy cream, reduce heat, and stir about 1 minute. You are ready to eat! Serve over chicken.

Cory Morrow

SHOW DATE: 2003

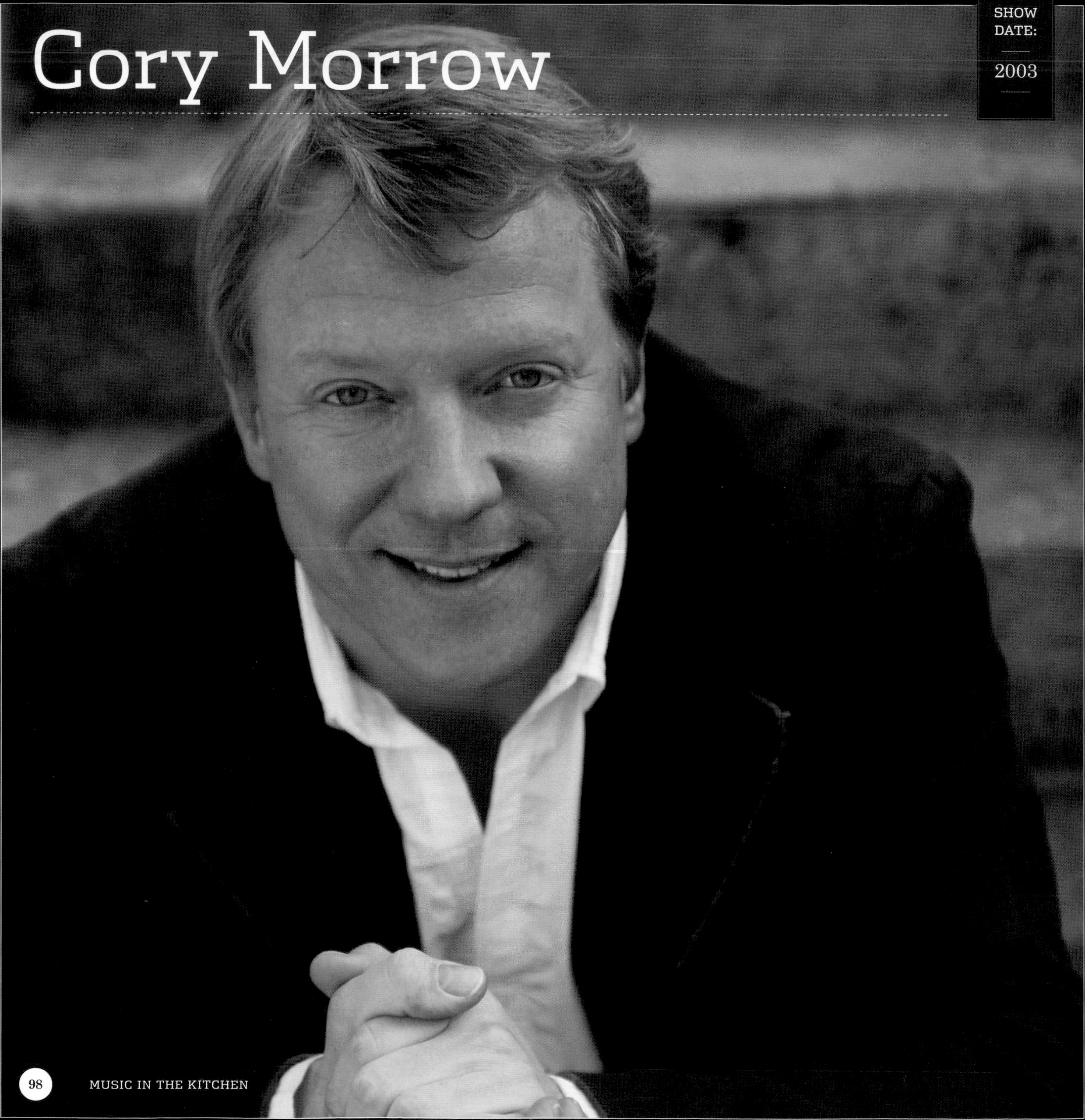

Granny's Chicken Casserole

cooking spray
asparagus tips
2–3 chicken breasts, steamed and chopped
2 or more cans of cream of chicken soup
3 T. softened margarine
1 T. lemon juice
breadcrumbs
yellow grated cheese

Grease a Pyrex dish with cooking spray. Line bottom with asparagus tips. Generously layer steamed chicken over the asparagus.

In a bowl, mix 2 or more cans of cream of chicken soup with softened margarine and lemon juice. Spread this mix generously over the chicken.

Spread breadcrumbs—toast some of your favorite bread and break it into small pieces—very generously and top with grated cheese.

Bake in the oven at 350° for 30 minutes. Voila! Granny's Chicken Casserole!

SERVING UP: Texas country

A FEW INGREDIENTS: In his more than fifteen years of writing and making music, native Texan and Austin resident Cory Morrow—along with college friend Pat Green—has stirred up a new recipe known as "Texas Country," a unique combination of country, swing, bluegrass, and blues. With his stripped-down, organic style Cory has sold over 200,000 albums independently, including *Outside the Lines*, which climbed several *Billboard* rankings: number twenty-eight on the Top Country Albums chart, number three on the Top Internet Albums chart, number eight on the Top Independent Albums chart, and number sixteen on the Top Heatseekers chart.

MORE TASTY MORSELS: corymorrow.com
CORY'S CHARITY: Dell Children's Medical Center of Central Texas, dellchildrens.net

Los Lonely Boys

SHOW DATES: 2004 2006

SERVING UP: Tejano, rock, blues

A FEW INGREDIENTS: Los Lonely Boys sound like they've been together all their lives—because they have. The three brothers—Henry, Jojo, and Ringo Garza—learned their chops from their father Enrique, a conjunto and country musician.

Los Lonely Boys recorded their debut album in 2003 in Austin at Willie Nelson's Pedernales recording studio. The single "Heaven" reached number one on the *Billboard* Adult Contemporary chart, and number sixteen on the *Billboard* Hot 100. The band has won fans and accolades for their musical mélange, including five Austin Music Awards in 2004, a Grammy in 2005 for Best Pop Performance by a Duo or Group, and Grammy nominations for Best New Artist, Record of the Year, and Best Rock Instrumental Performance that same year. In addition, Henry was named *Guitar World*'s 2005 Breakthrough Artist.

MORE TASTY MORSELS: loslonelyboys.org LOS LONELY BOYS' CHARITY: First Candle, firstcandle.org

Ringo's Rockin' Stir-fry

2 lb. boneless chicken thighs
water
fajita seasoning to taste
2 c. of white sushi rice
soy sauce to taste
1 bag baby carrots
1 bag of fresh ready-to-cook sugar snap peas
1 small orange bell pepper, sliced
1 small yellow bell pepper, sliced
1 T. sesame seeds

Cut chicken thigh meat into 1-inch-thick strips. Cook in cast-iron skillet on medium-high heat with 2 c. of water. Add a fistful of fajita spice or an amount to your liking. As water begins to evaporate, add more to keep chicken juicy. Continue to cook meat for about 30 minutes

Wash sushi rice until water runs clear. Put in pot. Add 2½ c. of water. Bring to a boil. Cover and simmer for 20 minutes. When rice is done, remove from heat. Let sit covered for 5 minutes.

Bring a few splashes of soy sauce and about ½ c. of water to a low boil in a pan. Sauté carrots on high heat for about 5 minutes. Stirring frequently, add sugar snap peas. Cook until they puff up, about 5 minutes. Add bell peppers and sesame seeds. Sauté additional 2–3 minutes until veggies are slightly tender.

Serve veggies over rice. Top with chicken. Enjoy!

Mary Cutrufello

SHOW DATES:

1997
1999

SERVING UP: Honky-tonk, rock

A FEW INGREDIENTS: Mary Cutrufello spent the 1990s in Texas, where her recipe for hard-driving honky-tonk and her hard-rocking guitar playing won her a loyal following, as well as kudos from the local media and two appearances on *Austin City Limits*. In 1996 Mary was featured on Jimmie Dale Gilmore's album, *Braver New World* and its subsequent tour. That same year Mary self-released her solo debut *Who to Love and When to Leave*, which showcased her gritty take on the honky-tonk tradition. After that came a move back to the rock music that Mary grew up on in the Midwest, and in 1998 she released the critically acclaimed *When the Night Is Through*. After being tragically sidelined with vocal nodes for a few years, Mary recovered and released *35* in 2006.

MORE TASTY MORSELS: marycutrufello.com

MARY'S CHARITY: National Trust for Historic Preservation, nationaltrust.org

Spicy Peanut Chicken over Rice

This recipe has a pretty big yield, but I find that the flavors marry if you don't eat it all right away. It's great the next day, and also freezes well. Keep the rice separate when freezing, though.

brown rice
1 T. peanut oil
1 medium onion, chopped
4 cloves garlic, minced
3 boneless, skinless chicken breasts, cut into small pieces
1 T. curry powder
½ tsp. salt
½ tsp. black pepper
1 tsp. crushed red pepper, or to taste (Here's the heat. You know what you like.)
6 c. chicken stock (You *are* using homemade stock, right?)
1 can tomato paste
5–6 roma tomatoes, diced
⅓ c. chunky peanut butter

Prepare the rice according to package directions. (Substituting chicken stock for the water is tasty.)

Heat the oil in a soup pot or Dutch oven over medium heat. Add the onion and garlic and sauté until translucent, about 5 minutes.

Add chicken and sauté until opaque.

Add curry powder, salt, pepper, crushed red pepper, chicken stock, tomato paste, tomatoes, and peanut butter.

Simmer to thicken. Serve over rice. Yield: 8 servings.

Pat Green

SHOW DATE: 2002

SERVING UP: Country

A FEW INGREDIENTS: Texas native Pat Green is a three-time Grammy nominee who prides himself on his fresh approach to stirring together a musical career from the grassroots up. His road to national recognition began with an appearance at Willie Nelson's Fourth of July Picnic in 1998, and Pat was soon playing sold-out shows in Texas, including at the Houston Astrodome and the Dallas Smirnoff Center. With ten studio albums, Pat's distinctive musical vision and songwriting style bolstered by a strong independent streak have taken the country by storm. His song "Wave on Wave" became a top three hit in 2003. In 2008, he released his first book, *Pat Green's Dance Halls & Dreamers*. The coffee-table book contains more than two hundred photographs of dance halls such as Gruene Hall, Luckenbach Dance Hall, Floore's Country Store and Schroeder Hall, as well as behind-the-scenes interviews with Texas music artists like Willie Nelson, Jack Ingram, Cross Canadian Ragweed, and Robert Earl Keen.

MORE TASTY MORSELS: patgreen.com
PAT'S CHARITY: American Red Cross, redcross.org

Chicken Squares

The Ultimate Bachelor's Meal

I'm the kind of guy who takes most cooking rather lightly. No recipe is sacred and everybody's tastes are different. So what I'm saying is, if you don't like how I make this just change it to suit your own belly.

- 1 skinless, boneless chicken breast
- 2 pkg. ⅓-less-fat cream cheese
- 1½ tsp. brown sugar
- 1 tsp. cayenne pepper
- salt and pepper to taste
- 1 can Pillsbury reduced-fat crescent rolls
- cooking spray
- ½ stick butter, melted
- breadcrumbs

Cook the chicken however you like: grill it, bake it, cook it in the microwave. Hell, it doesn't matter as long as it's fully cooked. I like to cook it with a little rosemary sometimes in the winter.

Chop the chicken into very small pieces and mix in a large bowl with the cream cheese until the chicken is evenly distributed. (For a lighter mixture, use only one package of cream cheese. But if you aren't worried about the fat content, leave the skin on the chicken, because damn, that's some tasty stuff.)

Add brown sugar, cayenne pepper, salt, and black pepper, and mix thoroughly. (This is where your own taste comes in: some folks might like a lot less cayenne pepper or a lot less sugar than is listed in the ingredients. Personally, I like the mixture of sweet and hot to be pretty equal. I also have used Tony Chachere's or Lawry's seasoning salt instead of the salt and pepper.)

Preheat the oven as directed on the Pillsbury crescent roll can. Each can of rolls makes 4 chicken squares. On a cookie sheet with some Pam on it, unroll each half of the raw dough and you will see 8 triangle shaped pieces. Each two-triangle section makes a rectangle that is diagonally perforated down the middle. Separate the sections and pinch the perforated edges together so that you have 4 rectangles. Take a couple tablespoons of the cream cheese and chicken mixture and place it at the center of each rectangle. Fold the rectangle in half and pinch it together on the sides. Using a fork, seal the open ends and completely enclose the chicken mixture. Brush melted butter on the top of each square and dust it with some breadcrumbs.

Finally, following the directions on the Pillsbury can, cook the squares. Once you take them out of the oven let them cool for 5 minutes—that concoction in the middle gets nuclear hot and will remove the top of your mouth if you aren't careful.

Served with a salad and a beer you have a good right-down-the-middle meal. Yummy good.

Patty Loveless

SHOW DATES:

1989
1994
1998
2001

Chicken in Yogurt Sauce

1 lb. boneless chicken breasts, halved
1 T. olive oil
½ c. onions, chopped
1 clove garlic, minced
1½ T. jalapeño peppers, seeded and finely chopped
⅛ tsp. cardamom
⅛ tsp. ground cloves
1 tsp. ground coriander
⅛ tsp. crushed red pepper
1 tsp. fresh ginger, finely grated
½ c. low-fat plain yogurt
¼ heavy cream

Cut chicken into 1-inch cubes and sauté in large skillet with olive oil for 2–3 minutes. Stir in onions, garlic, and jalapeño peppers; continue cooking for 2–3 minutes, or until chicken is no longer pink.

Reduce heat and stir in cardamom, cloves, coriander, crushed red pepper, grated ginger, and yogurt. Heat heavy cream in soup pot until hot and stir into pan. Serve over rice.

SERVING UP: Country, bluegrass

A FEW INGREDIENTS: Patty Loveless knows the key ingredient to a rich and satisfying career in country music is a heaping helping of classic country soul with a dash of bluegrass and mountain music. Patty's self-titled debut in 1987 marked her as a country traditionalist with decidedly contemporary appeal. Some of Patty's best-loved singles include "Blame it on Your Heart," "How Can I Help You Say Goodbye?," "Here I Am," "You Don't Even Know Who I Am," "Halfway Down," and "You Can Feel Bad." She received the CMA Awards for Female Vocalist of the Year and Album of the Year for her album *Fallen Angels Fly*. The Academy of Country Music presented the Female Vocalist of the Year Award to her two years in a row. Albums like *Trouble with the Truth*, *Long Stretch of Lonesome*, *Mountain Soul*, and *Sleepless Nights* solidified her reputation.

MORE TASTY MORSELS: pattyloveless.com
PATTY'S CHARITY: The Opry Trust Fund, opry.com/MeetTheOpry/OpryTrustFund.aspx

Richard Thompson

SHOW DATE: 2001

Olive Chicken

2 T. lemon zest
⅓ c. fresh lemon juice
2 T. olive oil
¼ c. + 2 T. rosemary
2 T. Italian parsley
salt and pepper to taste
3½ lb. chicken, cut into pieces
25 cloves garlic
¾ c. chicken broth
⅓ c. pitted green and black olives

Mix the lemon zest, lemon juice, and olive oil, herbs (save some parsley for garnish), salt, and lots of pepper. Marinate the chicken in this for a few hours before cooking.

Place the chicken and marinade in a roasting pan—one that can be brought to the table or can be transferred to a serving dish—add the garlic, and cook at 425° for approximately 40 minutes.

Remove from oven. Add chicken broth to the pan, and place on a stovetop burner set to medium-high. Stir, and scrape the bottom of the pan to loosen the browned bits. Add olives and cook for a few minutes. Garnish with the parsley and serve.

SERVING UP: Folk-rock, rock, electric folk

A FEW INGREDIENTS: Richard Thompson has been stirring the musical pot since he was a teenage founding member of Fairport Convention in the 1960s. Fast forward forty years or so to find Richard named one of the top twenty guitarists of all time by *Rolling Stone* magazine and the recipient of both the Ivor Novello Award for songwriting and the 2006 BBC Lifetime Achievement Award. His work has been recorded by such artists as Bonnie Raitt, David Byrne, and Elvis Costello. Richard's astounding body of work encompasses over forty albums, including his 1991 Grammy-nominated album, *Rumor and Sigh*. He also dabbles in composing: he wrote the soundtrack for the documentaries *Grizzly Man* and *Dreams with Sharp Teeth*.

MORE TASTY MORSELS: richardthompson-music.com
RICHARD'S CHARITY: The Organization for Tropical Studies, otis.duke.edu

Rosanne Cash

SHOW DATES:

1983
1986
1988
1992
1994
2003

Roast Lemon Chicken with Carrots and Onions

This recipe was adapted from Nigella Lawson.

3–3½ lb. whole organic chicken
butter
salt
olive oil
1 lemon
2 medium onions
4 large carrots

Preheat oven to 425°, and place chicken in roasting pan.

Rub butter and salt on chicken and drizzle with olive oil. Cut lemon in half and insert in cavity of bird and drizzle a little on outside as well. Chop onions and carrots, and spread around chicken. Place roasting pan in preheated oven and cook for 1¼ hours.

Transfer chicken and vegetables to platter; squeeze other half of lemon over chicken and add a bit more salt.

Add a little water to the juices in the pan, stir, then pour over chicken. Let sit a few minutes before serving. Yield: 3–4 servings.

SERVING UP: Country, folk, rock, blues

A FEW INGREDIENTS: A Grammy-winning singer-songwriter and the daughter of the legendary Johnny Cash, Rosanne has been serving up musical main dishes for over twenty-five years.

She has had eleven number one singles, and in 1988 she was named *Billboard*'s Top Singles Artist. Her most recent album, *Black Cadillac*, released in 2006, was nominated for a Grammy award for Best Contemporary Folk/Americana Album. Her first book, *Bodies of Water*, was published in 1995, and was followed by a children's book, *Penelope Jane: A Fairy's Tale* in 2000. Her essays and fiction have appeared in the *New York Times*, *Rolling Stone*, *The Oxford-American*, *New York Magazine*, among others. She is currently working on a book of nonfiction that will be published by Viking in 2008.

MORE TASTY MORSELS: rosannecash.com
ROSANNE'S CHARITY: PAX Real Solutions to Gun Violence, paxusa.org

Roy Rogers

SHOW DATE: 2002

SERVING UP: Country

A FEW INGREDIENTS: Roy Rogers is a slide guitarist who has been nominated for two Grammy Awards for his playing and six for his work as a producer for John Lee Hooker and Ramblin' Jack Elliott. He has been nominated for the W.C. Handy Award for Best Blues Guitarist on multiple occasions. Roy has appeared at festivals and special events around the world, including Montreux Jazz in Switzerland, the North Sea Jazz Festival in Holland, the Byron Bay Festival in Australia, and the Montreal Jazz Festival in Canada. Richard's music has been featured in numerous film and TV soundtracks, most notably *One Flew Over the Cuckoo's Nest* and *The Hot Spot*, which he recorded with Miles Davis, John Lee Hooker, and Taj Mahal and garnered a Grammy nomination.

MORE TASTY MORSELS: roy-rogers.com
ROY'S CHARITIES: Amnesty International, amnesty.org, New Orleans Musicians' Clinic, neworleansmusiciansclinic.org

Chicken and Rice with Parmesan

This is a basic recipe from my mother with added ingredients from me! I prefer to use all organic ingredients.

4 chicken breasts, skinned, boned, halved
olive oil
1 c. celery, chopped
1 c. crimini mushrooms, chopped
2 large cloves garlic, pressed
1 can celery soup
1 can mushroom soup
2 c. uncooked rice
3¾ c. chicken stock
1½ pkg. dry onion soup mix
salt and pepper to taste
shredded Parmesan cheese to taste

Sear and brown chicken breasts in olive oil.

In a 10 × 13–inch casserole dish, combine celery, mushrooms, garlic, celery soup, mushroom soup, rice, chicken stock, salt, and pepper. Mix thoroughly. Place halved chicken breasts in mixture. Top with onion soup mix and Parmesan cheese. Cover dish with foil.

Bake at 400° for 15 minutes. Decrease temperature to 350° for 65–75 minutes. Remove foil and bake for a final 10 minutes, or until golden crispy brown. Yield: 4–6 servings.

Ruthie Foster

SHOW DATE: 2003

SERVING UP: Americana, folk, gospel

A FEW INGREDIENTS: With her powerhouse voice and her stunning blend of contemporary folk music and old-school gospel and blues, Ruthie is often compared to Ella Fitzgerald and Aretha Franklin. After touring with the United States Navy Band Pride and spending a few years in New York City, Ruthie returned to her native Texas in 1993. Her live shows have taken her from the Kerrville Folk Festival to festivals in America and Europe. Her albums include *Crossover* (2001), *Runaway Soul* (2003), *Stages* (2004), *Woke Up this Mornin'* (2005), and *The Phenomenal Ruthie Foster* (2007).

MORE TASTY MORSELS: ruthiefoster.com

RUTHIE'S CHARITY: Town Lake Animal Shelter, ci.austin.tx.us/tlac/adopt.htm

Braised Chicken Curry (Gai Goh-Lae)

This recipe is from southern Thailand. Anything "southern" is a yes in my kitchen! I love to use this recipe as the "welcome to my home" meal. I am a true believer of what Dr. Maya Angelou claims when she says that the personality of a person, what they say, believe in, and who and what they love gets completely enveloped into their home, the walls, the curtains, everything. So this has become a special meal I prepare for close friends who come and bless my home with their presence.

Make the time to toast a little ground cumin, curry powder, cinnamon, and coriander in a small skillet beforehand then add a bit of curry paste to the mixture after it's browned a bit to get started.

Like most terrific recipes, if there are any leftovers, the second day of tasting is even better the first! For me this recipe is a nice mix of spicy southern cooking; it starts off a bit greasy but once the aroma from the seasonings kick in you'll want to open all your windows and call all your friends. Plus it's just a wonderfully yummy way to turn a house into a home. Happy eatin' y'all!

2 T. vegetable oil
2 lb. chicken thighs (or any combination of chicken pieces)
3 T. yellow curry paste (or 3 T. red curry paste plus 1 T. curry powder)
1½ c. unsweetened coconut milk
2½ c. chicken broth
2 T. fish sauce
2 T. freshly squeezed lime juice
1 T. palm sugar or brown sugar

Heat vegetable oil over medium-high heat in a 3-qt. saucepan. Brown chicken pieces in two batches, turning it once or twice until golden. This may get a bit messy, so you might want to invest in a skillet screen that cuts back on spattering grease! Transfer chicken to a medium bowl.

Reduce the heat to medium then add curry paste to saucepan. Stir and mash until the paste is softened, about 2 minutes. Return the chicken to saucepan, adding coconut milk and chicken broth. Bring to gentle boil, cooking for 15–20 minutes until chicken is tender and cooks through. Stir in fish sauce, lime juice, and sugar then remove from heat. Transfer to a serving bowl. Serve with any combinations of mixed vegetables and rice or even beans.

Taj Mahal

SHOW DATES:

1979
1993

SERVING UP: Blues, world music

A FEW INGREDIENTS: Trying to describe legendary musician Taj Mahal is like trying to describe a sumptuous feast. This multi-talented man is like an entire meal unto himself. Taj Mahal has been playing his distinctive brand of music—a combination of African, Cuban, Latin, Hawaiian, and Caribbean sounds layered on top of a solid country and blues foundation—for more than forty years.

He won a Grammy Award for Best Contemporary Blues Album in 1997 for *Señor Blues* and again in 2000 for *Shoutin' in Key*. More than just a musician, Taj Mahal is an explorer with an abiding interest in tracing American musical styles back to their roots in Africa and Europe. His global perspective reflects his passions and his travels.

MORE TASTY MORSELS: tajblues.com
TAJ MAHAL'S CHARITY: Special Olympics, specialolympics.org

Roasted Jerk Chicken

2 6–7½ lb. free-range chickens
2–3 lemons
jerk seasoning
curry powder
1 doz. medium red-skinned potatoes, halved
1 doz. dasheen, peeled
8 medium carrots, sliced lengthwise
1 elephant garlic bulb, peeled and sliced
1 clove garlic, peeled and crushed
1 bunch green onions, chopped
3 large yellow onions, cut into rings
4 bunches cilantro
2 boxes Bell's seasoning

Wash and rinse chicken the night before, remove giblets (neck, heart, and gizzard). Squeeze 2–3 lemons over chickens. Rub jerk seasoning very generously over chickens, including inside the body cavity. Shake a little more jerk seasoning along with curry powder and Bell's seasoning over chickens. Place chickens in large container in refrigerator overnight. Place all vegetables into large container and sprinkle with dry jerk seasoning until well coated. Then sprinkle 2 T. of Bell's seasoning and 2 T. of curry powder, and refrigerate overnight.

The next day, place chickens on a large platter and rub down with jerk rub and dry seasonings for good measure.

Place onions in roaster pan along with 2 bunches of cilantro, half of elephant garlic, and half of regular garlic. Place chickens in roaster and surround with potatoes, dasheens, carrots, onions, green onions, and both garlic around chicken.

Place any leftover garlic, onions, and cilantro in cavity of chickens. Add 6–8 oz. of water and cover with lid.

Preheat oven to 450° for 15 minutes. Reduce temp to 425°. Cook chickens for 25 minutes, then reduce temperature to 375° and cook until you can smell jerk chicken 2 rooms away, about an hour and a half. Chicken should fall from the bone and the vegetables should be soft but not mushy. Yield: 8 servings.

Deana Carter

SHOW DATE:

1999

Easy Baked Chicken

1 lb. chicken breast tenders
black pepper
red pepper flakes
¼ c. of soy or teriyaki sauce
1 small can of crushed pineapple
½ small white onion, chopped
splash of white wine (optional)

Spray glass baking pan with cooking spray to avoid sticking. Wash chicken and place flat in pan. Lightly coat the chicken with black and red pepper—you can leave out the red pepper if spice is not your thing. Add soy or teriyaki sauce to pan (or you can combine these, but don't make it too watery).

Distribute the pineapple evenly around and over the chicken so that it's lightly covered. Place onion pieces in and around chicken. Add splash of white wine.

Cover pan with foil and bake at 350° for about 45 minutes, making sure the chicken is done all the way through. When done, pull out of oven and keep covered until ready to serve. Bon appetit and God's blessings!

SERVING UP: Country

A FEW INGREDIENTS: Like strawberry wine, the music of Deana Carter is sweet and makes you want to come back for more. It's no surprise, then, that her song "Strawberry Wine," from her quintuple platinum debut *Did I Shave My Legs for This?*, began Deana's journey to commercial and critical successes; it shot to number one and won the Country Music Association Award for Single of the Year in 1997. To date, she has had three singles reach number one on the *Billboard* country charts: "Strawberry Wine," "How Do I Get There," and "We Danced Anyway."

Deana's music was also included on the soundtracks for the movies *Hope Floats* and *Anastasia*, the latter of which yielded nominations for both a Grammy and a Golden Globe for her song "Once Upon a December."

MORE TASTY MORSELS: deanacarter.com

DEANA'S CHARITY: University Kidney Disease Research Association, Los Angeles, California, universitykidneyresearch.org

Calexico

SHOW DATE:

2006

Boeuf Bourguignon

Submitted by John Convertino

I got this recipe from a true Parisian, my friend Naim Amor. It had been handed down to him from his father, a true Parisian as well. It is fun to make with Edith Piaf playing in the background, plenty of French wine, and a hearty appetite. This is it as it is written by the old man.

1 large onion
beef chuck, cut into 2-inch pieces
olive oil
1 T. flour
1 glass wine
salt and pepper to taste
herbs (thyme, bay leaf, etc.) to taste
water
potatoes, peeled and halved
2 carrots

Cook onion, cut in big chunks, in olive oil. Add meat and cook until golden. Add flour and a glass of (cheap) wine, and turn until well mixed. Add salt and herbs, and cover with water. Boil and reduce heat to a soft cook for 45 minutes. Add potatoes and carrots. Cook for 30 minutes. Serve with baguette.

OPTIONS

You can add a piece of bacon, it's popular but not an obligation. Mushrooms are another optional ingredient. And don't put in too many carrots—makes it too sweet.

SERVING UP: Rock, indie rock, alt-country

A FEW INGREDIENTS: Calexico stirs up music that reflects and celebrates their home of Tucson, Arizona, and the American Southwest. Their unique blend of Tex-Mex, folk-rock, and rumbling guitars, is as much art as it is music—it paints pictures of sun-scorched rocks and windswept deserts of the border country. Their debut album, *Spoke*, was released in 1996, and was quickly followed by *The Black Light*, which was released in 1998 and was selected by the *Wall Street Journal* as one of the best records of the year. Since 2000, they have released *Hot Rail*, *Feast of Wire*, and *Garden Ruin*, with each album using a different recipe for success.

MORE TASTY MORSELS: casadecalexico.com

Gary P. Nunn

SHOW DATES:

1983
1989
1995

SERVING UP: Country

A FEW INGREDIENTS: If Texas music and culture are the main course, Gary P. Nunn is the cold Lone Star beer that accompanies it. In 1972, Gary—along with Michael Martin Murphey, Jerry Jeff Walker, and Willie Nelson—helped usher in a new genre of country music dubbed "outlaw music." He led the Lost Gonzo Band and composed tunes that were recorded by Willie Nelson, Jerry Jeff Walker, Michael Martin Murphey, Rosanne Cash, David Allan Coe and others. His songwriting skills have earned him several gold and platinum records for writing, publishing, and performing. He was appointed Ambassador to the World by then Texas Governor Mark White in 1985, and has his name on the West Texas Walk of Fame.

MORE TASTY MORSELS: garypnunn.com

GARY'S CHARITY: Cal Farley's Boys Ranch® and Girlstown, U.S.A.®, calfarley.org

Pastitsio (Baked Macaroni with Meat Filling)

PASTA

1 medium onion, chopped
2 cloves garlic, chopped
1 T. olive oil
3 T. butter, divided
1½ lb. ground beef
1 can tomato paste
¾ c. water
salt and pepper to taste
dash of cinnamon
1 T. freshly grated nutmeg
1 lb. elbow macaroni
1 c. grated cheese (Parmesan, Reggiano, or Kassen)
Béchamel Sauce (prepare ahead; recipe follows)

Preheat oven to 425°.

Sauté onion and garlic in olive oil and 1 T. butter; add ground meat and cook until brown; add tomato paste thinned with ¾ c. water. Add seasoning: salt, pepper, dash of cinnamon, and 10 grates of nutmeg. Cook until meat is done, remove from heat. Cook macaroni in boiling salted water al dente, drain water, and return to pot. To keep the noodles from sticking add 2 T. butter to the pot and sprinkle grated cheese. Mix until butter is melted.

Put a small amount of meat sauce in the bottom of a 10 × 15–inch pan, cover with half of the noodles and sprinkle with grated cheese. Top with remaining meat sauce, then cover with remaining noodles. Add the rest of the cheese, pour the béchamel sauce evenly over noodles, and gently shake pan to allow sauce to penetrate.

Bake in 425° oven until top is golden brown, about 30 minutes. Serve with a green salad, and enjoy!

BÉCHAMEL SAUCE

4 c. milk
1 stick butter
½ c. flour
2 egg yolks
½ c. grated cheese
freshly grated nutmeg
salt and pepper to taste

Put milk in a pan and warm over low heat. In a bigger pot melt butter, but don't let it brown. Whisk in flour and cook 3–4 minutes, stirring constantly. Gradually add the warm milk and continue whisking until the sauce thickens. In a small bowl, beat 2 egg yolks, slowly adding some of the warm sauce to the eggs to temper, and stir. Add egg mixture to sauce along with grated cheese, nutmeg, salt, and pepper to taste, heat a couple of minutes.

It has been an honor to have *Austin City Limits* use my tune, "London Homesick Blues," as its theme song for more than thirty years of outstanding broadcasting.

—Gary P. Nunn

Holly Dunn

SHOW DATES:

1988
1992

SERVING UP: Country

A FEW INGREDIENTS: Like a ripe tomato squeezed too hard, Holly Dunn burst onto the country music scene in the mid-1980s with her debut single, "Daddy's Hands," which earned her one of three Grammy nominations. She was named Best New Female Vocalist in 1986 by the Academy of Country Music, received the Horizon Award in 1987 from the Country Music Association, was inducted into the Grand Ole Opry Cast, and was awarded Songwriter of the Year in 1989 by BMI. Holly has recorded ten albums and fourteen of her singles have reached the top ten on the *Billboard* chart, four of them hitting number one. Her *Greatest Hits* album was certified gold shortly after its release in 1991. Holly has retired from full-time performing and now focuses her talent and creative energy on painting.

MORE TASTY MORSELS: hollydunn.com
HOLLY'S CHARITY: Second Harvest Food Bank of Middle Tennessee, secondharvestnashville.org

Meatloaf-Hater's Meatloaf

I used to hate meatloaf until I tried this! It's never dry and the liquid smoke gives it great flavor.

1 small onion, diced
8 oz. raw mushrooms, diced
1 egg, beaten
1 lb. ground beef or turkey
1 c. seasoned breadcrumbs
1 T. liquid smoke
½ T. pepper
½ T. salt
½ T. garlic powder
1 c. tomato sauce or ketchup

Sauté onion and mushrooms until softened. Drain and set aside. In a large mixing bowl, beat 1 egg. Add all ingredients to bowl (except tomato sauce or ketchup) and mix together. This may require using your hands. If the mixture feels too dry, add a little tomato sauce or ketchup. If it feels too wet add more breadcrumbs. You should be able to form a loaf that sticks together.

Put your meatloaf mixture in a greased baking dish (square or rectangle) and form a loaf. Pour the tomato sauce or ketchup over the top and bake for 1 hour at 375°.

You may cover the top with foil if it is getting too brown. Yield: 8 servings.

Jason Mraz

SHOW DATE: 2003

SERVING UP: Pop, rock, adult contemporary

A FEW INGREDIENTS: Jason Mraz whisks pop and rock together with many other musical ingredients, including folk, jazz, country, reggae, and hip-hop. He has played with musicians such as the Rolling Stones, Bob Dylan, Dave Matthews Band, Alanis Morissette, and Jewel. His debut release, *Waiting for My Rocket to Come*, was certified platinum and reached number two on *Billboard*'s Top Heatseekers chart. He was also selected as Artist of the Year and received Song of the Year from the San Diego Music Awards in 2003. In 2005 he released *Mr. A–Z*, which earned him a Grammy nomination in the category of Best Engineered Album, Non-Classical. His single "I'm Yours" reached number one on Triple A Radio charts in 2008 and became his first top-ten hit on the *Billboard* Hot 100. In addition, Jason's album *We Sing. We Dance. We Steal Things.* was certified gold.

MORE TASTY MORSELS: jasonmraz.com.
JASON'S CHARITY: Make-a-Wish Foundation of America, wish.org

Mraz's Mom's Meatloaf

This is a family recipe that's easy to make. After you do it once you'll see how easy it is to substitute the ingredients and make it true to your own taste bud's craving. I prefer to use lean meat and organic vegetables whenever available.

1 lb. ground beef
½ lb. ground veal
½ lb. ground pork
2 eggs, beaten slightly
2 T. Worcestershire sauce
1 small green bell pepper, chopped
1 small Vidalia onion, chopped
1 c. Italian breadcrumbs
¼ c. ketchup
1 can organic tomato sauce
parsley flakes

Mix first 9 ingredients well with ¾ of tomato sauce. Form into loaf in loaf pan and top with remaining sauce. Sprinkle with parsley flakes.

Bake in loaf pan for 50–60 minutes at 350°. Use dripping to make tomato-based gravy. Yield: 1 loaf.

Miranda Lambert

SHOW DATE: 2005

Miranda's Mom's Almost-Famous Meatloaf

2 lb. ground beef or ground venison
1 lb. breakfast sausage
½ sleeve of saltines or Ritz crackers, crushed
½ c. brown sugar
1½ c. ketchup
1 T. mustard
1 T. Worcestershire sauce
½ onion, chopped
½ bell pepper, chopped
2 eggs
Gravy (recipe follows)

Mix up all ingredients well with hands and put into baking dish or cake pan. Bake at 350° for 1 hour. Remove pan from oven and drain grease (reserve for gravy drippings).

Mix 1 c. ketchup and ¼ c. brown sugar together in bowl. Spread over meatloaf and return to oven for 20 minutes or until topping thickens. Make extra glaze and save a little if you're making gravy! Yield: 1 loaf.

SERVING UP: Country

A FEW INGREDIENTS: In 2005 Miranda Lambert lit all four burners and then some with her nearly platinum-selling debut *Kerosene*, which reached the top of the country charts and the critics' polls. She was merely a teenager when the album came out and had written or co-written eleven of the CD's twelve songs.

Her follow-up album in 2007, *Crazy Ex-Girlfriend*, was a two-time Country Music Horizon Award nominee. Miranda became a household name as a finalist in the 2003 season of *Nashville Star*, the television series. She was nominated for the CMA Horizon Award and the ACM Top New Female Vocalist Award, as well as a Grammy nomination for Best Female Country Vocal Performance.

MORE TASTY MORSELS: mirandalambert.com
MIRANDA'S CHARITY: The Humane Society of East Texas, hsoet.org

GRAVY

½ c. grease
¼ c. flour
remaining ketchup and brown sugar mixture
½ c. water
salt and pepper to taste
ketchup to taste

Put about ½ c. of grease into a skillet on medium heat. Mix in ¼ c. flour and stir until it forms a paste. Add the remaining ketchup and brown sugar mixture (about ¼–½ c.) to skillet. Add ½ c. water. Stir in salt, pepper, ketchup to taste. Remove from heat when it starts to bubble. It will thicken upon standing. Serve with mashed potatoes!

Joe Cocker

SHOW DATE: 2000

Joe's Shepherd's Pie

1 medium onion, chopped
2 cloves garlic, crushed
2 T. oil
1½ lb. extra-lean ground beef
salt and pepper to taste
2 tsp. cayenne pepper
2 medium tomatoes, chopped
1½ c. water
1 beef bouillon cube
1 T. Worcestershire sauce
2 T. cornstarch
4 c. mashed potatoes (prepare ahead)
butter
shredded cheese

Sauté onion and garlic in oil, add the extra-lean ground beef, and cook until browned. Season with salt, pepper, and cayenne pepper.

Mix water, bouillon cube, and Worcestershire sauce. Add half of this mixture to the beef and simmer slowly for about 20 minutes. Add chopped tomatoes and cook 10 more minutes.

Add cornstarch to the remaining water mixture and stir well. Add this to the meat mixture and mix well. Cook 10 more minutes.

Place in shallow casserole dish or deep pie dish. Cover with mashed potatoes. Dot with butter and sprinkle with cheese. Place under broiler for a few minutes to brown top. Serve hot! Yield: 1 pie.

SERVING UP: Rock, blues

A FEW INGREDIENTS: With almost fifty years of stirring up the musical pot, Joe is truly one of the great and most recognized rock voices in history. Born in Sheffield, England, he has performed at Woodstock and on *The Ed Sullivan Show*. Joe's music has been featured in the movies *An Officer and a Gentleman* (the song, a duet with Jennifer Warnes titled "Up Where We Belong," won a Grammy), *9½ Weeks*, *Harry and the Hendersons*, *Bull Durham*, and *An Innocent Man*. In 1991 he recorded "Sorry Seems to Be the Hardest Word" for the Elton John and Bernie Taupin tribute album, *Two Rooms*, which has sold over three million copies to date. He has played for British royalty, Nelson Mandela's birthday, and at the inauguration of George W. Bush.

MORE TASTY MORSELS: cocker.com
JOE'S CHARITY: The Cocker Kids' Foundation, cocker.com

Monte Warden

SHOW DATES:

1988
1994

SERVING UP: Country, rockabilly, honky-tonk

A FEW INGREDIENTS: Austinite Monte Warden started gathering ingredients for his musical career when he was just fifteen years old. After coming to national attention as a member of the Wagoneers, Monte launched his solo career in the early 1990s, with his self-titled solo debut. It was named one of the one hundred best American albums of the twentieth century by *NME* magazine. Monte's most recent successes have come as a songwriter, selling millions of records, landing cuts in several movies and television shows, and composing songs for artists like Kelly Willis, Patty Loveless, George Jones, Bruce Robison, Travis Tritt, and George Strait, to name a few. He co-wrote Strait's smash "Desperately," which helped him win his first BMI Country Songwriting Award in 2005. In March 2006 he was awarded the prestigious BMI Million-Air Award, signifying over one million radio performances of his song, "Desperately." He's a local favorite too, having won seven Austin Music Awards.

MORE TASTY MORSELS: clickdesign.com/montewarden

MONTE'S CHARITY: Buddy Walk for Down Syndrome, buddywalk.org

Mama Burgers

My wife Brandi, whom we all call Mama, said she's never measured anything she puts into these burgers, but will do her best to come up with the recipe. They are the best burgers you've ever put in your mouth and anyone who disagrees with that statement is either a liar or a vegan and I have no time for either!

3 lb. lean ground beef or ground turkey
1 large yellow onion
5–6 cloves garlic
1 bunch fresh cilantro
3 jalapeños, seeded
salt and pepper to taste
Worcestershire sauce

Place meat in a large bowl. Place next 4 ingredients in a food processor and finely chop. Add to meat. Add salt, pepper, and enough Worcestershire sauce to make really juicy. Pat into thick burgers and grill on the outside grill or on a grill pan inside. Serve with your favorite toppings on a whole grain bun and enjoy! Yield: 8 burgers.

When my band, The Wagoneers, first appeared on *Austin City Limits* back in 1988, it was such a career highlight. Growing up in Austin, I'd also grown up watching that show and dreaming of being on there and performing my music someday. When I did, my whole family was there, including my elderly grandparents who made the drive all the way in from Houston to attend the taping. It immediately put me on the artistic map (and eased my grandparents' worried minds about the vocation I had chosen). *Austin City Limits* has always been and continues to be the gold standard for live music on television. I cherish my two tapings of the show.

—Monte Warden

Robbie Fulks

SHOW DATE:

1998

SERVING UP: Alt-country

A FEW INGREDIENTS: Robbie Fulks prefers throwing away the cookbook and creating his own recipes, with serious country music sprinkled with song spoofs, improvised rearrangements of his own music, and tongue-in-cheek humor. His debut album, *Country Love Songs*, was released in 1996, and was followed quickly by *South Mouth*, in 1997.

Robbie's single, "Fountains of Wayne Hotline," became a hit with fans and musicians alike. The song—which created an imaginary hotline songwriters could dial up for advice when having trouble—was called, "one of the most spot-on musical commentaries in recent years" by NPR.

MORE TASTY MORSELS: robbiefulks.com

ROBBIE'S CHARITY: American Cancer Society, cancer.org

Julia Child's Pot Roast

Raw basics, no fuss: the stuff of good cooking and good country music. But over the last twenty or so years, with the popularization if not beatification of Puck and Panisse, et al., it seems to me that California has done to American food what Nashville did to country: taken out the twang.

Julia Child never lost sight of the twang and the ecstasy (go ahead and use that, Wayne Hancock), even if her reputation as a Francophile and palate-uplifter implied otherwise. This pot roast (*boeuf a la mode*, if you sniff your finger) is so good that not only have I made it at least two dozen times, for all kinds of festive and family occasions (note distinction), I've continued to make it for others even after quitting meat myself. It never fails.

- 5 lb. rump roast (or any 5 lb. roast or round cut)
- salt and pepper
- 2 carrots, thinly sliced
- 2 celery stalks, thinly sliced
- 1 large yellow onion, thinly sliced
- 2 cloves garlic
- 1 T. thyme
- 2 bay leaves
- ¼ c. parsley, chopped
- 2 bottles red wine (e.g., Cotes du Rhone)
- ⅓ c. brandy
- ½ c. olive oil
- 4 T. cooking oil
- 4 or 6 marrow bones
- 3 or 4 slices of bacon
- 8–10 c. beef stock
- 1 T. cornstarch
- 2 T. Madeira or port

Rub the meat with salt and pepper. Put it in a bowl with half the vegetables and herbs under it and half over. Pour the wine, brandy, and olive oil over the meat. Cover and let it marinate overnight, 8–12 hours (or in the refrigerator for 24 hours). Turn and baste every so often.

Preheat oven to 350°. Drain the meat on a rack (preserving the marinade) and dry it thoroughly with paper towels. Heat cooking oil in a roaster that will hold the meat comfortably, with a few inches to spare between it and the pan. When the oil is about to smoke, put in the meat and brown all sides. Remove the meat, pour out the fat, return the meat, and pour in the marinade. Boil it down at high heat until it's reduced by about half, then add the bones and bacon. Add beef stock, enough to almost reach the top of the meat. Bring to a simmer, skim, cover tightly, and set on a lower rack in the oven.

Turn the meat every 20–30 minutes. It will be done in about 3 hours, or whenever the meat flakes off easily at the stab of a fork.

When the meat is done, remove it from the pan. Put it on the serving platter and keep it warm during the 10–15 minutes remaining. Skim the marinade then strain it, pressing the juice out of the vegetables with a potato masher or other tool. Boil down the marinade until it has reduced by half. Taste and correct seasoning. Unless the sauce is already thick, mix cornstarch and Madeira and beat it in, simmering for another 3 minutes. Cover meat with sauce and slice with an electric or a very sharp knife—it will be so tender that any blunter tool will only break it apart. Yield: 10 servings (or 3 servings, if your guests are Texan).

T. G. Sheppard

SHOW DATE: 1983

T. G. Sheppard's Baked Spaghetti

SERVING UP: Country, countrypolitan

A FEW INGREDIENTS: T. G. can be hot and saucy, with hit songs like "Last Cheater's Waltz" and "I Loved 'Em Every One," but he has a softer side, too, as he proved with "I Fooled Around and Fell In Love." It's a recipe that has worked for him, because T. G. is one of the most consistently played artists on country radio today, with seventeen number one singles to his credit. T. G. enjoys live performances more than anything else, which has made him a fan favorite.

MORE TASTY MORSELS: tgsheppard.com
T. G.'S CHARITY: St. Jude Children's Research Hospital, stjude.org

1 c. onions, chopped
1½ lb. ground chuck
¼ lb. sausage
garlic powder
2 T. cooking oil
1 (6-oz.) can tomato paste
1 (6-oz.) can tomato sauce
3½ c. tomato juice
1 tsp. salt
¼ tsp. pepper
1 tsp. oregano
8 oz. spaghetti
1 lb. sliced mozzarella cheese
½ c. Parmesan cheese

Brown onion, meat, sausage, and garlic powder in oil; drain off excess oil. Add remaining sauces and seasonings; simmer for 1 hour. In the meantime, boil the spaghetti.

In baking dish, put a thin layer of the meat sauce in the bottom, then a layer of noodles, another of sauce, and then cheeses.

Repeat until all ingredients are used, ending with cheese on top. Bake at 300° for 40 minutes. Yield: 4 servings.

Bloc Party

SHOW DATE: 2007

SERVING UP: Alternative rock, indie rock, art punk

A FEW INGREDIENTS: UK band Bloc Party whips up a sound similar to the Cure, Blur, the Smashing Pumpkins, the Pixies and Joy Division. The indie rock band, made up of members Kele Okereke, Russell Lissack, Gordon Moakes, and Matt Tong, released their debut album, *Silent Alarm*, in 2005. It was certified platinum a year later, and made *NME*'s Album of the Year list. Their second album, *A Weekend in the City*, was released in 2007 and peaked at number two in the UK and number twelve on the *Billboard* 200. They have played venues large and small all over the world including the Fillmore, Lollapalooza, the Fuji Festival, and Circo Voador in Sao Paulo, Brazil.

MORE TASTY MORSELS: blocparty.com

BLOC PARTY'S CHARITY: Lambi Fund of Haiti, lambifund.org

Pork with Ginger and Spring Onions

Submitted by Matt Tong

This is a variation of a recipe I saw in a Chinese cookbook, back in the days before the Internet when I couldn't afford cookbooks and had to go to bookstores and write down recipes into a notebook. I've tailored it somewhat because it looked a bit conservative to me. This is one of my favorite recipes because it's pretty hard to screw up and it's quite quick to do, and always impressive.

⅔ lb. to 1 lb. pork loin
2 T. sherry
2 T. light soy sauce
2 T. sesame oil
1 tsp. cornflour
8–10 spring onions
3-inch square of root ginger
1 tsp. salt
½ tsp. black pepper
1 tsp. dark muscovado sugar

Thinly slice the pork loin and put in a bowl. Pour in the sherry, soy sauce, and sesame oil. Add the cornflour and mix thoroughly. Leave the bowl in the fridge to marinate for half an hour while you prepare the rest of the ingredients.

Slice the spring onions into pieces approximately 3–4 inches in length. Thinly slice the root ginger. Don't worry about peeling it.

Heat a wok on a high heat. Don't worry about oil. Add the pork. Stir-fry the pork until it starts to expel some of its fat. This should take around 5–7 minutes and you'll know when it's ready because a sauce will start to form in the bottom of the wok. Add the ginger, salt, pepper, and sugar. Cook for another couple of minutes. Add the spring onion. Cook for another minute or so. You don't want it to get too soggy.

Serve with a bowl of rice and maybe a side of bok choi or something like that.

Suzy Bogguss

SHOW DATE: 1993

SERVING UP: Country, folk

A FEW INGREDIENTS: Suzy Bogguss has been cooking on all burners for nearly two decades, mixing up country, folk, pop, and jazz on nine studio albums and through countless miles on the road. She is a critically acclaimed vocalist, a sought-after songwriter, a successful record producer, and an accomplished guitarist. She has released one platinum album and three gold albums and has had six top-ten singles. In 1988 she won the ACM Top New Female Vocalist Award; in 1992 she received the CMA Horizon Award; and in 1994 she was honored with the CMA Album of the Year Award. A duet she recorded with Lee Greenwood, "Hopelessly Yours," went to number twelve on the country singles chart and received a Grammy Award nomination for Best Country Vocal.

Her 2003 album, *Swing*, includes performances by longtime friend Ray Benson, along with a number of other members of Asleep At The Wheel, past and present.

MORE TASTY MORSELS: bogguss.com

SUZY'S CHARITIES: Feeding America, feedingamerica.org, and the T.J. Martell Foundation, tjmartellfoundation.org

Rack of Lamb with Fig-Port Sauce

I love this dish with mashed potatoes and a combo of roasted green beans and baby carrots in garlic butter. Mmmmm . . . enjoy!

8 fresh mission figs, halved or quartered (dried or fresh)
1 c. tawny port
1 c. chicken stock
2 1¼-lb. racks of lamb, bones frenched
2 T. pure olive oil
salt and freshly ground pepper to taste
1 T. minced rosemary
1 T. minced thyme
1 tsp. balsamic vinegar

Preheat the oven to 450°. Place figs in port to soak. Bring chicken stock to boil and reduce by half.

Rub the lamb with 1 T. of the olive oil. Season with salt and pepper, and rub with rosemary and thyme.

Heat the remaining olive oil in a medium oven-proof skillet. Add the lamb, fat side down, and cook over high heat until browned, about 5 minutes. Turn and cook until lightly browned, about 1 minute. Add ½ c. of the port. Transfer the skillet to the oven and roast the lamb for about 15 minutes, or until a meat thermometer reads at least 125° (medium-rare).

Transfer the lamb to a carving board; cover loosely with foil. Add the remaining ½ c. of port and the figs to the skillet. Bring to a simmer, scraping up the browned bits from the bottom of the pan. Add the stock and vinegar and simmer over medium-high heat until thickened, about 5–7 minutes or until the liquid is reduced by half. Season with salt and pepper. Carve the racks into chops and set 3 or 4 on each plate. Top with the figs, spoon on the sauce, and serve. Yield: 4–6 servings.

Pam Tillis

SHOW DATES:

1993
1996
2000

SERVING UP: Country

A FEW INGREDIENTS: The daughter of country music legend Mel Tillis proved early on that she knows how to use the best of a favorite recipe and make it her own. Pam reached the top five on the *Billboard* country charts with "Don't Tell Me What to Do" from her second album *Put Yourself in My Place*, which was certified gold. Since then she has had more than thirty singles on the *Billboard* country charts, including her number one hit from 1995, "Mi Vida Loca (My Crazy Life)." She has released ten albums, and has earned three platinum and two gold certifications.

In 1994 she was named the CMA Female Vocalist of the Year. In 1999 she earned a Grammy Award for Best Country Collaboration with Vocals for "Same Old Train." Pam ranked at number thirty on CMT's *40 Greatest Women of Country Music* in 2002. On 2002's *It's All Relative*, a tribute to Mel Tillis, Pam sings a collection of her father's material—a project that finally found her embracing his legacy on her own terms.

Pam has also acted on stage and screen, and runs her own record label, Stellar Cat Records.

MORE TASTY MORSELS: pamtillis.com

PAM'S CHARITIES: The Red Cross, redcross.org, and Child Help, childhelp.org

Tillis's Georgia Ham

This is a Boston butt wrapped "en croute," or in crust. I added the au jus as my own touch—you could thicken this for gravy. Feel free to vary it, as everyone before you has done! It's also fantastic with mint jelly on the side.

- 5.5 lb. roast (if smaller, adjust proportions accordingly)
- 2 tsp. whole cloves
- 1 tsp. black peppercorns
- 2 bay leaves
- water
- Dough (prepare at least an hour before roast is done; recipe follows)
- Sage-Garlic Rub (prepare ahead; recipe follows)
- salt and pepper
- Au Jus (prepare ahead; recipe follows)

Put roast in stockpot. Add cloves, peppercorns, and bay leaves to water, and oover roast. (Save this water for the Au Jus.) Boil for 30 minutes then reduce heat and simmer. Check at 2 hours—temperature should reach 175°. Remove from heat.

Roll dough on floured counter to ½-inch thickness—roughly the size of a large pizza. Put on a large baking sheet and lay roast on top. Rub the top and sides of roast with the Sage-Garlic Rub. Salt and pepper well. Pull dough over top of roast and enclose, pinching edges.

Bake at 400° for 15–18 minutes, or until dough is a light golden-brown. Take out and brush with melted butter. Dust with paprika if desired. Serve with Au Jus.

DOUGH

- 1 pkg. fast-acting yeast
- ¼ tsp. salt
- ¼ c. + ¾ c. water
- ¼ c. + 2¼ c. flour

Mix all ingredients thoroughly in mixing bowl until spongy. Then sprinkle 1 T. flour on top. Set in a warm, draft-free spot (the oven works well—but don't turn on!). This will double in approximately 30 minutes.

Transfer to bread mixer. Add 2¼ c. flour and a little over ¾ c. water. Knead with dough hook until shiny, slightly sticky. Not a tight or stiff dough. Set aside until roast reaches 175°.

SAGE-GARLIC RUB

- 1 oz. sage, stems removed
- 4 large cloves garlic, minced in food processor
- 3 T. butter

Sauté sage and garlic in butter for 5 minutes and set aside.

AU JUS

While preparing everything else, reduce the liquid that the roast cooked in by at least ½, should take 2–3 hours. Salt and pepper to taste and serve on the side.

C. J. Chenier

SHOW DATE:

1992

Chenier's Creole Spaghetti Sauce

1 lb. shrimp, peeled
1 lb. smoked sausage
2¼ c. of water, divided
1½ lb. ground beef
Tony Chachere's Creole Seasoning to taste
1 large onion, chopped
1 bushel green onions, chopped
4 (8-oz.) cans tomato sauce
1 can whole-kernel corn
1 bag spaghetti

Boil shrimp and set aside.

In a 5-qt. pot, fry sliced sausage until brown. Add ¼ c. of water to sausage. Then put in ground beef (season ground meat with Tony Chachere's to taste), onions, and green onions. Fry until brown, stirring occasionally.

Drain grease from pot. Add tomato sauce, corn, and shrimp. Add 1 to 2 c. of water. Cook down to desired thickness.

Boil spaghetti. Put spaghetti on plate and scoop desired amount of meat sauce onto them and enjoy. Hei Toi!

SERVING UP: Blues, jazz, zydeco, rhythm and grooves

A FEW INGREDIENTS: When you want to spice things up, C. J. Chenier and the Red Hot Louisiana Band is just the right recipe. As much at home with ballads and the blues as he is with rock and roll and zydeco, C. J. has been burning up the stage since 1987 when he stepped up to inherit leadership of the Red Hot Louisiana Band from his father—Grammy Award–winning Clifton Chenier.

When Paul Simon got a taste of C. J. in 1990, he decided to feature him on his album *The Rhythm of the Saints*, and that year's *Born at the Right Time* tour. In 1992 C. J. played accordion on "Cajun Song," on the Gin Blossoms' breakthrough album, *New Miserable Experience*. C. J.'s 1994 solo debut, *Too Much Fun*, was named the Best Zydeco Album of 1995 by *Living Blues* magazine. In 1997 he won the Living Blues' Critics' Poll Award and an AFIM Indie Award for Best Zydeco Album for *The Big Squeeze*. C. J. has made appearances on the *Daily Show with Jon Stewart* and CNN.

MORE TASTY MORSELS: myspace.com/cjchenier
C. J.'S CHARITY: American Cancer Society, cancer.org

The Gourds

SHOW DATE: 2006

SERVING UP: Alt-country, progressive bluegrass

A FEW INGREDIENTS: Singer-songwriter Kevin Russell performs both as a solo artist and with the high-energy Austin band the Gourds. Kevin's multi-instrumental talent on guitar, mandolin, and banjo, adds spice to the band's eight albums. The music has been featured in the documentaries, *Growin' a Beard* (2003) and *Something's Brewin' in Shiner* (2004). They appeared on *Friday Night Lights* in 2005, and their songs have been featured on *My Name Is Earl*.

MORE TASTY MORSELS: thegourds.com

THE GOURDS' CHARITY: SIMS Foundation, simsfoundation.org

Kevin Russell's Crawfish Pie

I always wondered what that was Hank Williams was singing about and why my kin never made it along with their gumbo. It sounded like the perfect complement to that thick brown Louisiana stew. This is my version of this mysterious dish. It is always a big hit at my New Years Day feast. Even though crawfish is not in season at that time of the year, one can always find the tail meat frozen.

2 to 4 frozen pie crusts
1 stick of butter
1 large purple onion, diced
1 green bell pepper, diced
3 ribs of celery, chopped
2 lb. frozen crawfish tails, cooked
1 T. parsley, chopped
1 T. paprika
salt and cayenne
2 T. flour
½ c. water
1 egg, beaten
2 T. Tony Chachere's seasoning

Thaw the tails by running under tap water in a colander. Add the Tony Chachere's and toss. Eat a few just like that.

Melt half the butter in a large cast-iron skillet over medium heat. Throw your onion, bell pepper, and celery in the melted butter and let it cook for 8 or 10 minutes, until it starts really smelling good. Season with salt, cayenne, and paprika. Get those crawfish tails in there and stir it up good, let it go for another 10 minutes, stirring occasionally.

In a small bowl make a slurry of the water and flour. Add this to the mix and stir it up real good, bring it to a boil, and then drop the heat down to a simmer, until it thickens and comes together in a gooey goodness. Mix in the parsley and remove from heat. Let it cool down to room temperature.

Get out your pie crusts and separate. Fill the bottom crust up to the rim with crawfish mixture. Cut the bottom out of the remaining crust and carefully remove it from the tin. Turn it over and place it on top of the mixture filled crust, like a hat. Poke some holes in it with a fork. Brush the top with beaten egg.

Put this in a 375° oven for about 45 minutes, or until they get nice and golden brown. These can be made ahead of time easily if you've got a crowd coming. I serve 'em with black-eyed peas and that works pretty good.

Manhattan Transfer

SHOW DATE: 1998

SERVING UP: Jazz, pop

A FEW INGREDIENTS: Over the past three decades, the voice of nine-time Grammy winner and seventeen-time nominee Janis Siegel has been the undeniable flavor in the Manhattan Transfer's diverse musical catalog. She sang lead on some their biggest hits, including "Operator," "Birdland" (for which she also won a Best Arrangement Grammy), and "The Boy from N.Y.C." The Vocal Group Hall of Fame recognized the Manhattan Transfer's musical accomplishments and included them in its first class of inductees in 1999.

Janis has also had a very successful solo career with over a half dozen solo albums, and has been a part of many collaborative projects, amassing a large international fan base and consistently high critical praise along the way.

MORE TASTY MORSELS: janisseigel.com JANIS'S CHARITY: The Field Band Foundation, fieldband.org.za

Kone's Cioppino

Submitted by Janis Siegel

1 doz. clams
1 c. dry red or white wine
½ c. olive oil
1 large onion, chopped
4 cloves garlic, chopped
1 yellow pepper, chopped
¼ lb. dried Porcini mushrooms, soaked in warm water (reserve liquor)
6 ripe Italian plum tomatoes, peeled, seeded, and chopped coarsely
4 T. Italian tomato paste
2 c. robust red wine (Zinfandel or Pinot Noir)
1 tsp. salt
freshly ground black pepper
2 T. fresh basil, finely chopped
3 lb. Chilean sea bass, cut into serving pieces
1 lb. Dungeness crab meat
1 lb. raw shrimp, shelled
1 doz. smoked mussels or scallops
3 T. parsley, chopped

Steam the clams in the red or white wine until they open. Discard any that do not open. Strain the broth through two thicknesses of cheesecloth and reserve.

Heat the olive oil in a deep, heavy pot and cook the onion, garlic, pepper and mushrooms for about 3 or 4 minutes. Add the tomatoes and cook another 5 minutes.

Add the strained clam broth, the reserved, strained mushroom liquor, tomato paste and 2 c. of red wine. Season with salt and pepper. Taste and correct seasonings.

Add the fish and cook them through. Finally, add the shrimp, smoked mussels, crabmeat, basil, and steamed clams. Heat until the shrimp are nice and pink. Do not overcook.

If there doesn't seem to be enough liquid for a good stew-like consistency, add some of your favorite pasta sauce. Sprinkle with parsley and serve in deep bowls with plenty of sourdough bread and glasses of the wine you cooked with.

Marcia Ball

SHOW DATES:

1976
1979
1986
1990
1998

SERVING UP: R&B, blues

A FEW INGREDIENTS: When native Texan Marcia Ball heats up on the keyboards, things really come to a boil. Whether serving up blues, rock, zydeco, or an intimate ballad, she is a musical force to be reckoned with.

Marcia plays more than a hundred shows a year and appears at virtually every major festival in the United States—she has even performed at the White House. *No Depression* magazine described her style as "a little rock, a lot of roll, a pinch of rhythm, and a handful of blues."

Marcia received the Blues Music Award (formerly the W.C. Handy Blues Award) for Best Female Artist in 1998, for Blues Album in 2002 (for *Presumed Innocent*), for Contemporary Blues Album and Contemporary Blues Female Artist in 2005, and the Pinetop Perkins Piano Player of the Year Award in 2006 and 2007. She was nominated for a Grammy in 1998 for her album *Sing It!*

MORE TASTY MORSELS: rosebudus.com/ball

My Favorite Etouffee

Etouffee is the essence of seafood. Keep it simple.

3 large onions (or 2 large onions plus 1 c. celery)
1 bell pepper
3 clovers of garlic, chopped
1 c. of olive oil
1 stick of margarine
3 lb. raw small-to-medium shrimp or crawfish tails, peeled
3 T. paprika for color
1 c. parsley, chopped
1 heaping T. of flour to thicken
green onion tops, chopped
salt and red and black pepper to taste

In a large pot, sauté the onion, celery, bell pepper, and garlic in the oil and margarine until wilted. Add the seafood, sprinkle with the paprika. Salt and pepper lightly and stir. Cover and cook over medium-low heat for 10 minutes, stirring several times. It should make its own juice. Then, stir in the flour and the parsley. Cover and simmer 10 more minutes, again stirring several times. Taste and adjust salt and pepper.

Serve over white rice garnished with green onion tops and remaining parsley. Put the Tabasco and Louisiana hot sauce on the table. Bon appetit!

The Neville Brothers

SHOW DATES:

1979
1986
1995

Seafood and Okra Gumbo

We cook like we play music—toss in a little of this, a little of that. Never completely following a recipe but always ending up with something that tastes or sounds fresh . . . and like can't nobody else do.

SERVING UP: R&B, soul, jazz

A FEW INGREDIENTS: The Neville Brothers, otherwise known as the First Family of Funk, have been recording together since 1976 when they produced both their landmark project *The Wild Tchoupitoulas*—under the direction of their uncle George Landry, who headed a Mardis Gras Indian tribe as Chief Joy—and their self-titled album. Since then, they have released eight additional albums, including the most artistically successful release, *Yellow Moon*, in 1989. The brothers cook up beautiful music together and individually. Aaron has had a successful solo career, Art tours with a group called the Funky Meter, Cyril leads the Uptown All Stars, and Charles has recorded a series of critically acclaimed jazz records. But it is when they perform together as family that the music really sizzles.

MORE TASTY MORSELS: nevilles.com

THE NEVILLE BROTHERS' CHARITY: New Orleans Artists Against Hunger and Homelessness, noaahh.org

3 or 4 bell peppers, chopped
3 to 4 onions, chopped
1 whole pod garlic, peeled and chopped
2 bunches green onions, chopped
1 lb. okra, chopped
1 lb. hot sausage
1 lb. shrimp
1 lb. crab meat
several boiled crabs (optional)
1 jar oysters, drained
salt and pepper
2 or 3 drops liquid crab boil
1 bay leaf

Fill large pot with water; add bay leaf and season well with salt and pepper and a few drops crab boil. Slowly bring to a boil. Meanwhile, sauté hot sausage in skillet. Remove sausage. Add chopped onions, pepper, garlic, and okra to sausage fat; cook, stirring, until onions are wilted.

Drain excess fat. Return sausage to skillet. Add shrimp and crab meat. Cover and simmer over low heat until vegetables are tender and flavors blend.

Taste boiling water and correct seasoning; it should be spicy. Add shrimp and vegetable mixture to boiling water. If desired, add a few boiled crabs as well. Let simmer over low fire. About 5 to 10 minutes before serving, add oysters and cook just until edges curl. Serve at once over rice.

If desired, remove head from shrimp and boil heads only 10 minutes or so in water. Remove heads from water and discard. Add that water to gumbo water.

Quantities are approximate. Use enough seafood to make a thick, rich soup.

Blue Rodeo

SHOW DATE:

2002

Striped Bass with Curried Spinach

SERVING UP: Country, rock

A FEW INGREDIENTS: One of Canada's most popular bands, Blue Rodeo has been cooking up best-selling albums for twenty years. The band has been nominated for twenty-four Juno Awards (Canada's highest musical honor), winning eleven—five for Group of the Year. They have released eleven studio albums, one live album, a greatest hits collection, and an award-winning DVD. In addition, Blue Rodeo's music was featured in the movie, *Postcards From the Edge*.

MORE TASTY MORSELS: bluerodeo.com
BLUE RODEO'S CHARITY: Daily Bread Food Bank, dailybread.ca

filets of striped bass
⅓ c. olive oil (canola or sunflower if you prefer)
ground sea salt and ground peppercorns
1 lb. spinach leaves
3 cloves garlic, coarsely chopped
1 onion, chopped
½ tsp. turmeric
1 tsp. cumin seeds
½ tsp. black cumin seeds
1 tsp. anise seeds
½ tsp. cayenne powder
salt and pepper to taste
⅓ c. sweet Madeira
3 heritage tomatoes, chopped
3–4 T. coconut milk

Prepare the fish by rubbing in olive oil and salting and peppering on both sides. Place in oiled shallow baking pan, skin side up.

Prepare spinach by rinsing and removing stems. Shake away excess water, but leave a little wet.

Pour oil in wok and heat for 45 seconds on medium heat. Throw in chopped garlic, and sauté until translucent, about 1 minute. Add onion, turmeric, regular and black cumin, anise, cayenne, and salt and pepper. Cook for 3 minutes or until spices and onions are soft.

Add Madeira and tomatoes to wok. Stir and cook for 2 additional minutes. Add coconut milk. Stir and cook for 3 more minutes. Add spinach to wok, cover, and allow spinach to steam in mixture. (You may need to add a ½ to 1 cup of water to create more steam.) When spinach is soft, turn heat to low and leave covered.

Preheat broiler to high. Place fish on top rack. Broil until skin is bubbling, about 5 minutes. Move fish to lower rack and change oven temperature to 400°. Continue to bake for 3 to 4 minutes, depending on thickness. (The fish is done when it is easily separated by a fork but still moist.)

Turn heat up on the sauce in the wok and allow to boil for a couple of minutes.

Remove fish and sauce from heat, and plate. Serve the spinach around the fish and spoon the sauce over it.

Stanley Jordan

SHOW DATE:

1989

Bow-Tie Pasta with Smoked Salmon in Vodka Sauce

3 T. extra virgin olive oil
1 onion, finely chopped
5 cloves garlic, crushed and chopped
cayenne pepper (to taste)
1 pinch of basil flakes
2 (28-oz.) cans of crushed tomatoes
½ cup vodka
salt and pepper (to taste)
½ cup heavy cream
½ pound nova flakes
1 lb. bow-tie pasta

Put the olive oil in the pan and add the garlic and onions. Cook for a couple of minutes, until the garlic and onions are softened. Add the cayenne pepper, basil flakes, and crushed tomatoes. Bring to a boil and add the vodka and salt and pepper. Simmer for about 15 minutes over low heat. Stir in the cream and simmer until the sauce is heated. Add the nova flakes and stir lightly until blended.

Cook the pasta in a large pot of boiling water. Drain the pasta and add to the sauce. Stir well to coat.

SERVING UP: Contemporary jazz, jazz fusion

A FEW INGREDIENTS: Stanley Jordan's music is extraordinary, and his technique—including the ability to play two guitars at the same time—unbelievable. His debut album, *Magic Touch*, went gold. The key to his immediate acclaim was his mastery of a special "tapping" technique on the guitar's fret board, rather than conventional strumming and picking. His versions of "The Lady in My Life," first recorded by Michael Jackson, and the Beatles' "Eleanor Rigby" sent *Magic Touch* to the top of *Billboard*'s jazz chart for fifty-one weeks. In the past decade Stanley has begun to focus on music for inspiration and healing.

MORE TASTY MORSELS: stanleyjordan.com

STANLEY'S CHARITY: MusiCares, grammy.com/musicares/donate

Dr. John

SHOW DATE:

1993

SERVING UP: Blues, rock, New Orleans R&B

A FEW INGREDIENTS: Dr. John personifies the rich musical and cultural heritage of New Orleans. His very flavorful musical career began in the 1950s, but it was in 1968 that his persona, Dr. John the Night Tripper, complete with voodoo charms, was born and his breakthrough album, *Gris-Gris,* was released. Dr. John won Grammy Awards in 1989, 1992, 1996, and 2000, and has received six other nominations over the years, including a 2007 nomination for his Hurricane Katrina benefit album, *Sippiana Hurricane.* In 2004 he received a prestigious award from L'Académie Charles Cros for his song "N'Awlinz Dis Dat or D'udda." He remains committed to the plight of New Orleans alive in the people's hearts—in 2008 he released *City That Care Forgot.*

MORE TASTY MORSELS: drjohn.org

DR. JOHN'S CHARITY: New Orleans Musicians' Clinic, neworleansmusiciansclinic.org

Wild Duck and Goose Gumbo

This recipe is recommended for people with liver problems. I got the idea from Johnny Jambalaya from Thibodaux, Louisiana.

1 goose (speckled-belly, if possible)
2 ducks
1 Spanish onion, quartered
1 sweet onion, quartered
8 celery stalks, sliced
½ red bell pepper
½ yellow bell pepper
½ green bell pepper
1 bunch green onions, diced
3 cloves garlic
buckwheat pancake flour (for roux)
canola and flax seed oil (for roux)
file powder, Tabasco, lemon
Chili-spiced chicken sausage
Brown or white rice

Make marinade with file powder, lemon juice and Tabasco. Rub on goose and ducks for 10 minutes. Take chunks of the onion, slivers of green bell pepper, onion, and celery, and stuff in to goose and ducks. Place in large pot, legs down, in 325°–350° oven and cook until tender.

Make roux with buckwheat pancake flour, canola, and flax seed oil. Roux will cook fast on low heat. When roux is deep brown remove immediately. Watch that it doesn't turn black (medium roux is good)—if it does, start again. Add water, bell peppers, and garlic, then celery and onions. Carefully add ducks and goose to roux, and cook on medium-low heat very slowly to let flavors through.

Dice up chili spiced chicken sausage and keep temperature med-low to low. Let it cook 3½ hours. Let flavors combine. Taste broth. Make sure it's cooked. Then add green onions. Add a pinch of file powder when you serve over the boiled rice. Yield: 8 servings, depending on size of goose.

Mark Chesnutt

SHOW DATE: 1995

Braised Wild Goose

1 8-lb. wild goose
2–3 sprigs parsley
1 stalk celery
1 bay leaf
1 pinch thyme
1 qt. stock or consommé
fat salt pork
1 T. cornstarch
2 T. water

Clean, pluck, and singe a wild goose and stuff, if desired. Truss the legs and wings close to the body and cover the bird with a slice of fat salt pork. Roast the bird in a preheated oven at 400° until it is well-browned. Remove the fat from the roasting pan and add vegetables, bay leaf, a little thyme, and a qt. of stock. Cover the pan and continue cooking, basting often for 2–3 hours or until the bird is tender. Strain the gravy and thicken it with 1 T. cornstarch mixed with 2 T. of water. Serve with cranberry sauce or applesauce, and wild rice or corn fritters. Yield: 6 servings.

SERVING UP: Country

A FEW INGREDIENTS: Hailing from Beaumont, Texas, and learning his chops from his father Bob, a singer, fan, and collector of country music, Mark's musical career really started sizzling in 1990 with the release of his first single "Too Cold At Home." He won the CMA Horizon Award that year. His fans helped his records to climb the charts one right after the other making him one of the ten most played radio artists of the 1990s. He has had more than thirty songs on the *Billboard* Hot Country Songs chart, including eight number one singles. His first three albums and his 1996 *Greatest Hits* album have all been certified platinum, and 1994's *What a Way to Live* was certified gold.

MORE TASTY MORSELS: markchesnutt.com
MARK'S CHARITY: Garth House, garthhouse.net

James McMurtry

SHOW DATES:

1990
2006

SERVING UP: Rock and roll

A FEW INGREDIENTS: If you like your music with a bite of political commentary, James McMurtry, son of novelist Larry McMurtry, serves it up your way. James came to national attention in 1987 when he received an award in the New Folk songwriting category at the Kerrville Folk Festival. He later joined John Mellencamp, John Prine, Dwight Yoakam and Joe Ely to soundtrack the film *Falling from Grace*, which also produced the single "Sweet Suzanne." The Buzzin' Cousins, as the band was later christened, was nominated for Vocal Event of the Year by the Country Music Association in 1992. His 2005 CD *Childish Things* was nominated for an Americana Music Association Award for Best Album, and his single "We Can't Make It Here" was nominated for Best Song.

James plays regularly with his band in an around Austin, as well as keeping up a demanding touring schedule.

MORE TASTY MORSELS: jamesmcmurtry.com JAMES'S CHARITY: Hill Country Conservancy, hillcountryconservancy.org

Idiot Ridge Dove

I had to improvise this recipe when stranded at a remote ranch house with few provisions.

I own a small house on a dirt road in Archer County near a place the old people used to call Idiot Ridge. One of my uncles owns the adjacent pasture on which another of my uncles grazes cows and calves. On September evenings in the 1970s and 1980s, the stock tanks in that pasture used to attract clouds of thirsty mourning doves sweeping down from the wheat fields to the north on their way to roost in the post oaks to the south. In the 1990s my farming neighbors acquired bigger tractors, which allowed them to get their wheat stubble plowed in by mid-August, weeks before the opening of the dove season. With no spilled grain left to feed on, the birds move on.

One time in the late 1990s I decided to go bird hunting anyway, just to get out. I didn't have keys to any of the pasture gates, but I found the south gate open and drove in. The birds were few. I only had four when I drove back to find the gate locked. The pumper, the guy who keeps the oil pumping units going up and down and supposedly checks for flow-line leaks, must have been in the pasture when I drove in. I could see the overgrown feed road that took me across the pasture back to the house, but I still had no key to get my van out of the pasture. I knew my ranching uncle would be out in the morning to check on his cows, so I decided to make a supper of my meager kill and stay the night. I hadn't stayed there in a while so I faced a lack of provisions. There was no cooking oil, flour, butter, or anything that I might use to fry the birds into blackened hockey pucks, as had formerly been my custom. There was, however, a decent bottle of Bordeaux left by some benevolent unknown guest.

Since I had so few birds, I plucked and cleaned them whole, rather than "breasting" them as Texans do. I would need every morsel, and I had read that the only fat on a dove is under its skin, so I figured leaving the skin on would enhance the flavor. I had also recently read a book by one Russell Chatham of Livingston, Montana. Chatham owns a gourmet restaurant and bar in Livingston and likes to cook game. Chatham's recipe for wild duck calls for an oven preheated to 500°, into which one places a duck which has been allowed to reach room temperature, and cooks it for 20 minutes. I figured, 20 minutes for a duck, 8 minutes for a dove. I placed the birds in a shallow pan and poured some of the Bordeaux over them until they were sitting in a puddle of wine. I don't recall having any kind of spice. It worked though, best doves I ever cooked, just a trace of blood around the wing joints, tender, not a dry bite.

fresh doves (if you must use frozen birds, allow them to come to room temperature before cooking)
decent red wine, (a $10.99 bottle or better)
spices optional

Pluck and clean the doves whole. Do not breast, and do not remove skin. Save and clean the gizzards and hearts.

Preheat oven to 500°. Place birds on their backs in a shallow pan, not touching each other. Dribble the wine over the birds until they are coated and lying in a puddle of wine. Place the gizzards and hearts in the wine puddle. Place the pan of birds in the oven.

Pull them out in 8 minutes. If they seem a little rare, that's perfect. A dove is dark-meated, like a good steak.

Robert Earl Keen

SHOW DATES:

1989
1995
1997
2001

Bacon-Wrapped Dove Breasts

12 dove breasts
teriyaki marinade
salt and black pepper to taste
sliced fresh jalapeño peppers
6 slices bacon

Place dove breasts in a zip-seal plastic bag, cover with teriyaki, and marinate overnight in the refrigerator.

Remove breasts from bag and use a knife to slit the breast along the bone that runs the length of the breast. Insert one or two slices of jalapeño in each slit. Season breasts to taste with salt and black pepper. Wrap each breast with a half-slice of bacon. Secure bacon with a toothpick through each breast. Grill for 8 minutes but not on the hottest rack of grill, as the bacon and grease could catch fire.

Always best with real Mexican beer, like Carta Blanca or Bohemia. Enjoy! Yield: 12 breasts.

SERVING UP: Country, country rock, alt-country, folk, Texas country

A FEW INGREDIENTS: Like the mystery ingredients that makes so many recipes that much better, native Texas son Robert Earl Keen, is the secret behind the success of so many musicians and their art. His songs have been recorded by George Strait, Lyle Lovett, Shawn Colvin, the Dixie Chicks, and the Highwaymen. He consistently plays sold-out shows for audiences that have numbered as many as twenty-five thousand.

Robert began playing guitar in College Station while attending Texas A&M University, where he lived next door to Lyle Lovett. The two became friends and co-wrote "This Old Porch," a song that each of them later recorded. After a brief stint in Nashville, he returned to Austin and released his national debut album, *West Textures*, in 1989. That album included one of his signature numbers, "The Road Goes on Forever."

MORE TASTY MORSELS: robertearlkeen.com

ROBERT'S CHARITY: Hill Country Youth Orchestras, hillcountryyouthorchestras.com

Keep the Beet

VEGETABLES AND LEGUMES

Loretta Lynn

SHOW DATES:
1983
1998

SERVING UP: Country, honky-tonk, alt-country, gospel

A FEW INGREDIENTS: When it comes to a successful career in music, Loretta wrote her own cookbook. This coal miner's daughter (the title of her hit single and album, best-selling autobiography, and Oscar-winning film) has earned the status of a true American icon. Songs like "Wine, Women, and Song," "Happy Birthday," and "Blue Kentucky Girl," each a top-ten hit, were early hints of Loretta's undeniably female point of view—a perspective unique at the time when they were released. Without her it would be all but impossible to imagine the likes of Shania Twain's "Any Man of Mine," Deana Carter's "Did I Shave My Legs for This?" or many Dixie Chicks' hits. She had an activist streak in her, too: her single "Dear Uncle Sam" was among the very first popular recordings to focus on the human costs of the Vietnam War.

Loretta has had fifty-two top-ten hits, sixteen of which reached number one. Her numerous awards include a Grammy Hall of Fame Award, Female Artist of the Year for both the Academy of Country Music and the American Music Awards, and an ACM award for Top Vocal Duo that she shared with Conway Twitty.

MORE TASTY MORSELS: lorettalynn.com
LORETTA'S CHARITY: American Diabetes Association, diabetes.org

Loretta's Country Collard Greens

1 bunch of fresh collard greens, chopped
1 tsp. vegetable oil
1 smoked ham jowl
1 small onion, diced
1 clove garlic, minced
1 c. water
1 tsp. sugar
¼ tsp. garlic powder
½ tsp. season salt
2 T. apple cider vinegar
2 c. chicken stock

Wash and chop collards, discarding thick stems. Over medium-high heat add vegetable oil to a Dutch oven with a lid and sauté the smoked ham jowl. Add onions and garlic. Cook just until onions are starting to turn clear.

Pour in water and add a few collard greens. Sprinkle with a bit of sugar, garlic, season salt, and vinegar. Keep layering; the greens will start cooking down as you add more.

Pour in chicken broth and turn your heat to medium-low. Cook for 90 minutes, or until greens are tender. You can always steal a quick taste as you are cookin' to make sure the greens have cooked long enough, and to see if you need to add more seasoning.

Kathy Mattea

SHOW DATES:

1987
1990
1993

SERVING UP: Country, bluegrass

A FEW INGREDIENTS: Kathy Mattea carved out a slice of musical history in the 1980s and 1990s as a traditional country artist with a love of free-ranging innovation. She has twice been named Female Vocalist of the Year by the Country Music Association, and in 1990 Kathy won the first of two Grammys, earning the award for Best Female Country Vocal Performance for "Where've You Been," co-written with her husband Jon Vezner.

An early spokesperson and advocate for AIDS awareness and research, Kathy's dedication to activism is currently focused on bringing public attention to environmental issues; she is a grassroots presenter of the Climate Project's global-warming slideshow, and she works to curtail mountaintop-removal coal mining in her native Appalachia. Her latest CD, *Coal*, artfully blends her passion for her home and her music.

MORE TASTY MORSELS: mattea.com

KATHY'S CHARITY: MusiCares, grammy.com/musicares

Roast Veggies in Pastry

This is a recipe I figured out all on my own, standing in the produce section at the store. I made this and took it to Suzy Bogguss's house for dinner, and we had it with a delicious rack of lamb . . . mmmmmm.

- 1 eggplant
- salt
- 1 yellow pepper, cut in small strips
- 1 red pepper, cut in small strips
- extra virgin olive oil
- 1 yellow onion
- 2 leeks
- butter
- 1 tsp. sugar (optional)
- toasted pine nuts
- phyllo dough
- blue cheese crumbles

Take the eggplant, halve it, and slice it about ½" thick. Sprinkle it with salt and leave in a colander for at least 1 hour. Rinse, drain, and squeeze all the moisture out by pressing between paper towels or dish towels.

Toss the eggplant with the pepper strips, drizzle with olive oil, and roast on a rimmed baking sheet in the oven at 400° until well-browned and soft, about 10–20 minutes. Be sure and check them and stir every 5 minutes. Let cool to room temperature.

To caramelize the onions and leeks, slice them very thin. Melt butter and olive oil in a skillet over medium-high and add the onions and leeks. As soon as they begin to start cooking, turn them down to low, and cook another 20 minutes or so, stirring occasionally. You can add 1 tsp. of sugar, if you like. They should be really soft and brown. Let cool to room temperature.

Pull eggplant apart into bite-size pieces, and mix eggplant and peppers with the onions. Add toasted pine nuts.

Unwrap the phyllo and spread on a dish towel. Cover with a damp dish towel. (This will keep it from drying out.) Pull off one paper-thin layer at a time, and spread on work surface (re-cover phyllo stack immediately with damp towel). Brush with melted butter. Repeat 4 times.

Line the vegetable mixture along one side of the phyllo, about 1 inch from the edge. Lay blue cheese crumbles along the top. Fold ends over and roll into log. Brush with butter.

Place in preheated 400° oven, and bake for 25–30 minutes, or until golden brown. Let stand for 5 minutes, then slice and serve. Yum!

Kimmie Rhodes

SHOW DATE: 1997

SERVING UP: Country

A FEW INGREDIENTS: Native Texan Kimmie Rhodes has recorded and released twelve solo CDs, written and produced three musicals and hundreds of songs, and co-written a book with Joe Gracey, *The Amazing Afterlife of Zimmerman Fees: A Metaphysical Story and Cookbook*. Kimmie's album *West Texas Heaven* was chosen by *USA Today* as one of the top-ten country records of 1996. Kimmie's songs have been recorded by a wide variety of artists including Willie Nelson, Wynonna Judd, Trisha Yearwood, CeCe Winans, Joe Ely, Waylon Jennings, and Emmylou Harris.

Kimmie has also composed music for films and television. Her soundtrack credits include "A Heart That's True" from *Babe: Pig in the City*, "I'm Not an Angel" featured in *Mrs. Winterbourne*, and a song on the soundtrack of *Daddy's Dyin' . . . Who's Got the Will?* "Shine All Your Light," co-written with Beth Nielson Chapman, was recorded by Amy Grant for the *Touched By An Angel* TV series. Kimmie also co-wrote "Ordinary Heart" with Emmylou Harris, who performed the song for the soundtrack to the movie *Happy, Texas*, and was nominated for a Grammy for the performance.

MORE TASTY MORSELS: kimmierhodes.com KIMMIE'S CHARITY: Hospice Austin, hospiceaustin.org

Babette's Eggplant Gratin

Adapted from The Amazing Afterlife of Zimmerman Fees: A Metaphysical Story and Cookbook *by Kimmie Rhodes, featuring recipes from Gracey-Rhodes family and friends*

This dish is usually served in single portions as a starter course, but it's also good as a main course with fettuccini on the side and grated fresh Parmesan on top. If done correctly it will be very thin and light.

1 head of garlic
1 (28-oz.) can crushed tomatoes
1 large eggplant
olive oil
1 large chunk of Gruyère cheese
salt and pepper to taste

Peel and chop the entire head of garlic. Add the garlic to the tomatoes in a saucepan and cook slowly, uncovered for about 1 hour until the sauce is thick. Preheat oven to 400°.

Wash the eggplant and slice thinly, about ⅛-inch thick is good. (It's important that the slices be thin because otherwise they soak up too much oil during cooking and also the dish is wonderfully delicate if the slices are thin. It's the "secret" to the dish.)

Sauté the eggplant slices until tender in olive oil, and drain on paper towels. Line a large, shallow casserole dish with a thin layer of the cooked eggplant slices, then a thin layer of the thickened tomato sauce on top of that, and then a layer of grated cheese.

Repeat these layers one more time and then end with a generous layer of breadcrumbs on top of the last layer of cheese.

Bake for about 45 minutes, or until the whole casserole bubbles and the breadcrumb topping is crusty and dark golden-brown. Season with salt and pepper. Yield: about 8 servings.

The Allman Brothers Band

SHOW DATE:

1995

"Big House" Corn Casserole

Submitted by Kirsten West, an Allman Brothers Band favorite

2 T. sugar
1½ T. flour
1 tsp. baking powder
1 tsp. salt
3 eggs
1 c. whipping cream
2 T. melted butter
1 c. fresh-shucked corn
1 (14-oz.) can creamed corn
3 T. chopped onion
1 c. shredded Mexican cheese

Preheat oven to 350°. Combine sugar, flour, baking powder, and salt. Whisk together eggs, whipping cream, and butter. Gradually add the sugar mixture to the egg mixture, whisking until smooth. Stir in the corns, onions, and cheese. Pour into a 2-qt. baking dish and bake for 55 minutes.

SERVING UP: Southern rock, blues rock

A FEW INGREDIENTS: The Allman Brothers Band have a thirty-nine-year tradition of blending the new and the old: playing songs that stir fans' souls because they bring back so many great memories, casting classic blues tunes in a new light, and turning up the flame with something completely fresh that is destined to become a classic. Their classic album, *The Allman Brothers Band at Fillmore East* (1971), is the stuff of rock legend, and to date they have had ten gold albums, four of which have been certified platinum or multiplatinum. But the recipe for the Brothers is not just a musical concoction, it's a family experience—they consider their fans worldwide to be part of their Peachy Extended Family.

MORE TASTY MORSELS: allmanbrothersband.com
THE ALLMAN BROTHERS BAND'S CHARITY: Big House Foundation, bighousemuseum.org

Joe Ely

SHOW DATES:

1980
1985
1991
1996
2000
2008

SERVING UP: Country, rock, honky-tonk

A FEW INGREDIENTS: Joe Ely is as Texan as chili made with beef, beer, and a secret spice that'll set your insides on fire. Joe's first band, the Flatlanders, which consisted of Joe, Jimmie Dale Gilmore, and Butch Hancock, had a sound that was a visionary melding of country and rock. Not one to be pigeonholed however, his next project, the Joe Ely Band, toured with the Clash. This was just the beginning of Joe's genre-crossing career—he has since performed with Bruce Springsteen, Los Super Seven, James McMurtry, Lyle Lovett, John Hiatt, and Guy Clark, and he has worked on film, too; in the late 1990s Ely wrote music for Robert Redford's movie *The Horse Whisperer*.

MORE TASTY MORSELS: ely.com
JOE'S CHARITY: American Youthworks, Austin, Texas, americanyouthworks.org

Joe Ely's Black-eyed Peas

Some say to prepare black-eyed peas on New Years Day to ensure good luck, but for Sharon and Joe Ely, "Every day is New Years for us!"

1 lb. black-eyed peas, dried
1 pan of water
5–6 cloves fresh garlic
1 T. sugar
1 jigger of olive oil
1 T. Better Than Bouillon soup base
1 can chicken broth
1 tsp. oregano or Italian seasoning

Add 1 lb. of black-eyed peas to a pan and cover with water and soak for 1 hour. Add garlic. Turn on the burner to low and cook for 1½ hours.

Add 1 T. of sugar and 1 jigger olive oil. Simmer for another hour.

Add 1 can of chicken broth and the bouillon; add more water as needed. Add a couple of shakes of oregano or Italian seasoning. Cook until the peas and juice thicken. Serve with 2 slices of yellow onion. That's it!

Bruce Hornsby

SHOW DATES:

1994
1999
2000

Missy's Sweet Potato Fluff

Recipe created by Melissa Smith.

4 c. cooked sweet potatoes, peeled and mashed
⅓ c. of butter, melted
2 eggs, beaten
½ c. milk
1 tsp. vanilla extract
½ c. sugar
½ c. chopped nuts
½ c. shredded coconut
3 T. butter or margarine, melted (for topping)

Preheat oven to 375°. In a large bowl, combine mashed sweet potatoes, ⅓ cup butter, eggs, milk, vanilla extract, and sugar. Spread into a greased 1½-qt. casserole dish.

Combine nuts, coconut, and 3 T. butter. Sprinkle over sweet potato mixture.

Bake for 25 minutes. Enjoy!

Austin City Limits is one of the few shows where audiences can see someone do more than just their hit single, like they do on Letterman and Leno's shows. It is great, and I'm a huge fan.

—Bruce Hornsby

SERVING UP: Jam band, bluegrass, rock, jazz

A FEW INGREDIENTS: Since the release of his first album in 1986, Bruce Hornsby has whisked together a musical life that includes a pinch of almost everything in the kitchen. A twelve-time nominee, Bruce has won three Grammy Awards, and sold over eleven million copies of his albums. The title cut from *The Way It Is* was the most played song on American radio in 1987, winning the ASCAP Song of the Year Award. In 1989 he co-wrote the classic "The End of the Innocence" with Don Henley, a top-ten song. He has a reputation as a great musical collaborator and has played on over one hundred albums, with musicians such as Bob Dylan, Don Henley, the Grateful Dead, and Bonnie Raitt. Bruce has toured the globe and played many unique, history-making events, such as Farm Aid, the modern incarnations of Woodstock, the Newport Jazz Festival, and the Telluride Bluegrass Festival.

MORE TASTY MORSELS: brucehornsby.com BRUCE'S CHARITY: ALS Association (DC/MD/VA Chapter), alsinfo.org

John Gorka

SHOW DATE:

1993

SERVING UP: New folk

A FEW INGREDIENTS: *Rolling Stone* once called John Gorka "the preeminent male singer-songwriter of the new folk movement," and he has the raw talent and resume to back that title up.

John has released a dozen albums in his long career. A favorite songwriter of many musicians, his songs have been recorded and performed by the likes of Mary Chapin Carpenter, Mary Black, and Maura O'Connell. John has toured with many prominent musicians, Nanci Griffith and Mary Chapin Carpenter among them.

MORE TASTY MORSELS: johngorka.com

JOHN'S CHARITY: The Carter Center, cartercenter.org

John Gorka's Family Pierogi

Pierogi are filled dumplings that come from Eastern Europe. This recipe comes from my father's side of the family, which is the Polish side—both of his parents were born in Poland. The pierogi we are making here feature two different fillings: potato-cheese and sauerkraut-and-bacon. Prepare the two fillings before making the dough, as it is the same for both types.

POTATO-CHEESE FILLING

1 lb. ricotta cheese
¼ head fresh garlic
½ bunch green scallions
2 medium potatoes, boiled and mashed
3 T. half-and-half
basil (use liberally)
black pepper
oregano (little bit)
salt (go easy)

Boil potatoes and drain. Mash potatoes and add half-and-half while mashing. Mix cheese into potatoes, and add spices to taste. Yield: filling for 15 dumplings.

SAUERKRAUT-AND-BACON FILLING

4 strips of bacon
1 can Bavarian-style Kraut
¼ head garlic, chopped fine
½ bunch green scallions, chopped fine

Fry or microwave bacon until crispy and drain fat, let cool, crumble into roughly ¼-inch square bits. Drain liquid from sauerkraut and add to a 12-inch skillet on medium heat. Mix in garlic, onions, and bacon. Simmer until sauerkraut is translucent and slightly brown. Let cool. Yield: filling for 15 dumplings.

DOUGH

The dough is the tricky part for me. I will sometimes use more flour than listed below, so I won't have to roll the dough so thin that the pierogi break when boiled.

3 c. flour
¼ tsp. salt
2 T. butter
2 eggs
1 c. warm water
olive oil
salt

Mix flour and salt in a big bowl. Make a space in the middle of bowl and put butter and eggs there. Slowly stir up mixture, adding warm water to make a stiff dough. Don't make too loose; you may not need all the water. Knead dough until very smooth. Let stand in bowl for 10 minutes covered by a dish towel.

Divide dough into 2 halves, and roll out with a rolling pin. Leave unrolled half in covered bowl. Shape dough by hand and roller to make a large rectangle that is longer vertically than it is wide.

Roll out on floured, flat surface until dough is ¹⁄₁₆-inch thick. Roll out from center of dough to the edges. Divide dough in half, scoring but not cutting a horizontal line across the middle with a knife. Use approximately 1 T. of filling for each pierogi.

Space fillings evenly in rows and fold top half of dough over the bottom half. Usually I have more in the top rows than in the bottom row because dough is often more in the shape of a tall oval than a rectangle with precise 90-degree angles.

Cut into rows using a pizza cutter or knife. Cut rows into individual pierogi and press edges with fingers. Fork to seal in the fillings. Put them on trays covered with floured paper towels. Bring 2 large pots of water to a boil, adding olive oil and salt.

Add pierogi and boil for 8–10 minutes, slightly longer if your dough is really thick. Serve with melted butter and champagne. Some may prefer one type or another but the two flavors seem to compliment each other well.

Take pictures because they are gone really quickly and you may not believe they were real. Yield: dough for 30 dumplings.

Buddy Guy

SHOW DATES:

1991
1998
2003

Buddy Guy's Red Beans and Rice

1 lb. dried red beans
1 onion, chopped
2 cloves of garlic, chopped
2 stalks of celery, chopped
1 bell pepper, chopped
2 bay leaves
1 or 2 large ham hocks (optional; bacon is a suitable substitute)

Look through red beans for any rocks and then thoroughly rinse them. Put beans in a large pot and fill with water until there is about 2½ inches of water above the beans. Bring to a boil and then turn the heat down and let the beans simmer on medium-low heat for 2 hours.

Stir occasionally so the beans don't stick to the bottom of the pot. Add the onion, garlic, celery, bell pepper, bay leaves, and meat, if applicable. Let simmer on a very low flame for one more hour.

Serve with rice. Yield: 6–8 servings.

SERVING UP: Chicago blues, rock

A FEW INGREDIENTS: Buddy Guy cooks on all four burners, all the time. He's a Rock and Roll Hall of Fame inductee, an influence to guitar gods like Hendrix, Clapton, and Vaughan, and a pioneer of the electric blues. As a session musician in his early days, Buddy backed the likes of Muddy Waters, Howlin' Wolf, Little Walter, and Sonny Boy Williamson. During the 1970s and 1980s, he released no fewer than twenty albums, but it was in the 1990s when he reached commercial and critical success. Three of his albums—*Damn Right, I've Got the Blues*, *Feels Like Rain*, and *Slippin'*—all earned Grammy Awards in rapid succession. Even at the age of seventy-two, Buddy keeps on stirring things up—he recorded with Carlos Santana on "I Put a Spell on You," and partnered up with John Mayer on a recording of the Otis Redding-penned "I've Got Dreams to Remember."

MORE TASTY MORSELS: buddyguy.net
BUDDY'S CHARITY: Magnolia Baptist Church and Fairview Baptist Church, Baton Rouge, Louisiana

Omar and the Howlers

SHOW DATE:

1987

Red Beans and Rice

Submitted by Omar Kent Dykes

- 1 small bag dry red kidney beans
- 4 c. water
- 2 tsp. salt
- 2 tsp. black pepper
- 1 tsp. garlic powder
- 2 tsp. Creole seasoning
- dash of cayenne pepper
- ½ tsp. chili powder
- 2 tsp. onion powder
- 1 tsp. sugar
- 1 tsp. vinegar
- 1 whole sausage link, sliced
- white rice
- onion and bell pepper, diced (optional)

Wash beans and place in large pot with 4 c. of water. Add all seasonings and half of the sliced sausage. Boil beans over medium high heat for about 1 hour, stirring occasionally. If you need to add more water to the beans as they cook, add small amounts of hot water. When beans are almost soft, add remaining sausage and turn the heat down to low. Cook another hour or so, until beans are soft. Serve over rice.

Add diced onion and bell pepper, if desired. (My original recipe contained onion and peppers, but my wife and son preferred these beans without vegetables. I adapted the recipe suited to their taste.)

SERVING UP: Blues, R&B

A FEW INGREDIENTS: If you're hungry for some rough and tumble blues, accompanied by some rock and roll and maybe even a side dish of western swing or polka, Omar and the Howlers serve it up. Omar Dykes has gained a loyal following in Texas, the southern U.S., and Europe. In 1980 the Howlers recorded their debut album, *Big Leg Beat*, and followed up with their second album, *I Told You So*, and their first video, "Border Girl," in 1984. *Hard Times in the Land of Plenty* (1987) was a breakthrough album for the band—it sold more than half a million copies and earned an Edison Award. In the 1990s the band returned to Austin where they produced *Monkeyland*, and Omar recorded his first all-blues solo album, *Blues Bag*. For 2003's *Boogie Man*, Omar rang up some friends—including Darden Smith, Chris Layton and Tommy Shannon of Double Trouble, Jeff Beck, and Frank Zappa—and got them to contribute.

MORE TASTY MORSELS: omarandthehowlers.com

OMAR'S CHARITY: Health Alliance for Austin Musicians, healthallianceforaustinmusicians.org

Janie Fricke

SHOW DATES:

1980
1983

Rice and Bean Casserole

Here's my favorite healthy dish. You may add cooked spinach, or cut-up cooked chicken.

- 1 large onion, chopped
- 3 cloves garlic, minced
- 2 T. defatted chicken stock
- 2 c. brown rice, cooked
- 2 c. black beans, cooked
- 1 T. chili powder
- 1 (4-oz.) can chopped green chiles
- 1 c. part-skim ricotta cheese
- ¼ c. skim milk
- 1½ c. grated part-skim mozzarella
- vegetable cooking spray

Sauté onion and garlic in stock for 5–7 minutes until onions are clear. Remove from heat and place in bowl. Add rice, beans, chili powder, and chiles.

In a separate bowl, combine ricotta and milk, blending until smooth. Add 1 cup of mozzarella cheese.

Spray a 1½ qt. casserole dish with cooking spray. Spread a layer beans and rice on the bottom of the dish. Cover with a layer of the cheese mixture.Repeat until dish is full, ending with rice mix.

Bake covered at 350° for 30 minutes. Uncover, top with remaining ½ cup of mozzarella, and bake uncovered for 5 minutes longer, until cheese is melted. Serve hot. Yield: 6 cups.

SERVING UP: Country pop

A FEW INGREDIENTS: Janie's career first started to simmer in the 1970s—as one of the most successful jingle singers in the country. Hers was the voice for corporate giants like Coca-Cola, 7Up, United Airlines, and Red Lobster. Soon after, she became a key ingredient in country music, dominating the country charts with smash hits such as "Don't Worry 'Bout Me Baby," "He's a Heartache," and "You're Heart's Not in It." Her many awards include CMA Female Vocalist of the Year, ACM Top Female Vocalist of the Year, and a star on the Country Music Hall of Fame Walkway. She was nominated twice for Grammys and all told has released twenty-three albums and thirty-six hit singles.

MORE TASTY MORSELS: janiefricke.com

JANIE'S CHARITY: Art for Autism Awareness in Lancaster

Grupo Fantasma

SHOW DATE:
2007

Chela's Rice

Submitted by Chela, Johnny Lopez's mother

2 T. olive oil
1½ c. long grain rice
½ white onion, diced
2 garlic cloves, minced
½ green bell pepper, diced
2 tomatoes, diced
¼ c. cilantro, chopped
3 c. chicken stock
2 tsp. tomato or chicken bouillon—Knorr is the best

In large skillet heat olive oil on low for 2 minutes—oil is ready when single grain of rice sizzles when tossed in. Add rice and stir constantly until brown, about 3–5 minutes. When the brownout is attained, add onions and garlic, stirring until caramelized. Add bell pepper, tomato, and cilantro. Now you add the chicken stock and bouillon—Knorr if you're smart! On medium heat bring mixture to a boil, stirring constantly.

Once the rice is boiling, cover and turn heat down to low. After 5 minutes, add ½ cup water or chicken stock to rice if it begins to look dry. Keep covered for 5–10 minutes checking periodically to make sure that it's not drying out. Turn heat off, uncover, fluff and serve.

SERVING UP: Latin, funk

A FEW INGREDIENTS: With ten members and a four-piece horn brigade, Grupo Fantasma fuses Afro-Latin funk, cumbia, salsa, merengue, and more into an intoxicating full meal. It's a sound that demands the audience to move—no one stays seated when Grupo Fantasma is in town. Their self-titled debut CD, released in 2001, earned them an NPR special, and provided the soundtrack to John Sayles's film *Casa de los babys*.

They have also played at New Orleans Jazz Fest, Bonnaroo, the Montreal Jazz Fest, and the North Sea Jazz Fest in the Netherlands. In 2007 they took the stage in London, performing with Prince for whom they also played backup at the CBS Superbowl Bash and the ALMA Awards.

MORE TASTY MORSELS: grupofantasma.com
GRUPO FANTASMA'S CHARITY: People Organized in Defense of Earth and Her Resources, poder-texas.org

Damian "Jr. Gong" Marley

SHOW DATE: 2006

SERVING UP: Reggae, raga, dancehall

A FEW INGREDIENTS: Jr. Gong has a unique gift; he blends eclectic musicality with a classic reggae sensibility and tops it off with dashes of hip-hop, R&B, and dancehall. His label album debut *Halfway Tree* won the Grammy in 2002 for Best Reggae Album. His musical specialty is "toasting," a Jamaican vocal technique that is similar to rapping and relies on talking or chanting over a beat.

In 2005 he won the Best Reggae Album Grammy again, this time for his album *Welcome to Jamrock*, and Best Urban/Alternative Performance for the title track, making him the only Jamaican reggae artist to win two Grammys in one awards show. In fact, he has recorded tracks with hip-hop giants Cypress Hill and Snoop Dogg. In 2004, Damian, along with his brothers, performed in the 27-city Bob Marley Roots Rock, and Reggae Festival.

MORE TASTY MORSELS:
damianmarleymusic.com

DAMIAN'S CHARITY: Ghetto Youths' Foundation, ghettoyouths.com/foundation.html

Vital Ital

Ital is food that should be natural or pure and from the earth. Therefore, avoid ingredients that are chemically modified or contains additives. Thanks to the *Roaring Lion* newsletter for this recipe, which I've adapted.

1 medium-sized coconut
1 qt. hot water
1 c. red peas
1 clove garlic
2 scallion or leek stalks
a few sprigs of thyme
salt to taste
¼ tsp. black pepper
3 c. rice

Grate coconut manually or in a blender. Using 2 c. of hot water at a time, express milk by squeezing the milk through a sieve after each addition until the water is finished. (Coconut can also be grated in the blender.)

Place peas in a saucepan with the coconut milk and add the clove of garlic. Cook until peas are tender, but not over cooked. Add scallion or leeks, thyme, salt, black pepper, and rice, adding more water if necessary in order to boil rice properly. Cook over medium heat, covered until the water is absorbed and rice is cooked.

CALLALOO

1 bunch callaloo or spinach (use more as needed)
1 onion
1 tomato
1 green pepper
dash of black pepper
salt if desired
olive oil

Wash callaloo thoroughly. Cut callaloo into small bits. Chop all remaining ingredients and place in pan with olive oil. Sauté for one minute, then add callaloo. Sprinkle with black pepper and salt, cover tightly, and let steam for 10 to 15 minutes. Serve with rice and peas.

ITAL YUDDIN'

2 c. cornmeal
2 c. wheat flour
3 potatoes, grated
½ lb. of yam or dashine, grated
4 carrots, grated
4–6 c. coconut milk
1 tsp. nutmeg
1 tsp. vanilla
1 tsp. cinnamon
1 tsp. clove
1 tsp. ginger
1 c. honey or brown sugar

Mix cornmeal, flour, grated potatoes, grated yam, and grated carrots in a large bowl, gradually adding coconut milk until you get a fairly soft batter.

Add a tablespoon of nutmeg, vanilla, cinnamon, clove, and ginger. Stir it up, adding a cup of honey or brown sugar to your desired sweetness. For an extra touch, raisins or nuts can also be added.

Pour mixture into two greased 9-inch pans or a large square baking tin. Bake at 350° for 1 hour or until done. Cut into triangles and serve.

Kelly Willis

SHOW DATES:

1991
1994
2000

Creamy Corn and Garlic Risotto

Adapted from Betty Crocker's Quick & Easy Cookbook

3¾ c. chicken broth
4 cloves garlic
1 c. uncooked medium-grain white rice
3 c. frozen corn
½ c. grated Parmesan cheese
⅓ c. shredded mozzarella cheese
¼ c. fresh parsley, chopped

Heat ⅓ cup of the broth to boiling in a skillet. Cook garlic in the broth for 1 minute, stirring occasionally. Stir in rice and frozen corn. Cook 1 minute, stirring occasionally.

Stir in remaining broth. Heat to boiling, then reduce to medium heat. Cook uncovered for 15 to 20 minutes, stirring occasionally, until rice is tender and creamy. Remove from heat.

Stir in cheeses and parsley, then serve. Yield: 4 servings.

SERVING UP: Alt-country

A FEW INGREDIENTS: Kelly Willis, whom NPR called "Alternative-country's golden goddess," began heating things up in high school with her rockabilly band, Kelly Willis and the Fireballs. She sang "I Don't Want to Love You (But I Do)" in the movie *Thelma and Louise* and also had a small part in *Bob Roberts*. Her 1999 album *What I Deserve* was praised by critics and hailed by *Time* magazine as "the smartest, most consistently worthwhile CD" released that year.

MORE TASTY MORSELS: kellywillis.com
KELLY'S CHARITY: The Hope Food Pantry at Trinity United Methodist Church, Austin, Texas, tumc.org/hope

My Morning Jacket

SHOW DATES:

2005
2008

SERVING UP: Indie rock, experimental, psychedelic rock, country rock, jam band

A FEW INGREDIENTS: My Morning Jacket is known for their mix of indie rock, country rock, Southern rock, psychedelic, and jam band styles, and their enthusiastic and energetic live shows. Formed in 1998 in Louisville, Kentucky, the band's debut album *The Tennessee Fire*, was released in 1999 and became a hit overseas, particularly in the Netherlands. The band toured in Europe and was featured in a Dutch documentary. After two more albums, October 2005 saw the release of the critically acclaimed album *Z*, which includes ballads such as "Wordless Chorus" and "Knot Comes Loose." They've played with the Boston Pops and at Boston Symphony Hall.

MORE TASTY MORSELS:
mymorningjacket.com

MY MORNING JACKET'S CHARITY: Juvenile Diabetes Research Foundation, jdrf.org

Quinoa Eggs with Cheese, Please!

Submitted by Jim James

1 c. quinoa
2 c. water
6 eggs
splash of milk or Rice Dream
olive oil
salt and pepper to taste
4 pieces of havarti cheese
love
fun

Place quinoa and water in a small pan. Bring to a boil. Cover and cook until all water is absorbed, about 10–15 minutes.

Place the eggs in a bowl with Rice Dream or milk and "scramble" them. You know how! Throw the eggs in a hot frying pan with olive oil, just like you would normally scramble eggs, but throw in the quinoa about 30 seconds later, while the eggs are still wet. With a spatula, mix that stuff up real good. Salt and pepper to taste.

Dump the egg-quinoa mix on a plate and cover with cheese. Let that mess melt a little bit. Eat the hell out of that tasty shit! Boo-yeah! Yield: 2–3 servings.

Billy Joe Shaver

SHOW DATES:
1980
1983
1985

SERVING UP: Outlaw country

A FEW INGREDIENTS: Despite an accident that caused him to lose parts of three fingers when he was young, Billy Joe Shaver has built a musical career and established himself as one of the icons in outlaw country music.

Waylon Jennings's 1973 album, *Honky Tonk Heroes*, was penned almost exclusively by Billy Joe, and everyone from Elvis to Bob Dylan has covered one of his songs. In the 1990s, he and his son Eddy (who passed away in 2000) put together a band called Shaver, and their heavy-metal approach to honky-tonk music set audiences on fire. In 1999 he performed at the Grand Ole Opry and in 2006, he was inducted into the Texas Country Music Hall of Fame. In 2005 Billy Joe's autobiography, *Honky Tonk Hero*, was published by the University of Texas Press.

MORE TASTY MORSELS: billyjoeshaver.com

BILLY JOE'S CHARITY: M. D. Anderson Cancer Center, mdanderson.org

Billy Joe's Synthetic Huevos Rancheros

Note about recipe from Billy Joe: "I don't cook."

2 flour tortillas
3 eggs
1 jar of Ragu

Warm tortillas. Fry eggs. Pour bottle of Ragu over tortillas and eggs.

Michael Martin Murphey

SHOW DATES:

1987
1991
1996

SERVING UP: Country, cowboy, folk, gospel

A FEW INGREDIENTS: Michael Martin's career as a singer-songwriter, has sizzled since the 1970s. His song "Wildfire" is one of the most played songs in radio history—in any format—and his awards and honors are numerous and varied: in 1983 he was named Best New Vocalist by the Academy of Country Music; he has been inducted into the Western Music Association Hall of Fame; the Cowboy Hall of Fame's Western Heritage Awards has honored him six times; he has received the Will Rogers Cowboy Philosopher Award; six of his thirty albums have gone gold; and he wrote New Mexico's state ballad, "The Land of Enchantment."

MORE TASTY MORSELS:
michaelmartinmurphey.com
MICHAEL'S CHARITY: The Osteogenesis Imperfecta Foundation, oif.org

Cowboy Hashbrowns

This recipe was created by Michael Martin's favorite chuckwagon cook, John Schaffner. The dish has been served at many trail rides, concerts, special events, and church gatherings that MMM and John have worked together. According to Murphey, the recipe will provide a scrumptious helping of "authentic cowboy cookin' and is extremely tasty." His dad, P. L. Murphey, named the recipe!

3½–4 lb. washed, unpeeled potatoes, diced
½ onion, diced
Zesty Italian dressing
⅛–¼ c. soy sauce
salt and pepper

Heat a 12-inch cast-iron Dutch oven over a bed of coals. Soak diced potatoes in cool water until ready to use.

Take the preheated Dutch oven off the coals, remove the lid, and pour in enough Zesty Italian dressing to cover the bottom. (The Dutch oven should be hot enough that the dressing sizzles when it is poured in.)

Drain the water from the potatoes and dump them and the diced onions into the Dutch oven until it is level. Pour soy sauce over the top of the potatoes.. Add salt and pepper to the top. Replace the oven lid.

Place the Dutch oven back over the bed of coals and cover the top of the lid with coals. (Important hint: The coals for cooking with a Dutch oven should be from good, dry hardwood so that they stay hot long enough to complete the cooking.)

In 45 minutes to an hour they should be cooked and ready to serve. Stir the potatoes somewhat as you serve them, to mix in all the flavors.

Dixie Chicks

SHOW DATES:

1999
2001
2007

SERVING UP: Country

A FEW INGREDIENTS: One day perhaps they'll replace the phrase "selling like hotcakes" with "selling like Dixie Chicks albums"; two of the band's albums, *Wide Open Spaces* and *Fly*, made it to diamond certification, signifying sales of ten million each. Dixie Chicks are the only country group in history and the only female group of any genre to release back-to-back diamond albums.

Dixie Chicks have won more than ten Grammy Awards and sold over one hundred million dollars in concert tickets. Outspoken songs like "Goodbye, Earl" highlight their make-our-own-rules philosophy. Their 2006 album *Taking the Long Way* and the single "Not Ready to Make Nice" won Grammies for Record of the Year, Album of the Year, Best Country Performance by Duo or Group, and Best Country Album.

MORE TASTY MORSELS: dixiechicks.com DIXIE CHICKS' CHARITY: Thoughtful House Center for Children, thoughtfulhouse.org

Acorn Squash–Sweet Potato Purée

Submitted by Emily Robison

A lighter version of this recipe can be done by using two acorn squash instead of sweet potatoes, replacing the regular yogurt with light yogurt, and removing the butter from the recipe. It is a nice alternative to regular sweet potatoes for the holidays, and is great for homemade baby food!

1 large acorn squash
2 large sweet potatoes
water
2 T. butter
⅓ c. Fage Greek yogurt
cinnamon
allspice
ground sea salt
pepper

Preheat oven to 300°.

Wash, cut into quarters, and deseed the acorn squash.

Wash and quarter the sweet potatoes. Place the pieces of the squash and potatoes skin side up in a deep baking dish and fill with about ¾" of water.

Cover the dish with foil and bake at 300° for about an hour or until the squash and potatoes are soft.

When they are done, remove all the skin on both the squash and sweet potatoes and place the softened squash and potatoes into a mixing bowl. Add the butter and yogurt and purée the mixture (this can be done easily with a hand mixer). Add spices to your taste and continue to blend. Serve like mashed potatoes. Yield: 4 servings.

Ryan Bingham

SHOW DATE:

2008

Bingham's South Texas Taters

5 large potatoes
5 jalapeño peppers
2 onions
1 stick of butter
1 (12-oz.) can of beer (Tecate preferred)
½ oz. shredded cheese of choice

Peel potatoes and cut into any size desired. Do the same with jalapeños and onions.

Cut up butter and place into medium sized casserole dish with potatoes. Pile on the pepper and onions. Pour in the beer.

Cover dish with foil and bake until potatoes are soft.

Remove from oven and add cheese. Cover again with foil until cheese is melted. Serve.

SERVING UP: Alt-country

A FEW INGREDIENTS: With the 2006 debut album *Dead Horses*, Ryan Bingham started measuring out the ingredients for his own recipe for success, one that was seasoned with his love of traditional country music. The following year saw the release of his major label debut, *Mescalito*, which was peppered with a little finger-picking, some mandolin and harmonica, some Rolling Stones-flavored blues.

Ryan has performed on Bob Harris's country show on BBC's Radio 2, on the *Tonight Show with Jay Leno*, and on *Late Night with Conan O'Brien*.

MORE TASTY MORSELS: binghammusic.com
RYAN'S CHARITY: Surfrider Foundation, surfrider.org

Drive-By Truckers

SHOW DATE: 2008

Drunken Baby Carrots

Submitted by Shonna Tucker

This is a simple but delicious side dish. If you like carrots, you're gonna love these!

2 tsp. olive oil
1 lb. baby carrots, washed and trimmed
1 clove garlic, chopped
1 tsp. dried or ¼ cup fresh rosemary
salt and pepper to taste
1 c. veggie or chicken stock
1 c. red wine

Heat olive oil in large pan over medium heat.

Add carrots. Stir often to keep from burning for about 5 minutes. Add garlic, rosemary, salt, and pepper. Cook for about another 2–3 minutes. Add stock and wine. Bring to a boil. Reduce heat and cover. Let simmer for about 15 minutes, stirring occasionally. Uncover and simmer for about another 5 minutes or until carrots are fork tender. Serve hot. Enjoy!

SERVING UP: Rock, alt-country, cowpunk, southern rock

A FEW INGREDIENTS: If you like an extra helping of southern influence with your rock and country music, Drive-By Truckers delivers. Their 1998 debut album, *Gangstabilly*, was followed by 1999's *Pizza Deliverance* and 2001's *Southern Rock Opera*, which received a four-star review in *Rolling Stone* magazine. Their eighth album, *Brighter than Creation's Dark* cracked the top forty on the *Billboard* Hot 100 chart.

The band also performed as backup musicians for Bettye LaVette's 2007 album, *The Scene of the Crime*, which went to number one on *Billboard*'s Blues Chart and was nominated for a Grammy Award for Best Contemporary Blues Album.

MORE TASTY MORSELS: drivebytruckers.com
DRIVE-BY TRUCKER'S CHARITY: Nuci's Space, Athens, Georgia, nuci.org

Thank you, *Austin City Limits*. I had a blast taping the show and playing the festival. You rock! Hope to see you guys again real soon!

—Shonna Tucker, Drive-By Truckers

The Polyphonic Spree

SHOW DATE: 2004

SERVING UP: Choral symphonic rock, psychedelic pop

A FEW INGREDIENTS: If you're mixing up a recipe like the Polyphonic Spree, chances are you'll have to go back to the store for more ingredients. At different times in the evolution of this Dallas band, the lineup has included between thirteen and twenty-seven members, including a ten-person choir. Polyphonic Spree started getting widespread attention from critics and fans when their song "Light & Day/ Reach For the Sun" was used in a joint commercial for Volkswagen and Apple. In 2004, they were featured on the TV shows *Scrubs* and *Las Vegas*, as well as the soundtrack for the movie *Eternal Sunshine of the Spotless Mind*. They have toured extensively and were invited to perform at the Nobel Peace Prize Concert honoring Wangari Maathai.

MORE TASTY MORSELS: thepolyphonicspree.com

THE POLYPHONIC SPREE'S CHARITY: Save Darfur Coalition, savedarfur.org

Hangover Hash

Submitted by Jennie Kelley

This spicy and full-flavored breakfast dish is a wonderful way to start the day after a long night out (or a great way to wrap up a long tour before some much-deserved R&R). For the full experience, accompanying the dish with fresh mimosas is highly recommended!

3 T. extra-virgin olive oil, divided
8 oz. mushrooms, thinly sliced (button or baby bella)
¾ red onion, chopped
salt and pepper to taste
1 lb. lean ground turkey
¼ c. low-sodium chicken stock
3 tsp. ground cumin
3 tsp. chili powder
½ bunch flat-leaf parsley, finely chopped
4 oz. Manchego cheese, grated
1 T. butter
6 large cage-free brown eggs
Pico de Gallo (prepare ahead; recipe follows)

Drizzle 1 tablespoon of the olive oil into a large saucepan over medium-high heat. Sauté the mushrooms and ¾ of the red onion with a dash of salt and pepper until soft, about 5 minutes.

Set the mushrooms and onions aside and lower the heat to medium. In the same pan, add the remaining olive oil and coat the entire base of the pan. Add the ground turkey in small bits to cook thoroughly. To keep the lean turkey moist, cook slowly and add chicken stock if it seems to be drying out or overcooking.

Add the ground cumin and chili powder, then salt and pepper to taste. When the meat has just browned, add the mushrooms and onions back to the pan and simmer for about 5 minutes to cook the meat through entirely. Drain and plate on a large serving tray. Sprinkle with parsley and Manchego, then cover with foil and set aside until the eggs are ready.

Lightly butter a large nonstick, oven-safe pan and place over medium heat. Crack in 6 eggs and season with salt and pepper. When the egg whites just begin to set, place the pan in a preheated oven and broil to cook completely (approximately 1 to 2 minutes, depending on yolk preference). Remove and immediately place the eggs on the hash, maintaining the integrity of the yolks. The Pico de Gallo can be added on top or served on the side. Serve immediately. Yield: 4–6 servings.

PICO DE GALLO

2 tomatoes, chopped and drained (heirloom is recommended but not required)
1 large bell pepper, chopped
1 large jalapeño, finely diced
¼ red onion, chopped
salt and pepper to taste
2 limes, freshly squeezed
½ bunch cilantro, roughly chopped

This can be done the day of, but it's recommended that you prepare this the night before so the flavors can fully combine. Regardless, it should definitely be made before starting on the hash.

In a medium bowl, combine the tomatoes, bell pepper, jalapeño, and red onion. Add salt and pepper to evenly coat the vegetables. Add the lime juice and cilantro, then stir everything together. Refrigerate for at least 30 minutes.

Hit Singles

Hal Ketchum

SHOW DATES:

1992
1994
1998

Chicken Enchiladas

4 skinless, boneless chicken breast halves
1 onion, chopped
½ pt. sour cream
1¾ c. shredded cheddar cheese, divided
1 T. dried parsley
½ tsp. dried oregano
½ tsp. ground black pepper
½ tsp. salt (optional)
1 (15-oz.) can tomato sauce
½ c. water
1 T. chili powder
⅓ c. green bell pepper, chopped
1 clove garlic, minced
8 (10-inch) flour tortillas
1 (12-oz.) jar taco sauce

Preheat oven to 350°.

In a medium, nonstick skillet over medium heat, cook chicken until it is no longer pink and juices run clear. Drain excess fat. Cube the chicken and return it to the skillet. Add onion, sour cream, cheddar cheese, parsley, oregano and ground black pepper. Heat until cheese melts. Stir in salt, tomato sauce, water, chili powder, bell pepper, and garlic.

Roll even amounts of the mixture in the tortillas. Arrange in a 9 × 13–inch baking dish. Cover with taco sauce and remaining cheddar cheese. Bake uncovered in the preheated oven 20 minutes. Cool 10 minutes before serving.

SERVING UP: Country

A FEW INGREDIENTS: Forget the main course and go straight to Hal Ketchum, who has been called "the most effervescent voice in country music." Hal continues to write his own recipe for artistic success, blending painting, master carpentry, and a wildly successful recording career. His first single, "Small Town Saturday Night," hit number two on *Billboard*, and his debut album, *Past the Point of Rescue*, went gold in 1991. He's had fifteen hits in the top ten, five of those in the top five. He's also a favorite of fellow musicians; artists as varied as Neil Diamond and Trisha Yearwood have covered his songs.

MORE TASTY MORSELS: halketchum.com.
HAL'S CHARITIES: St. Jude Children's Research Hospital, stjude.org, World Vision, worldvision.org

Little Feat

SHOW DATE: 1991

Paul's Chicken Tostada

leftover chicken
salsa to taste
raisins
1 or 2 tortillas (flour or corn)
cheese (I find a nice sharp cheddar works for me)
lettuce
tomatoes
sliced avocado
grated carrots
beans
Tabasco sauce (optional)
mayo and ketchup (optional)

Wondering what to do when you have leftover chicken? Here's a quick fix: cut up all the leftover chicken and put it in a saucepan, and then add your favorite salsa to taste, either homemade or bottled (I like La Victoria medium). Then add raisins—yes raisins, kind of a Tex-Mex concoction—and heat it up real good!

Heat up either a corn or flour tortilla, either on the griddle or just on the burners until it's a little crispy, then lay it out on a plate, put your hot chicken-and-salsa mix on top and then add some cheese so it can melt a little bit. Then add the salad fixins' on top and serve with more salsa or a salad dressing made from mayo and ketchup with some Tabasco sauce thrown in for good heat! Enjoy. Yield: 1 or two tostadas.

SERVING UP: A fusion of rock, funk, and boogie

A FEW INGREDIENTS: Little Feat has been serving up a rich musical gumbo of rock, folk, funk, country, and what they call "New Orleans swamp boogie" since 1969. Their self-titled debut released in 1971 featured the popular hit "Willin'."

After countless lineups and decades of touring and recording, the band was recently celebrated with a reissue of their classic live album *Waiting for Columbus* and a huge box set called *Hotcakes and Outtakes: 30 Years of Little Feat*. Another recent work, an album titled *Join the Band*, included musical collaborations with Jimmy Buffett, Dave Matthews, Bob Seger, Emmylou Harris, Vince Gill, and others—and it all makes musical sense.

MORE TASTY MORSELS: littlefeat.net
LITTLE FEAT'S CHARITY: The ALS Association, Greater Los Angeles Chapter, webgla.alsa.org

Nanci Griffith

SHOW DATES:

1985
1989
1992
1995
1998
1999
2001

SERVING UP: Folk, country

A FEW INGREDIENTS: Austin-born Nanci Griffith is known as much for her brilliant, confessional songwriting as she is for her beautiful voice.

Her career started to bubble in the late 1970s and early 1980s with the release of her first two independent recordings: *There's a Light Beyond These Woods* and *Poet in My Window*.

With a career that has spanned three decades, she's received a total of five Grammy nominations—including a win for *Other Voices, Other Rooms*, which celebrated the work of other songwriters. Her CD *Last of the True Believers* was nominated for a Contemporary Folk Grammy in 1986, and "Love at the Five and Dime," a song Nanci wrote for Kathy Mattea, was nominated for Country Song of the Year. The remaining nominations were for her dazzling performances on albums by the Chieftains.

Her album *Ruby's Torch* was cookin' in 2006, and we can look forward to many new albums of songs penned by Nanci Griffith on the menu soon.

MORE TASTY MORSELS: nancigriffith.com

Quick Chili and Enchiladas

I can't really claim this as an original recipe but on a "chilly" winter day, it never fails to please my household. For the chili, I use Wick Fowler's 2-Alarm Chili Kit using 2 lb. of ground turkey breast and adding chopped fresh tomatoes occasionally. (In a pinch, a can of Wolf Brand chili in a can will do, but nothing beats Wick Fowler's because you made it yourself.) Follow the instructions on the package. There is always leftover chili in my freezer to supply the makins' for enchiladas.

Sometimes the leftover chili is too thick for the enchiladas, so when you reheat it, you can add water and cumin (a tsp. at most) so that it is liquid enough to spoon over the enchiladas.

1 doz. soft corn tortillas
3 T. cooking oil
approx. 3 c. shredded Colby cheese, divided
onion, chopped
sautéed mushrooms, chopped (optional)
2 fresh jalapeños, chopped (optional)
leftover chili (prepare ahead; see introductory note)

Preheat oven to 350°. Heat oil in a skillet. With kitchen tongs, place individual tortillas briefly in the oil, just long enough to soften them. Remove and place on paper towel, then place in 11 × 17–inch baking dish. Set aside.

In a medium bowl, mix together ¾ c. shredded cheese, ¾ c. onions, mushrooms (optional), and jalapeños (optional) for the enchilada filling. Spoon 2 T. of this mixture into a flat tortilla in the baking dish.

Roll 'em up with the seam on the bottom. Spoon your leftover chili evenly on top of the rolled enchilada. Sprinkle remaining cheese and chopped onion on top and bake in the oven for 20 minutes. And that's the whole enchilada!

Riders in the Sky

SHOW DATES:
1981
1987
1993

SERVING UP: Cowboy music

A FEW INGREDIENTS: For three decades, Riders in the Sky has kept alive the tradition of cowboy music—handed down to them from the Sons of the Pioneers, Gene Autry, and Roy Rogers—while putting their own brand on the genre.

The Western Music Association has named Riders in the Sky Entertainers of the Year seven times. The group wrote the score for the 2002 Academy Award-winning short *For the Birds* and composed the theme song for the Internet cartoon show "Thomas Timberwolf." But they are most often linked to the lovable cowboy Woody in *Toy Story 2*; in 2001 Riders in the Sky wrote the song "Woody's Roundup," which appeared on the soundtrack and helped them earn their first Grammy—the Best Musical Album for Children Award. Two years later, they roped in their second Grammy in the same category, for *Monsters Inc. Scream Factory Favorites*, the companion CD for that award-winning movie.

MORE TASTY MORSELS: ridersinthesky.com

RIDERS IN THE SKY'S CHARITIES: American Cancer Society, cancer.org, Gilda's Club Worldwide, gildasclub.org

Tooranch Chili

Submitted by Too Slim (Fred LaBour)

This recipe will feed 8 to 10 hungry ranch hands, and it's easy to half if you have fewer mouths to feed. Trust Too Slim: "It's idiot-proof and tastes great!" Try it topped with cheese, onions, or jalapeños and served with chips.

2 lb. ground turkey or beef
1 large or 2 medium onions, chopped
1 (16-oz.) jar salsa (live it up, get a spicy one!)
1 (10-oz.) pkg. frozen corn
2 (16-oz.) cans kidney beans, drained
2 (16-oz.) cans pinto beans, drained
2 (16-oz.) cans black beans, drained
2 (16-oz.) cans diced tomatoes
2 pkg. dry chili seasoning

Brown the ground meat and onion. If you are using low-fat turkey, you might want to add a tsp. or two of oil to the pan.

While the meat is browning, combine remaining ingredients in a large pot and cook over medium-high heat. Stir occasionally and bring to a simmering boil.

Stir in the browned meat and onion. Cover and cook on low for one hour, or transfer the chili to a slow cooker and cook on low for 4–6 hours.

Tracy Lawrence

SHOW DATE: 1993

Pulled-Pork Enchiladas

1 small pork shoulder
8 large flour tortillas
1 medium onion, chopped
1½ tsp. cumin
1 tsp. salt
1½ tsp. cayenne pepper (optional)
1 small bell pepper, chopped
2 regular cans tomato sauce
½ lb. cheddar cheese, grated

Cook pork shoulder until tender and done. Pull meat from shoulder in strands. Fill each tortilla with pork.

Mix onion, cumin, salt, cayenne, bell pepper, and 1 can of tomato sauce. Spoon mixture over meat in tortillas. Roll tortillas, and place face down in deep pan. Cover with remaining tomato sauce and cheese. Bake at 350° until cheese is melted. Serve Hot! Yield: 8 servings.

SERVING UP: Country

A FEW INGREDIENTS: Tracy moved to Nashville in 1990, where he developed his own style: country with a cutting edge. His first album, 1991's *Sticks and Stones*, catapulted him to the top of the charts, yielding three number one hits and one top-ten hit. Since then he has had two platinum records and two double-platinum records, and was named the Academy of Country Music's Top New Male Vocalist in 1993. Tracy has starred in two CMT specials, one of which included footage of him on a USO tour to Kosovo to entertain troops. He also co-produced nine of the thirteen songs on *The Civil War: The Nashville Sessions*, a collection of songs written for the Broadway theater production *The Civil War: An American Musical Event*.

MORE TASTY MORSELS: tracylawrence.musiccitynetworks.com

TRACY'S CHARITY: Tracy Lawrence Fund, tracylawrence.musiccitynetworks.com

Widespread Panic

SHOW DATES:

2000
2005

SERVING UP: Southern rock

A FEW INGREDIENTS: Widespread Panic is known for their nonstop touring (they play as many as two hundred and fifty shows a year) and their ability to fill big concert arenas across the country. Their major label debut came in 1991 with their self-titled album. Widespread Panic has sold more than three million albums, and released a total of fifteen CDs and five DVDs. They also started the Tunes for Tots annual benefit concert, which raises money to buy musical instruments for children.

In 2002 the band had a double helping of great success, receiving gold certification for their concert DVD *Live at Oak Mountain* and headlining two nights of the first Bonnaroo Music Festival, where they played for a crowd of upwards of seventy thousand people.

MORE TASTY MORSELS: widespreadpanic.com

WIDESPREAD PANIC'S CHARITY: ArtDocs: Artists Receiving Treatment, Doctors Offering Crucial Services, artdocs.com

"Chilly"

Submitted by John Bell

This recipe was inspired by the Widespread Panic song "Chilly Water," and was submitted on behalf of Widespread Panic.

This can be cooked slowly (3–8 hours in a crockpot) or in 1–2 hours (in a big stovetop pot), depending on personal time considerations and sense of ritual.

1 (15-oz.) can black beans
1 (15-oz.) can navy beans
1 (15-oz.) can red kidney beans
2 (14.5-oz.) cans diced tomatoes
1 (10-oz.) can Ro-Tel Chili Fixin's
1 c. onion, diced
1 c. carrot, finely diced
⅔ c. celery, diced
⅔ c. bell pepper
½ c. fresh cilantro, minced
2 bulbs fresh garlic
salt and ground pepper to taste
6 Morningstar Farms Veggie Breakfast Sausage Patties
olive oil or cooking spray
Italian seasoning to taste
garlic powder to taste
chili powder to taste
favorite hot sauce to taste

Drain beans in a colander. Put the still dripping beans into crockpot. Add 1 can of diced tomatoes and 1 can of Ro-Tel Chili Fixin's. Put in crockpot on high and cover.

Begin sipping on beer, wine, or beverage of choice. (Careful with your knives!)

Set aside ¼ of the vegetables, cilantro, and fresh garlic to use later. Dump the rest in the crockpot. Add a little salt and pepper (about 1 tsp. each). Stir it up, cover, and do something else for 2 hours.

Finely chop the six "sausage patties" (after blasting them for 1 minute in microwave). Sauté and brown in olive oil (or spray oil, which can help prevent over-oiling). Stir in a little pepper and Italian seasoning while browning.

Add "meat" about ½ hr before serving to best preserve its fake meat texture. Add remainder of above-mentioned vegetables and cilantro. Add the second can of diced tomatoes.

Use spices throughout the process according to personal taste. Other "secret" ingredients you might try: bay leaf, sun-dried tomatoes, chocolate, red wine (but use any of these sparingly—sun dried tomatoes you can be heavier with). Yield: 4–6 servings.

Joss Stone

SHOW DATE: 2004

SERVING UP: Soul, R&B

A FEW INGREDIENTS: Few chefs shoot to the top of their careers in their teens, but Joss Stone had all the ingredients ready early. Born in England, Joss released a cover album of soul classics titled *The Soul Sessions* when she was sixteen. Her 2004 CD, *Mind, Body, and Soul*, showcasing her original material, went multiplatinum and featured the song "You Had Me." The album and the single were nominated for Grammy Awards in 2005 while Joss was nominated for Best New Artist. In 2006 she joined Stevie Wonder, John Legend, and India.Arie in the Super Bowl XL pregame show, and in 2007 her album *Introducing Joss Stone* achieved gold status.

MORE TASTY MORSELS: jossstone.com.
JOSS'S CHARITY: Amigos Charity, amigos.org.uk

Veggie Lasagna

8 T. olive oil
1 large red onion, diced
4 cloves garlic
9 T. butter
1 (10.5-oz.) bag Quorn Mince
1½ cans chopped tomatoes
1 tsp. of Dijon mustard
7 T. flour
6 T. sun-dried tomato purée
1 can kidney beans
1 can butter beans
1½ pt. milk
salt and pepper
½ lb. mature cheddar cheese
splash of red wine
fresh basil
1 handful chopped white grapes
1 box lasagna sheets
1 handful grated cheese

It is essential that you put on some soul music to cook to; I am listening to Van Morrison but also love to cook to Dusty Springfield.

Preheat the oven to 425°.

Warm the olive oil in a deep pan, fry the diced onion, and add the garlic. Whilst this is cooking, melt the butter into another saucepan in preparation for the cheese sauce.

When you feel the onion and garlic are fried off to your satisfaction, add the Quorn Mince, and the 1½ cans of chopped tomatoes. (What's great here is you don't have to wait for the Quorn to defrost before you add the tomatoes.)

Now we are back to the cheese sauce. Add mustard to the melted butter and stir. Now add the flour, and mix while the pan is off the heat, making a roux sauce.

Add the sun-dried tomato purée to the Quorn mix, and give that a stir up. If you feel it's getting too dry you can add water. Then add the kidney beans and butter beans.

Back to the roux: mix the milk in slowly, in parts. If you don't mix it in increments it will go lumpy, which is the shittiest thing. Beat it at every stage until it comes to a boil. Add salt and pepper to taste. Once the roux sauce has come to a boil you can add the cheese, and keep mixing it—don't ever ignore the cheese sauce because if you turn your back on it for one minute it will fuck you! Once the cheese has melted into the sauce you can pop that to one side, off the heat. If you have any lumps in the bastard cheese sauce feel free to use a whisk to beat them to hell, as you must have a smooth sauce.

A splash of red wine and a few leaves of basil are always nice in the Quorn-tomato goodness, though not necessary. Once you feel the sauce is perfect, add 1 handful of chopped white grapes to the Quorn-tomato Bolognese. (Please bear in mind I have small lady hands, so no huge man-handfuls please!)

Grab a large ceramic baking tray, and oil the base of the tray to ensure the lasagna does not stick. Lay a lasagna sheet into the baking tray. Pour a generous helping of the tomato sauce over the lasagna sheet, add a little cheese sauce with a ladle, and then repeat the process until the dish reaches about half an inch from the top. Sometimes the lasagna will not fit the pan exactly, so feel free to break the lasagna sheets into smaller bits to make it fit.

Once you feel you have enough lasagna in your life, pour the remaining cheese sauce on top and cover the dish with grated cheese.

Pop in the oven for half an hour. Once the lasagna is browned, remove and serve. Thank God I'm not a model because this dish is not healthy, but hey, it tastes great! I hope you've had a good time cooking with me.

Jimmy LaFave

SHOW DATE: 1996

Italian Spaghetti with Pine Nuts

1 lb. spaghetti, dried
dash olive oil
¼ c. butter
salt and ground pepper
1 garlic clove, crushed
1 small onion, very finely chopped
⅔ c. pine nuts
2 T. fresh parsley, chopped
1 (8-oz.) carton sieved tomatoes
4 T. chopped basil
grated fresh Parmesan cheese

Cook the spaghetti in boiling water with a dash of olive oil—stirring occasionally, until tender. Drain and set aside.

Melt the butter in a large frying pan and sauté the garlic and onion for about 3 minutes or until the onion has softened.

Add the pine nuts and stir-fry until evenly golden.

Add the tomatoes, basil, garlic, parsley, salt and pepper and cook for 5 minutes stirring occasionally. Then add the spaghetti and stir to coat in the tomato sauce. Cook another 5 minutes and serve straight from the pan. Top with the sprinkled slivers of Parmesan cheese.

SERVING UP: Red dirt music

A FEW INGREDIENTS: Originally from Oklahoma, Jimmy LaFave has been mixing up his recipe for country music in Austin since 1986. In 1995 and 1996 Jimmy was chosen Best Singer-Songwriter at the Austin Music Awards. That same year he performed at the Rock and Roll Hall of Fame tribute to Woody Guthrie. He has toured extensively in the U.S., Canada, and Europe. His latest release, *Cimarron Manifesto* features special guest appearances by Carrie Rodriguez, Ruthie Foster and Kacy Crowley.

MORE TASTY MORSELS: jimmylafave.com
JIMMY'S CHARITY: The American Indian College Fund, collegefund.org

What Made Milwaukee Famous

SHOW DATE:

2005

Rigatoni with Black Pesto, Sweet Corn, Goat Cheese, and Squash

Submitted by Jeremy Bruch

This is easy, summery, and insanely delicious—warm or cold. The pesto can be made in bulk and frozen in ice cube trays for times when basil is hard to find.

PASTA

1 box rigatoni pasta
1 squash, sliced lengthwise and quartered
olive oil
Black Pesto (prepare ahead; recipe follows)
1 ear sweet corn, cut from cooked cob
1 pkg. of goat cheese, broken into small pieces
dash of salt

Cook pasta as directed, drain, and set aside. Sauté squash in a little olive oil until tender.

Add pesto, corn, and squash to pasta, and toss well. Add goat cheese and toss again lightly.

Now, try to stop eating it. Go ahead. Try.

BLACK PESTO

¼ c. smokehouse almonds
1 c. olive oil
1 bunch opal (purple) basil
2 cloves garlic

Combine almonds, oil, basil, and garlic in a food processor.

SERVING UP: Indie rock

A FEW INGREDIENTS: You might not expect a band named What Made Milwaukee Famous to hail from Austin, Texas, but indeed it does. The band performs regularly at local shows and every year at the South by Southwest music festival, and Austinites love 'em almost as much as they love barbecue and Lone Stars. The world is quickly catching on to the energetic, forceful, and impassioned pop rock the band is known for. Their debut CD, *Trying to Never Catch Up*, was recommended by the *Austin Chronicle* as an Album of the Year in 2006. The band has been named in *Billboard* and *Rolling Stone* as a band to watch. They have also appeared on WXPN's *World Cafe Live* in Philadelphia, Steve Lamacq's music show on BBC Radio, and at the Austin City Limits music festival.

MORE TASTY MORSELS: whatmademilwaukeefamous.com

JEREMY'S CHARITY: Eager to Learn Program, Austin Public Library, Austin, Texas, ci.austin.tx.us/library

Bob Schneider

SHOW DATE: 2000

SERVING UP: Alternative

A FEW INGREDIENTS: Bob Schneider approaches music the way a great chef approaches cooking. He mixes together a little funk, tosses in some country, seasons with rock, and tops it off with some folk music. Several of his tunes have appeared in movies and on TV. His song "Blue Skies for Everyone" was included in the movie *Gun Shy*, "The World Exploded into Love" was featured on the first episode of the television sitcom *Men in Trees*, and "Bullets" appeared on the *Jay and Silent Bob Strike Back* soundtrack. Bob is committed to playing smaller venues and thrives on the energy of the stage. He plays regularly at the Saxon Pub and Antone's in Austin, Texas, when he's not touring with other acts such as the Dixie Chicks, who he joined on the road in 2006.

MORE TASTY MORSELS: bobschneidermusic.com

BOB'S CHARITY: Austin Food Bank, austinfoodbank.org

Bob's Baddass Veggie Chili

¼ c. olive oil
2 large onions, chopped
1 (12-oz.) pkg. Quorn meatless and soy-free grounds
⅛ c. instant espresso powder
⅛ c. chili powder
⅛ c. ground cumin
⅛ c. dried oregano leaves
1 (28-oz.) cans crushed tomatoes with added purée
⅛ c. honey
3 large cloves garlic, minced
3 (15-oz.) cans black beans, rinsed and drained
1 c. water
1 tsp. salt
⅛ tsp. chipotle chili powder or chili powder
pinch of ground cinnamon

Heat the oil in heavy large pot over medium-high heat. Add the onions and meatless ground and sauté until onions are tender and the ground is cooked through.

Add the espresso powder, ¼ c. chili powder, cumin, and oregano and cook for about another minute. Add the tomatoes, honey, and garlic.

Bring the whole thing to a simmer. Set the heat to medium-low, cover, and let it do its thing for 30 minutes or so. Then add the beans, water, salt, chipotle chili powder, and cinnamon. Bring all that to a boil on the high heat.

Reduce heat to medium let it simmer and thicken for at least 30 minutes, but the longer the better and make sure to keep stirring every once in a while. Add salt to taste.

Top with sour cream and/or shredded cheddar.

Dolly Parton

SHOW DATE: 2000

SERVING UP: Country

A FEW INGREDIENTS: Dolly Parton is one of the most successful country artists in the world, with twenty-six number one singles and forty-two top-ten country albums. In addition to serving up tasty country music, her acting career has been simmering since 1980 when she starred in *9 to 5* and received a Golden Globe nomination for Best Actress. The theme song for the movie, which she wrote and sang, earned her an Oscar nomination and two Grammys, and was number seventy-eight on the American Film Institute's television special *100 Years, 100 Songs*. Her song "I Will Always Love You" was rerecorded by Whitney Houston and became one of the best-selling singles of all time. Dolly was named the Top Female Box Office Star by the *Motion Picture Herald* in both 1981 and 1982. Her other major films were *The Best Little Whorehouse in Texas* (for which she received another Golden Globe nomination), *Rhinestone*, and *Steel Magnolias*. She is also the only musician who has her own successful theme park: Dollywood. With her quick wit, flamboyant style, and voluptuous figure, Dolly is an American icon.

MORE TASTY MORSELS: dollyparton.com DOLLY'S CHARITY: Dolly's Imagination Library, imaginationlibrary.com, which works with local sponsors in the U.S., Canada, and the UK to inspire a love of reading and books among preschool children. To date, over fifteen million books have been mailed directly to children's homes.

Mama Dean's Chili and Spaghetti

Excerpted from Dolly's Dixie Fixin's: Love, Laughter, and Lots of Good Food

I met my husband Carl Dean on the day I arrived in Nashville. I was doing a bit of laundry at the Wishy Washy laundromat and there he was, the most handsome man I'd ever laid eyes on. The first time he brought me home to meet his Mama and Daddy was also the same night he told them we were getting married! Mama Dean made her special spaghetti, now a sentimental dish that I make for Carl a lot because it reminds us of the early days when we first got together.

3 onions, chopped
6 garlic cloves, minced
3 T. vegetable oil
3 lb. ground beef chuck
⅓ c. chili powder
2 T. sweet paprika
2 tsp. ground cumin
1 tsp. ground coriander
1 tsp. ground allspice
1 tsp. dried oregano, crumbled
½ tsp. cayenne
½ tsp. cinnamon
¼ tsp. ground cloves
1 bay leaf
1 (16-oz.) can tomato sauce
2 T. red wine vinegar
2 T. molasses
3 c. water or stock
1 lb. spaghetti, cooked

In a large heavy-bottomed pot, sauté the onions and the garlic in the oil over moderate heat, stirring, until the onions are softened. Add the beef and cook, breaking up the meat with a spoon, until the beef loses its pink color. Add the chili powder, paprika, cumin, coriander, allspice, oregano, cayenne, cinnamon and cloves, and cook the mixture, stirring, for 1 minute. Add the bay leaf, 3 c. of water, the tomato sauce, vinegar, and molasses and simmer the mixture, uncovered, stirring occasionally and adding more water if necessary to keep the beef barely covered, for 2 hours, or until it is slightly thickened, like a stew. Discard the bay leaf and season the chili with salt and pepper. Ladle the chili over the spaghetti and serve. Yield: 6 servings.

Want some great new recipes? Check Dolly's new cookbook! Details can be found at imaginationlibrary.com.

Ralph Stanley

SERVING UP: Country, bluegrass, mountain music

A FEW INGREDIENTS: Ralph Stanley has been keeping things cooking since 1946. He has more than two hundred albums under his belt, most recorded with the Stanley Brothers and the Clinch Mountain Boys, two of the most celebrated bluegrass music groups in the world. In January 2000 he became the first artist of the new millennium to be inducted into the historic Grand Ole Opry. The Library of Congress honored him with the Living Legend Award, and he was the first recipient of the Traditional American Music Award from the National Endowment for the Humanities. In 2002 Ralph won Grammy Awards for Best Country Male Vocalist Performance and Album of the Year for his work on the *O Brother, Where Art Thou?* movie soundtrack, and he is featured in a documentary about the music of the film called "Down From The Mountain."

MORE TASTY MORSELS: ralphstanley.net
RALPH'S CHARITY: Shriners Hospitals for Children, shrinershq.org

Meatballs Americana

1½ lb. lean ground chuck or round
1 tsp. salt
¼ tsp. pepper
¾ c. oats
1 c. evaporated milk
3 T. onion, finely chopped
1 T. green pepper, chopped
Spaghetti Sauce (prepare ahead; recipe follows)

Mix all ingredients except Spaghetti Sauce and form into balls—about ⅓ cup of mixture for each. Place in greased baking dish. Pour Sauce over meatballs. Bake uncovered at 325° for about 45 minutes. (Actual time will depend on the size of the meatballs so be sure to check for doneness.) Baste during cooking. If your meat is not very lean, you can use a baster to remove some of the grease from the sauce as it bakes.

SPAGHETTI SAUCE

2 T. Worcestershire sauce
2 T. brown sugar
3 T. vinegar
½ c. water
1 c. ketchup
5 T. chopped onions

Combine all ingredients.

The New Orleans Social Club

SHOW DATE:

2006

Jambalaya

- 2 bay leaves
- 1 tsp. salt
- 1 tsp. cayenne pepper
- 1 tsp. dried oregano
- 1 tsp. dried thyme
- 2 tsp. black pepper
- 3 T. butter
- 1 c. diced tasso or smoked ham
- 1 lb. sliced andouille or chorizo sausage
- 4–6 chicken thighs boned and cubed (or equivalent amount of breast if you prefer)
- 1½ c. onions, diced
- 1 c. celery, diced
- 1 c. green peppers, diced
- 3 cloves garlic, minced
- 4 medium tomatoes, peeled and diced
- ½ c. tomato sauce
- 4 c. chicken stock
- 2 c. uncooked rice
- 1 lb. shrimp, deveined

Combine seasonings and set aside in a Dutch oven or stockpot.

Melt butter, add tasso and sausage, sauté 5 minutes. Add onions, celery, and peppers. Sauté 5 minutes, stirring regularly. Add chicken, and cook another 5 minutes.

Add seasoning and garlic, stirring regularly and cook 3 minutes. Add tomatoes and sauce, stirring, add the rice, combine, then add stock and bring to a boil. Remove from stove, cover and place in 350° oven for 30 minutes. If you'd like to add shrimp, put in 1 lb., deveined, during the last 5 minutes of cooking. Yield: 8–10 servings.

SERVING UP: New Orleans funk

A FEW INGREDIENTS: After the devastation of Hurricane Katrina, a group of musicians who called the Big Easy home—including Ivan, Cyril, and Charles Neville of the Neville Brothers, two members of the Meters, Raymond Weber, and Henry Butler—decided to band together to restore the city's musical heritage. The New Orleans Social Club, as they have come to be known, whisked together a CD filled with old and new songs, and called it *Sing Me Back Home*. The CD also included tunes by Marcia Ball, Dr. John, the subdudes, and other friends.

MORE TASTY MORSELS: burgundyrecords.com/nosc

THE NEW ORLEANS SOCIAL CLUB'S CHARITY: New Orleans Musicians' Clinic, neworleansmusiciansclinic.org

the subdudes

SHOW DATE: 1992

SERVING UP: American rock, blues, soul

A FEW INGREDIENTS: Blending artful storytelling with soulful harmonies, the subdudes' music is a New Orleans-style gumbo of rock, blues, roots, Cajun, and soul sounds. From their self-titled 1989 debut to 2007's critically acclaimed *Street Symphony*, the subdudes have perfected their own unique recipe. The band got together in 1987 for what they thought would be a one-time performance in New Orleans, but the show—featuring mostly acoustic music with strong vocal harmonies and the use of a tambourine instead of drums—was so successful, the subdudes took off. After a six-year hiatus, the band continues to tour and win over new fans with their rootsy music.

MORE TASTY MORSELS: thesubdudes.com THE SUBDUDES' CHARITY: Autism Society of America, autism-society.org

Weenie Jambalaya

Submitted by Jimmy Messa

When I was a little kid, my mom (Mae Messa), used to cook this for us as a special treat sometimes, down in Chalmette, Louisiana. I still make it and I love it! I hope you like it, too.

- 5 or 6 Hormel Little Sizzlers pork sausages, cut into ¼ inch disks
- olive oil
- 1 medium yellow onion, chopped
- 1 medium green bell pepper, chopped
- 5 or 6 high-quality hot dogs (such as Nathan's), cut into ¼ inch disks
- 3 or 4 cloves garlic, chopped
- 1 (15-oz.) can Del Monte stewed tomatoes, well drained and chopped (you should use some of the tomato water from the can as your rice cooking water)
- Cajun seasoning (such as Tony Chachere's or similar)
- salt and pepper to taste
- ½ c. Mahatma short-grain rice
- 1 c. (or a tiny bit less) water

In a pretty big (2- or 3-qt.) heavy-bottomed saucepan, fry the Little Sizzlers until brown over medium heat. They will release a good bit of oil. When browned, remove from pan.

Add a small amount of olive oil, 1 or 2 T. at most, to the pan. When it returns to temperature, add the onions and bell pepper. Fry until the onions are translucent, about 5 minutes.

Add the hot dogs and cook for about 3 to 5 minutes more. Add the garlic, cook for about 2 minutes more (do not let the garlic burn!). Return the Little Sizzlers to the pot along with the chopped tomatoes. Cook till the tomatoes are just heated through, about 2 minutes.

Sprinkle on a generous amount (according to your taste) of the Cajun seasoning, salt, and pepper. Stir so everything in the pot is seasoned.

Add the rice and stir so that everything is well mixed. Fry the rice for about 30 or 40 seconds. Add the water, stir, and then turn up the heat to bring to a boil. As soon as it starts to boil, cover the pot and turn the heat down to very low.

Cook, covered, for 20 minutes. If, after 20 minutes, the rice still seems a little wet, cook uncovered for a couple of minutes more.

This dish is even better the next day, so I sometimes cook it and leave it in the refrigerator overnight, then microwave individual servings in bowls. This goes great with a salad, Louisiana hot sauce, and buttered French bread. Enjoy!

Shelby Lynne

SHOW DATES:

1991
2000

Southern Italian Sausage Sandwich

6 turkey sausages
2 red bell peppers
1 white onion
4 cloves of garlic
sweet fresh basil
dried oregano
1 can tomato paste
¾ c. dry Marsala wine
6 sourdough baguettes

Before I start I'll go ahead and tell you that I don't measure much when I cook. And I cook a lot in a cast-iron skillet, but whatever you have is OK.

Brown sausages in skillet, remove. Slice peppers and onions, chop garlic and basil. Add to skillet.

Allow peppers and onions to cook down then add garlic, basil, and oregano. When onions are translucent and peppers are limp add ½ can of tomato paste for color and sweet flavor.

Then add the Marsala wine and the sausages back into the pan and let simmer for about 20 minutes.

I hollow out a little of the bread, spoon sausage on, and serve open faced. You know what you do now. Eat it! Yield: 6 servings.

SERVING UP: Alt-country, roots

A FEW INGREDIENTS: Although she is perhaps best known as a country artist, Shelby Lynne's music takes a bite from blues, southern soul, roots rock, western swing, jazz, and adult contemporary pop. Early in her career, in 1988, she sang a duet with George Jones called "If I Could Bottle this Up," which became a top-fifty hit. She won the ACM's Top New Female Vocalist in 1990, and in 1991 she was given the CMA Horizon Award. In 2000, she released *I Am Shelby Lynne* for which she won the Grammy for Best New Artist. Her next two projects, *Love, Shelby* and *Identity Crisis*, reached number one and number five, respectively, on the U.S. charts. In 2001 she performed at Radio City Music Hall at a tribute to John Lennon, and she had the role of Carrie Cash in the 2005 film *Walk the Line*. Her songs are among those featured on sister Allison Moorer's 2008 album, *Mockingbird*.

MORE TASTY MORSELS: shelbylynne.com

Sweet Sounds

DESSERTS

B. B. King

SHOW DATES:

1983
1993
1996

SERVING UP: Blues

A FEW INGREDIENTS: B. B. King is an internationally known blues singer. With over one hundred albums to his name, the international "King of the Blues" still loves the South. "I claim Indianola, Mississippi, and Memphis, Tennessee, as my home. I was born on a plantation in Indianola and my career was launched in Memphis. Both places are rich in music heritage and famous for their down-home cooking," he says.

MORE TASTY MORSELS: bbking.com

B. B.'S CHARITY: Juvenile Diabetes Research Foundation, jdrf.org

Classic German Chocolate Cake

The following delicious low-fat, low-calorie recipe is adapted from *1001 Desserts for Diabetics.*

1 c. granulated sugar
¾ c. packed light brown sugar
½ c. prune purée
1½ c. low-fat milk
1 T. lemon juice
4 oz. German sweet chocolate, melted
1 tsp. vanilla
2 eggs
2 egg whites
2 c. all-purpose flour
1 tsp. baking soda
½ tsp. salt
Coconut Frosting (recipe follows)

Mix sugars and prune purée, milk, lemon juice, melted chocolate, and vanilla in large bowl. Beat in eggs and egg whites. Combine flour, baking soda, and salt in a small bowl and add to mixture.

Pour batter into two greased and floured 9-inch round cake pans. Bake at 350° until cakes spring back when touched, about 25 minutes. Cool in pans on wire rack for 10 minutes; remove from pans and cool completely.

Place 1 cake layer on serving plate; spread with ¾ c. Coconut Frosting; top with second cake layer. Frost top and sides of cake. Yield: 16 servings.

COCONUT FROSTING

⅓ c. sugar
1 T. cornstarch
2½ T. margarine
3 T. light corn syrup
⅔ c. evaporated fat-free milk
1 tsp. vanilla
¼ c. coconut, shredded
½ c. toasted pecans, chopped

Combine all ingredients, except coconut and pecans, in medium saucepan. Heat to boiling; stir in coconut and pecans. Cool until thick enough to spread, stirring occasionally. Yield: about 1¼ cups.

Jerry Lee Lewis

SHOW DATE: 1984

Buttermilk-Chocolate Pudding Cake

Submitted by Phoebe Lewis

2 c. sugar
1 c. salad oil
2 eggs, beaten
2 c. all purpose flour
½ tsp. baking soda
¼ c. cocoa
½ c. buttermilk
1 c. water
1 tsp. vanilla extract
Buttermilk-Chocolate Frosting (recipe follows)

Combine sugar, oil, and eggs; beat well. Combine dry ingredients; add to sugar mixture, a small amount at a time, stirring well after each addition. Blend in buttermilk, water, and vanilla. The batter will be thin.

Spoon batter into a lightly greased 13 × 9 × 2–inch pan. Bake at 350° for 25 minutes. Spread Buttermilk-Chocolate Frosting over hot cake and allow to cool in pan. Cut into squares to serve. Yield: 10 to 12 servings.

BUTTERMILK-CHOCOLATE FROSTING

1 (16-oz.) pkg. powdered sugar
¼ c. cocoa
¼ c. melted butter or margarine
1 tsp. vanilla extract
⅓ c. buttermilk

Combine powdered sugar and cocoa, blending well. Stir in remaining ingredients. Yields: Enough frosting for 1 13 × 9 × 2–inch cake.

SERVING UP: Rock and roll, country, rockabilly

A FEW INGREDIENTS: If the meal is ready and what you really need is music to jumpstart the party, Jerry Lee Lewis's hot licks and toe-tapping tunes are just the ticket. A musical pioneer on the piano, Jerry has been inducted into both the Rock and Roll Hall of Fame and the Rockabilly Hall of Fame. In 2004 *Rolling Stone* ranked him number twenty-four on their "100 Greatest Artists of All Time" list.

In his career that stretches as far back as 1957, he has had twenty-two albums and forty-seven singles make the top-twenty charts in the U.S. and Britain. Nine of his albums have been certified gold. His classic "Great Balls of Fire" was elected to the Grammy Hall of Fame in 1998, and "Whole Lotta Shakin' Goin On" received the same honor in 1999. He received a Lifetime Achievement Grammy Award in 2007. In 1989 Dennis Quaid starred as Jerry in a movie biopic, *Great Balls of Fire*.

MORE TASTY MORSELS: jerryleelewis.com

JERRY'S CHARITY: American Society for the Prevention of Cruelty to Animals, aspca.org

Johnny Gimble

SHOW DATES:

1980
1981
1990
1993

SERVING UP: Texas swing

A FEW INGREDIENTS: Johnny Gimble always fiddles with the recipe and it comes out great. Considered one of the best fiddle players in history, Johnny joined the Texas Playboys in the 1940s and has played his way into the hearts and souls of fans and fellow musicians ever since. Some of the stars he has recorded with include Merle Haggard, Charley Pride, Chet Atkins, Joan Baez, and Paul McCartney. He currently has his own show, *Gimble Music Ranch* on Willie Nelson's Outlaw Music Channel, and has appeared in *Nashville*, *Honeysuckle Rose*, *Songwriter*, and *Honkytonk Man*. Johnny has been named "Fiddler of the Year" by the Academy of Country Music eight times and won a Grammy in 1994 for his performance with Asleep at the Wheel, and the National Fellowship Heritage Award by Endowment for Arkansas.

MORE TASTY MORSELS: johnnygimble.com
JOHNNY'S CHARITY: The Friends Foundation, Dripping Springs, Texas, thefriendsfoundation.org

Apple Cake

Submitted by Barbara Gimble, Johnny's wife

Johnny likes this to be his birthday cake.

2 c. flour
1 c. sugar
½ c. brown sugar
1 tsp. allspice
½ tsp. salt
3 eggs lightly beaten
1 c. salad oil
1 T. vanilla
4 c. diced apples (Golden Delicious and Tasty, cooked)
1 c. raisins
1 c. chopped pecans

Mix the flour, sugars, allspice, and salt. Set aside. Blend the eggs with the salad oil and vanilla. Fold into the flour mixture. Gently add the fruit and nuts.

Spread into greased 13 × 9 × 2–inch baking pan. Bake at 350° for 50–60 min. Do the wooden toothpick thing in the center.

Serve in squares, topped with dollop of fresh whipped cream or crème fraîche or vanilla ice cream.
Yield: 1 cake.

Marty Stuart

SHOW DATES:

1979
1987
1990
2000

SERVING UP: Country

A FEW INGREDIENTS: Like a great casserole, Marty Stuart's career is many-layered, combining a passion for country music with his interests in photography, writing, and producing records for fellow musicians. From his 1982 debut album *Busy Bee Café*, to his more commercially successful outing *This One's Gonna Hurt You* (which reached number twelve on the country charts), to 2005's *Live at the Ryman*, Marty has been busy mixing up country, rockabilly, and honky-tonk for decades. He has been a member of the Grand Ole Opry since 1993 and serves on the board of the Country Music Foundation. In 2005 he won the AMA Lifetime Achievement Award for Performing.

MORE TASTY MORSELS: martystuart.net
MARTY'S CHARITY: MusiCares, grammy.com/musicares

Applesauce Cake

Submitted by Hilda Stuart, Marty's mom

This is Marty Stuart's very favorite cake.

4 c. plain Martha White flour
2 c. sugar
4 tsp. regular baking soda
2½ c. applesauce (chunky or plain)
1 tsp. cloves
1 tsp. cinnamon
1 tsp. nutmeg
1 (15-oz.) box raisins
1 c. chopped pecans
2 sticks margarine or butter, melted and cool

Combine flour, sugar, baking soda, applesauce, spices, raisins, and pecans. Add cooled margarine or butter. Mix with spoon; batter will be thick. Spoon batter into a well-greased 15 × 4–inch loaf pan or Bundt pan. Bake at 275° for 1½ hours, or until toothpick comes out clean. Makes a good breakfast snack.

Bellamy Brothers

SHOW DATES:
1982
1988

SERVING UP: Country, rock

A FEW INGREDIENTS: In a career that has already spanned more than thirty years, the Bellamy Brothers, Howard and David, wrote the recipe for success for a country music duo—a recipe that has since been followed by acts like Brooks and Dunn, Montgomery Gentry, and Big and Rich. The Bellamys' career started to heat up with the debut of their pop single "Let Your Love Flow" in 1976. In the late 1970s, they moved toward their country roots with another hit, "If I Said You Had a Beautiful Body (Would You Hold it Against Me)," one of many of their number one singles. The Bellamy Brothers hold the record in both the Academy of Country Music and the Country Music Association Awards for the most nominations received by a duo, and they have also been nominated for numerous Grammy Awards.

MORE TASTY MORSELS: bellamybrothers.com
BELLAMY BROTHERS' CHARITY: The Salvation Army, salvationarmyusa.org

Kumquat Refrigerator Pie

Submitted by Daniel and Sylvia Bellamy

This recipe for Kumquat Pie is a favorite of the whole Bellamy family. It has been passed down for generations. I believe it was originally made by Aunt Hattie. Her daughter and the Bellamy's cousin, Sylvia Young, kindly gave us the recipe some years back and now Daniel and I make it for the family during Christmas. Kumquats are grown on our ranch in Florida.

1 9-inch pie crust, cooled (prepare ahead; recipe follows)
1 can condensed milk
1 (8-oz.) container Cool Whip
½ c. lemon juice
1 (8-oz.) pkg. of regular cream cheese
⅓ c. puréed kumquats

Prepare crust. Beat condensed milk and Cool Whip. Add lemon juice and cream cheese and beat until thickened. Add kumquats and pour into cool pie shell, and chill in refrigerator for 1 hour. Yield: 1 pie.

PIE CRUST

¼ c. sour cream
1 (4-oz.) block real butter
1⅓ c. of all-purpose flour

Stir sour cream and butter together, then mix in flour. Stir all this into a ball and refrigerate for just a few minutes, then roll into crust. Cook at 350° for about 20 minutes.

The Charlie Daniels Band

SHOW DATES:

1976
1981
1989

The Charlie Daniels Band. Photograph by Scott Newton © 2008. Courtesy of KLRU-ACL.

Wonderful Sugar Cookies

Submitted by Charlie Daniels

This is a recipe that we've made at Christmas time with our son for thirty years. A real family tradition! Of course you can make them at any holiday and use the appropriate cookie cutters for the occasion.

2½ c. all-purpose flour
1½ c. powdered sugar
1 c. butter
1 egg
1½ tsp. vanilla
1 tsp. baking soda
1 tsp. cream of tartar

Mix all ingredients together. Refrigerate for 3 hours. Divide in half and roll out one half at a time. Roll thin, about ¼ to ⅛ inch thick. Use seasonal cookie cutters. Sprinkle with granulated sugar, either white or colored sugar if desired. Bake at 375° for 7–8 minutes.

SERVING UP: country, southern rock, outlaw country, country rock

A FEW INGREDIENTS: Charlie Daniels achieved with one single what most musicians pray for in an entire career. "The Devil Went Down to Georgia," topped both country and pop charts, won countless awards including a Grammy, was featured on the *Urban Cowboy* movie soundtrack, and propelled his album to triple-platinum sales. Many of Charlie's other albums have gone on to platinum, double-platinum, and even triple-platinum status, including *Full Moon and Simple Man* and *A Decade of Hits*.

In 1996 he was honored with the release of a boxed set of his classics. In 1998 he received the Pioneer Award from the Academy of Country Music. And in his long career he has recorded with artists as diverse as Bob Dylan, Leonard Cohen, Ringo Starr, and Johnny Cash.

MORE TASTY MORSELS: charliedaniels.com CHARLIE'S CHARITY: The Angelus, theangelus.com

Neko Case

SHOW DATE: 2003

SERVING UP: Indie rock, alt-country

A FEW INGREDIENTS: Sometimes it is hard to know where to file a recipe—it's so good you want to have it as an appetizer, but it's really a full meal, not to mention a tasty dessert. That describes Neko Case's music to a T. Neko's stunning vocals and songwriting were first showcased on *Mass Romantic*, the New Pornographers' first album. In addition to touring and recording with the New Pornographers, Neko often cooks up music with other Canadian performers, including the Sadies and Carolyn Mark. In fact, the Society of Composers, Authors, and Music Publishers of Canada considers her an "honorary Canadian." Neko's 1997 album, *The Virginian*, had critics comparing her to honky-tonk singers like Loretta Lynn and Patsy Cline. Her 2006 release, *Fox Confessor Brings the Flood*, was number one on the Amazon.com music editors' picks and number two on NPR's *All Songs Considered*. That same year Neko was named Female Artist of the Year at the Plug Independent Music Awards.

MORE TASTY MORSELS: nekocase.com NEKO'S CHARITY: Greyhound Adoption League of Tucson, Arizona, galgreys.com

Neko Case. Photograph by Dennis Kleiman.

Houndstooth Chocolate Chip Cookies

I can't stand a "puffy cake" cookie. I spent a year of my life perfecting the cookie of my dreams and am happy to share the recipe with you! Keep in mind that you may have to tweak the recipe a bit to suit your altitude and depending on whether you use a gas or electric oven. When I developed this recipe I was using a gas oven at about four thousand feet. I also have to say that the electric mixer is essential.

2¼ c. flour
½ tsp. baking soda
½ heaping tsp. salt
2 sticks of butter (softened to room temp)
1 c. light brown sugar
½ c. sugar
3 T. malt (the secret ingredient!)
3 tsp. vanilla extract
2 eggs (at room temperature)
½ to 1 bag of Ghirardelli or Guittard Chocolate Chips

Set your oven at exactly 350° and line your cookie pans with parchment paper. (You can reuse the same parchment up to 5 or 6 times.)

OK, here we go, this will sound drawn out, but every detail counts.

Whisk together dry ingredients of flour, baking soda, and salt.

Separately, in mixer bowl, combine butter (After much trial, I have decided that Land O Lakes Salted Butter is the best, but salted organic butter is great, too. This is the key to the flavor of the cookies.), sugars, and malt together until kinda fluffy. Whip it, baby! Then, on low-speed add vanilla and eggs, and then immediately add the previously combined dry ingredients—in two segments so the eggs don't get over-mixed. I'd say add the dry ingredients even before the eggs have mixed in all the way with the butter-sugar-malt blend. Not over-mixing is what makes these cookies chewy and not cakelike.

Add chocolate chips and stir with a wooden spoon.

Now, take a regular dinner spoon and drop 12 lumps on the cookie sheet. Bake anywhere from 9 to 12 minutes, depending on how light you like the bottoms of your cookies (and depending on your specific oven and altitude).

Use a thin metal spatula when you remove the cookies from the cookie sheet because they will be very soft. They may actually seem undercooked, but fear not! When you transfer them to a cooling rack, they actually keep cooking themselves! It's called "carry-over cooking." (I heard that on *Emeril*. Busted!) They become a little flatter as they cool, too. Their chewiness becomes apparent the next day. I think it's the malt that binds to the other sugars and helps them caramelize, hence, chewy!

Diamond Rio

SHOW DATE: 1994

SERVING UP: Country

A FEW INGREDIENTS: The best recipes blend ingredients in a way that brings out the best of everything—the same can be said of Diamond Rio, with their beautiful harmonies. The band, originally calling themselves the Tennessee River Boys, performed at first at Nashville's Opryland theme park in the 1980s. Redubbed Diamoned Rio in 1989, they hit the ground running with the release of their debut single, "Meet in the Middle," which reached number one on the *Billboard* Hot Country Songs chart. They quickly had four more top-ten hits from their self-titled album: "Mirror, Mirror," "Mama Don't Forget to Pray for Me," "Norma Jean Riley," and "Nowhere Bound." In the more than two decades since, Diamond Rio has had thirty-three more chart-toppers, and three of their albums have been certified platinum. They have also been honored with Group of the Year awards from the Country Music Association, two Top Vocal Group awards from the Academy of Country Music, and thirteen Grammy Award nominations.

MORE TASTY MORSELS: diamondrio.com

DIAMOND RIO'S CHARITY: Big Brothers and Big Sisters of Middle Tennessee, Nashville, Tennesee, bbbsmt.org

Devilish Love Bar

Submitted by Marty Roe

This is the cake that me and my brother Scott always requested our mom to make for our birthdays (though we leave out the nuts). It is a family birthday tradition!

- 1 c. water
- 2 sticks margarine
- ¼ c. cocoa
- 2 c. flour
- 2 c. sugar
- 1 tsp. baking soda
- 2 tsp. vanilla
- 2 eggs, beaten
- ½ c. buttermilk
- Fudge Icing (recipe follows)

Bring water, margarine, and cocoa to a boil. Pour hot mixture into remaining ingredients. Bake in greased and floured 12 × 15–inch sheet pan . Bake at 350° until set, about 20 minutes. Pour Fudge Icing over hot cake and sprinkle chopped nuts on top. Cut into bars when cool.

FUDGE ICING

- ½ c. buttermilk
- 1 stick margarine
- ½ c. cocoa
- 1 box confectioners' sugar
- nuts, finely chopped

Bring buttermilk and margarine to a boil. Add the remaining ingredients and blend with a mixer.

Femi Kuti

SHOW DATE:

2007

Photograph by Scott Newton © 2008, Courtesy of KLRU-ACL

Puff Puff

The recipe can be eaten as a snack or served with juice.

¼ c. warm water
2½ T. yeast
pinch of salt
1 T. sugar
ground nutmeg to taste
½ lb. flour
vegetable oil for frying

Put warm water in a small bowl. Add yeast, a pinch of salt, a little sugar, and ground nutmeg. Sir and leave for 30–60 minutes to rise. Now sift your flour into a big bowl, and add the remaining sugar. Mix it very well. Add your yeast mixture. Stir with your bare hands—use both hands. Add enough water to make it a little light and slippery, then cover for another hour to rise.

Wash your frying pan very well. Add vegetable oil to pan. Allow it to heat up for at least 3 minutes. Use your hand to shape the dough into balls, and place them in the pan. Turn the balls every 3–5 seconds to allow sides to brown. Remove from the pan with a slotted spoon.

SERVING UP: Afro-dance, R&B

A FEW INGREDIENTS: Femi Kuti's Afro-beat is one of the most exciting new sounds to emerge from Nigeria. Borrowing the best ingredients from his father, Fela Anikulapo-Kuti, and his powerful musical recipe—a funky, jazzy, heavily percussive style—Femi adds his youthful, energetic perspective. Femi and his band, the Positive Force, have toured extensively, crossing Africa and Europe in 1996 and 1997. His first solo album, *Shoki Shoki*, was released in 1999 and received critical acclaim from the *New Yorker*, *Rolling Stone*, and *Vibe*. In addition to his music, Femi is also a goodwill ambassador for UNICEF.

MORE TASTY MORSELS: myspace.com/femikuti
FEMI'S CHARITY: Street Child Africa, streetchildafrica.org.uk

Shawn Colvin

SHOW DATES:
1995
2000

SERVING UP: Folk-rock

A FEW INGREDIENTS: Forget fast food. Shawn Colvin's music is everything a home-cooked meal should be, prepared with love and tenderness, and so seductive that you can't help but come back for seconds or thirds. Her 1991 album, *Steady On*, won a Grammy Award for Best Contemporary Folk Album, but 1996's *A Few Small Repairs* was the CD that put her career in high gear. The single "Sunny Came Home" became a top-ten pop single and won the Grammys for both Song and Record of the Year. "Nothin' on Me" was used as the theme song for the Brooke Shields sitcom *Suddenly Susan*. Her beautiful voice and storytelling style have earned her six subsequent Grammy nominations. She has made guest appearances on *The Larry Sanders Show* and voiced a character on *The Simpsons*.

MORE TASTY MORSELS: shawncolvin.com
SHAWN'S CHARITY: Marathon Kids, marathonkids.org

Swedish Pancakes

Submitted by Shawn and Kay Colvin

This "puff" pancake is something my sister and I would beg Mom to make for breakfast on the weekends. When we were kids, there was something magical about how the pancake puffed up into some sort of mystical landscape. Of course, they also tasted great!

4 eggs
2 c. whole milk
2 tsp. salt
1 tsp. sugar
1¼ c. flour
2 T. butter, melted

Using a hand mixer, beat eggs, milk, salt, and sugar together. A little at a time, beat in the flour. Pour mixture in a greased 9 × 3–inch baking dish.

Pour the melted butter into the batter and swirl it around with a spatula. Place in a 450° oven for about 15 minutes, or until the pancake puffs up and browns around the edges. Serve with butter and syrup.

The String Cheese Incident

SHOW DATE: 2001

The String Cheese Incident. Photograph by Scott Newton © 2008. Courtesy of KLRU-ACL.

Pistachio Chocolate Cake

Submitted by Kyle Hollingsworth and Nonna Dot

1 box golden or butter cake mix
½ c. orange juice
4 eggs
½ c. oil
1 pkg. pistachio pudding mix
¾ c. chocolate syrup

Preheat oven to 350°. Grease and flour Bundt pan.

Combine cake mix, orange juice, eggs, oil, and pudding mix. Mix until smooth (there are small nuts in the batch). Pour ¾ of batter in Bundt pan. Add chocolate syrup to remaining batter, stir, and add to other batter in pan.

Bake at 350° for 45–50 minutes. Sprinkle with powdered sugar (optional). Yield: 1 cake.

SERVING UP: Progressive bluegrass, country, neo-psychedelic, jam band

A FEW INGREDIENTS: With a college degree in jazz piano performance, Kyle Hollingsworth is a prolific musician with the ability to write and perform in a variety of styles, from rock to classical, ragtime to bebop. He is best known as keyboardist-singer-songwriter for independent music pioneers The String Cheese Incident. The band has been recognized not only for their musical creativity, but for being one of the first musical acts to use the Internet as an effective distribution and marketing tool. With their fans in mind, the band created their own ticketing and merchandise company and a fan-friendly travel agency. The String Cheese Incident was also among the first performers to encourage environmentally friendly shows and tours. In fact, their support has helped launch several nonprofits including Conscious Alliance, Rock the Earth, and Head Count.

MORE TASTY MORSELS: kylehollingsworth.com, stringcheeseincident.com
KYLE'S CHARITY: Conscious Alliance, consciousalliance.org

Sarah McLachlan

SHOW DATE: 2008

Sarah McLachlan. Photograph by Scott Newton © 2008. Courtesy of KLRU-ACL.

Currant Cake

Excerpted from Sarah's cookbook, Plenty

½ c. cream or half-and-half
1 heaping T. molasses
¾ c. butter
¾ c. Demerara sugar
3 eggs
2 c. currants
2⅔ c. flour
2 tsp. baking powder
¼ tsp. salt

Preheat oven to 325°. Heat the cream and mix in molasses. In a separate bowl, cream the butter until light and fluffy. Gradually add the sugar to the butter. Add the eggs, one at a time, beating well after each addition. Stir in the cream and molasses mixture, then add the currants. Sift the dry ingredients together and add to the wet mixture. Pour into a greased loaf pan and bake for about 1 hour or until a knife inserted in the middle comes out clean. Yield: 6–8 servings.

SERVING UP: Pop, ballads

A FEW INGREDIENTS: With a voice like warm honey, Sarah McLachlan is an artist you can serve with any meal. Winner of three Grammy Awards—for Best Female Pop Vocal Performance in 1997 for "Building a Mystery," in 1999 for the live version of "I Will Remember You," and Best Pop Instrumental Performance in 1997 for "Last Dance." She has also won eight Juno Awards, including Female Vocalist of the Year (1998), Songwriter of the Year (along with Pierre Marchand—1998 and 2004), Album of the Year for *Surfacing* (1998), and the International Achievement Award (2000).

Every one of Sarah McLachlan's studio and live albums and videos has been certified gold, platinum, or multiplatinum. In 1997 Sarah founded and headlined the pioneering Lilith Fair tour. In 2004 she released the socially conscious video "World On Fire," which was nominated for a Grammy for Best Short Form Music Video and raised money for eleven charitable organizations around the world.

MORE TASTY MORSELS: sarahmclachlan.com SARAH'S CHARITY: The Sarah McLachlan Foundation, sarahmclachlanmusicoutreach.com/smf/content.html, and the SPCA, spca.bc.ca

Encore Buffet

Groovin' with Soups, Stews, Salads, and Breads

Main Attractions: Poultry, Meats, Seafood, and Game

Keep the Beet: Vegetables and Legumes

Hit Singles

Sweet Sounds: Desserts

One More Time

JOAN BAEZ

Zucchini Curry Soup

Use organic ingredients when possible.

4 zucchini, cut into thick slices
1 onion, chopped
1 T. curry powder
3 c. chicken stock
¾ c. half-and-half
salt and pepper
½ c. yogurt or sour cream (optional)
½ c. chopped chives (optional)

Put zucchini, onion, curry powder, and chicken stock in a saucepan. Bring to a boil, cover and simmer for 25 minutes, stirring occasionally. Purée mixture in blender, strain, return to saucepan, and add half-and-half. Season to taste with salt and pepper. Reheat to serving temperature. Serve with a dollop of yogurt or sour cream, and sprinkle with chives. Enjoy! Yield: 4–6 servings.

FEMI KUTI

Ogbono Soup and Eba

Submitted by Onome Udi

About this recipe: Ogbono is the kernel of the bush mango or wild mango tree. It is used as a soup thickener. Ogbono soup contains all the vitamins the body needs: carbohydrates, proteins, vitamins, etc. Eba is a carbohydrate paste made from garri, a popular West African food derived from cassava tubers. Ugwu leaf is pumpkin leaf. Fresh spinach can be used as a substitute if ugwu is not available. Bitter leaf is derived from the leaves of a small evergreen shrub found all over Africa called Vernonia. Periwinkles are sea snails or other edible snails; where snails are not available, clams or mussels may be used.

- meat
- palm oil
- water
- ogbono
- dry pepper
- Maggi seasoning
- salt to taste
- ugwu leaf
- bitter leaf
- periwinkle
- Eba (prepare ahead; recipe follows)

Fry the meat in the palm oil. Boil water in a pot. In a bowl, combine ground ogbono with the pepper. Put this mixture in the boiling water and leave it for some time. Then add the remaining ingredients, including the fried meat, to the pot and let it simmer for around 30 minutes. Then it is ready to eat. Serve with Eba.

EBA

- water
- garri

Boil water. Sprinkle in the garri a little at a time, stirring constantly, until it doesn't have seeds.

FEMI KUTI

Ogbono Soup

Submitted by Udofot Richard Kingsley

This is a traditional African dish.

meat and fish
stock fish
palm oil
ogbono
pepper
crayfish
vegetables
Maggi seasoning to taste
salt to taste

Prepare the meat and fish by boiling them. In another pot, heat the palm oil. Add the ogbono and the pepper to the oil. Add the ogbono mixture to the boiling pot. Then add the crayfish, vegetables, and seasonings, and allow to boil for about 35 minutes.

Egusi Soup and Eba

Submitted by Opeyemi Awomolo

This dish is served with Eba. See the recipe on page 273.

crayfish or dry fish
palm oil or vegetable oil
ground pepper
ground tomatoes
ground melon
vegetables
crab
beef
shrimp
Maggi seasoning to taste
salt to taste

Boil your crayfish or dry fish to soften. Then add your palm oil or vegetable oil and allow to steam for a while. Then add pepper and tomatoes. Then add the melon, vegetables, the other meats (cooked to your liking), Maggi seasoning, and salt. Leave it to boil for about 15 minutes, and then it is ready to serve.

FEMI KUTI

Egusi Soup and Pounded Yam

Submitted by Tiwalade Ogunlowo

This recipe is prepared for visitors in the Yoruba-speaking area in Nigeria.

fresh beef
dry fish
salt to taste
Maggi seasoning to taste
palm oil
onion
ground melon
ground pepper
ground dry crayfish
bitter leaf
yam

Wash your meat and fish properly, and boil them with salt and Maggi for 30 minutes.

Pour your palm oil into a separate pot. Place it on the fire for 3–4 minutes. Add your shredded onion. Allow it to steam. Add your ground melon and stir. Pour the meat, fish, and water into this pot. Stir very well. Allow it to steam for another 5 minutes. Add a small amount of water. Add ground pepper, crayfish, more Maggi seasoning, and salt to taste. Leave for 2 minutes then add your bitter leaf. Leave for another 3 minutes. Stir and it is ready.

In a separate pot, boil the yam. Use a mortar and pestle to pound the softened yam vigorously until there are no more seeds in it. Add 5 spoons of water and pound thoroughly again. Serve these together.

TIMBUK3

Good-For-You Green Stew

Recipe submitted by Barbara Kooyman

Here's a recipe for one of my everyday dishes. This is a tasty side dish, or you can eat it all by itself with a friend.

olive oil
1 large sweet onion, chopped
1 jalapeño, chopped
cumin seeds
1 or 2 potatoes, peeled and cubed
1 bunch Swiss chard
salt and pepper to taste
2 tomatoes, quartered

Put a good splash of olive oil in a frying pan, and turn the burner on medium-high. Throw in the chopped onion and jalapeño.

Now smash a bunch of cumin seeds to release their goodness (don't hold back!), and throw them in with the onions and jalapeño. Stir occasionally and watch for the onions to get brown.

At that point, throw the potato in and cook it until it starts sticking to the bottom of the pan, not quite burning but getting there. (That brown stuff on the bottom of the pan will come in handy later on.)

Wash up a bunch of Swiss chard. I like the red-stemmed chard because it makes me think I'm about to do something good for my blood, and we all know how important blood is. Chop up that chard, still wet from the washing, and throw it in the pan.

Now add some salt and pepper. My favorite number is 9, so I like to do things in multiples of 9. Another favorite number of mine is 3 (I like 7 and 4, too), so put in 3 rounds of 9 shakes of salt—that'd be 27 shakes—and 9 grinds of fresh black pepper. Of course, if you're a pepper freak, you can add another 9 grinds.

The water from the freshly washed chard will start to work on the brown stuff on the bottom of the pan, and now we're talking flavor. The last thing to do, after the chard wilts, is to lay the quartered tomatoes in the pan, put the cover on, reduce the heat, and let it simmer for about 10 to 15 minutes. Then it's done. I hope your tongue enjoys it as much as the rest of your body.

SHOW DATE: 1989

SERVING UP: Folk, pop

A FEW INGREDIENTS: Austin resident Barbara Kooyman's career started to marinate in the later 1980 as part of Timbuk3, a band she formed with her then-husband, Pat MacDonald. The first album, *Greetings from Timbuk3*, included the hit single "The Future's So Bright, I Gotta Wear Shades." Timbuk3 was nominated for a Grammy Award for Best New Artist in 1987. The group broke up in 1995, and since then Barbara has released two solo albums: *Ready* and *Undercover*.

She also launched Sparrows Wheel, a philanthropic record company that, for each album sold, gives five dollars to the public radio station of the purchaser's choosing. Barbara hopes to show that music should always come before business.

MORE TASTY MORSELS: barbarakooyman.net

BARBARA'S CHARITY: Artists for Media Diversity, a4md.org

OLD CROW MEDICINE SHOW

Roast Chicken with Citrus and Bacon

Submitted by Ketch Secor

This is a time-tested favorite with added flair. The bacon wrap adds crunch and flavor while the citrus brings zest to the meat. Perfect for a Sunday dinner or just a casual setting.

2½–5 lb. chicken (roaster or fryer)
¼ c. canola oil
1 clove garlic, minced
salt and pepper
1 medium unpeeled orange, sliced
1 small unpeeled lemon, sliced
5 strips raw bacon
1 tsp. chipotle chili pepper

Rinse the bird and pat dry. Remove giblets. (Stuffing the cavity is optional as it simply extends cooking time.)

Rub with oil, garlic, salt, and pepper, covering the entire skin of the bird. Place chicken in a small roasting pan, breast-up. Cover chicken with citrus slices, topping them with the bacon strips laid perpendicular to the breastbone. Sprinkle chili powder.

Before covering the pan with foil, consider adding your favorite cubed vegetables to garnish the bird.

Bake at 350°, 25 minutes per pound or until thermometer reads 170° in the breast and 185° in the thigh.

Remove foil and let sit 10 minutes before serving. (Optional: Save liquid from pan and make gravy; the bacon flavor will really come through.) Yield: 3–4 servings.

B. J. THOMAS

Baked Fish with Herb Bread Topping

Submitted by Nora Thomas Cloud

3 c. fresh, plain breadcrumbs
3 T. green onions, sliced
¼ c. flat-leaf parsley, chopped
1 tsp. dried herb (thyme, sage, or oregano will work)
2 T. whole-grain mustard
¼ c. fresh squeezed lemon juice (2 large lemons)
1 tsp. lemon zest
2 T. mirin
2 T. soy sauce
1 T. olive oil, plus more for drizzling the fish
3 lb. fresh fish (salmon, bass, halibut, or any firm-fleshed fish)
salt and pepper to taste

Place breadcrumbs, green onion, parsley, dried herb, mustard, lemon juice, lemon zest, mirin, soy sauce, and olive oil in a medium bowl. Mix until even. Place fish on a baking dish lined with parchment paper or foil. Lightly rub both sides of fish with olive oil and salt and pepper. If the fish has skin, place skin side down. Evenly top fish with the breadcrumb mixture. Bake at 400° for about 15 minutes, or until the fish flakes easily with a fork. Baste the fish with the accumulated juices. Turn the oven to broil and cook for 5 minutes longer, until the top is a nice golden brown. Yield: 6 to 8 servings.

MANHATTAN TRANSFER

Konish Crabkakes

Submitted by Janis Siegel

Baby Konehead is my nickname, hence the name of this dish.

1½ T. butter
⅓ c. yellow bell pepper, diced
⅓ c. red bell pepper, diced
1 lb. fresh Dungeness crab meat, broken up
1 c. whole-grain breadcrumbs, divided
½ c. tartar sauce
½ T. Worcestershire sauce
1 egg, beaten
1 T. chopped fresh parsley
1 tsp. fresh thyme
cayenne pepper (optional)
olive oil and butter, mixed

Melt butter in small skillet and sauté peppers until soft. Allow peppers to cool and combine with next seven ingredients in a bowl. You may need more crumbs or more tartar sauce, depending on the consistency you like. Form mixture into patties. Tiny ones are nice for hors d'oeuvres or appetizers, big ones are good for obvious reasons. Coat patties with crumbs. Heat oil and butter in a medium sized skillet and sauté patties till browned.

Serve with tartar sauce, tomato chutney (my fave), or homemade aioli. Yield: approximately 4 servings.

MAURA O'CONNELL

Salmon Enchanted Evening

2 (approximately 12-oz.) large fillets of salmon with skin
1½ c. crumbled feta cheese
½ c. raw baby spinach
1 tsp. lemon zest
4 large tomatoes
2 T. crushed garlic

Wash and dry salmon. Blanche spinach by plunging it into boiling water and removing immediately. Place spinach in a colander to drain. Coarsely chop spinach and mix with feta cheese and lemon zest.

Place one filet of salmon skin side down on a baking tray or oven-safe dish that has been sprayed with cooking spray or brushed with olive oil. Spread the spinach and cheese mixture over first salmon fillet. Place second salmon fillet on top, skin side up. Chop tomatoes finely and mix with garlic. Spread tomato-garlic mixture over salmon, completely covering top and sides.

Bake in 350° oven for 40–45 minutes. Serve with rice and salad. Bon appetit!

THE OAK RIDGE BOYS

Ginger Shrimp in Coconut Sauce

Submitted by William Golden

My oldest grandson, Lee Rush Golden, has an aspiration to be a chef. One night he brought over the ingredients and prepared this dish for my wife and me. We loved it and I am sure you will too.

- 1 T. vegetable oil
- 1 T. ginger, minced
- 2 cloves garlic, minced
- 1 jalapeño pepper, seeded and minced
- ¾ lb. medium-size shrimp, deveined and peeled
- 1 c. coconut milk
- ⅛ tsp. ground pepper
- 1½ tsp. lime juice
- ½ tsp. salt
- 1 T. cilantro, chopped
- 2 c. rice, cooked

Put vegetable oil in a saucepan and sauté the ginger, garlic, and jalapeño for one minute over medium heat. Add shrimp and cook until pink. Add coconut milk, ground pepper, lime juice, and salt. Bring to a boil. Stir in cilantro and serve over rice.

SARA HICKMAN

Pad Thai

1 pkg. of Thai rice noodles
⅓ c. firm tofu
1½ c. scallions, chopped
1⅓ c. bean sprouts
2 T. vegetable oil
1½ c. smashed peanuts
3 cloves garlic, minced
2 T. tamarind
2 T. sugar
4 tsp. fish sauce
½ tsp. ground, dried chili pepper
1–2 eggs
½–¼ lb. shrimp
2 limes, quartered

Begin by soaking the dry noodles for 10–15 minutes in lukewarm water. In the meantime, julienne the tofu, making long pieces. Cut up scallions in to small pieces, saving some for garnish later. Rinse the bean sprouts, saving half for garnish, as well. Mince the garlic.

I prefer to use a wok, but any large skillet will work fine. Get the wok or skillet very hot and pour in oil. Toast the peanuts in the oil, remove and set aside. Add garlic and tofu, stirring until slightly browned. Check the noodles: they should be limber but not expanded. Drain the noodles and add to the hot wok, keeping flame steady. (If your wok is not hot enough, you will see extra water, so turn up the heat, if needed.) Keep stirring or things will start to stick!

Add tamarind, sugar, fish sauce, and chili pepper. Make room for the egg by pushing all ingredients to the side of the wok. Just crack the egg on the side of the wok, scrambling it quickly on the hot surface. Fold the egg into the noodles. Add shrimp. Make sure you stir well after adding all ingredients. Add bean sprouts and scallions. Stir, stir, stir! By now, the noodles should be soft and tangled with yummy ingredients!

Transfer hot pad thai from wok to serving plate with tongs. Sprinkle with broken peanuts. Serve with sides of scallions, lime wedges, and raw bean sprouts. In Thailand, condiments like sugar, chili pepper, vinegar, and fish sauce are also on the table so the guest can add to their taste. By all means, experiment and have fun! Enjoy! Yield: 2 big or 4 small servings.

JOAN BAEZ

Corn Soufflé

- 1 can corn, drained
- 1 can creamed corn
- 1 box "Jiffy" Corn Muffin Mix
- 1 (8-oz.) container sour cream
- 1 stick butter, melted
- 1 egg, beaten

Mix together first 5 ingredients in a medium-sized bowl. Stir in egg. Pour into a greased, round casserole dish and bake uncovered at 350° for 55 minutes, or until a knife or toothpick comes out clean. Yield: 8–10 servings.

DELBERT McCLINTON

Cucumber, Onion, and Avocado Salad

- 1 cucumber, peeled and thinly sliced
- 1 medium red onion, thinly sliced
- ⅓ c. fresh dill, chopped
- 1 clove garlic, crushed
- 2 T. sugar
- 1 tsp. salt
- 1 ripe but firm avocado, peeled, pitted, and chopped
- ¼ c. red wine vinegar

Place first six ingredients in a bowl and toss. Refrigerate for 25 minutes. Add the avocado to the cucumber mixture and refrigerate for 15 more minutes. Remove from the refrigerator and drain. Toss with red wine vinegar. Serve.

THIEVERY CORPORATION

Curried Squash and Peas

Submitted by Loulou Ghelichkhani

For this fragrant and highly spiced stew, butternut squash teams up with ginger, garlic, and potent curry spices. Rice or couscous make a natural date for this dish. After exotic tours and travels, coming home to a gray East Coast winter becomes very difficult. So I always try to make food with an aromatic spice that delivers an intense level of heat. My daughter finds real comfort in curry. Perhaps being named Shiva, she somehow requires it to find a balance as well!

1 oz. butter or coconut oil
1 c. onions diced
2 garlic cloves, minced
1 chili pepper, minced
1 c. red bell pepper, diced
1 medium carrot, sliced or cubed
1 tsp. your favorite curry
2 tsp. ginger, minced
1 dash cumin
3 c. butternut squash, cubed
1 c. chickpeas, precooked or soaked until tender
6 c. filtered water
salt and pepper to taste

In a large saucepan, heat the oil over medium heat. Add the onion, garlic, peppers, carrot, curry, cumin, and ginger and cook, stirring for about 5–8 minutes or until onion and carrots look a bit golden. Still stirring, gently add the water, a cup at a time. Reduce the heat to low and add the remaining two ingredients: the squash and the chickpeas. Let this stew simmer for about 30 minutes.

I usually check at this point to see if the carrots and squash are really soft. If so, the stew is ready. If not, monitor the broth level—the ratio of it to the top of the vegetables should be pretty even. Add a cup of water and let it simmer for another 10 minutes, if needed. Once the stew is ready, let it cool off for a few minutes. Then serve the vegetables next to the couscous or rice, and separate the broth in little bowls to be served on the side, as soup or just for your friends to add as they eat.

Make sure to make a good amount of rice or couscous. You can always add the leftovers to some salad the next day. Enjoy with a nice glass of red wine or some black tea. Yield: 4 servings.

FEMI KUTI

Rice, Vegetables, and Plantains

Submitted by Bose Ajilo

vegetables
vegetable oil
red pepper
meat and fish, boiled
salt
Maggi seasoning
curry
thyme
plantains
rice

Parboil vegetables. In another pot, heat the oil, add the pepper, and cook for 10 minutes. Add the already boiled meat and fish and all seasonings. Fry the plantains in hot oil. Boil rice for 40 minutes. Combine all and you are ready to eat.

LOST GONZO BAND

Bob Livingston's Tofu Migas

I ate my first tofu migas in California in 1970. I had gone out West to seek my musical fortune and I fell in with some very health-conscious folks living up in the Hills of Beverly. They ate very healthy, mostly vegetarian, and had long, well manicured, hair. Being raised on bacon and eggs, it was a lifestyle I was unaccustomed to. Back in Lubbock, they called folks like these "rabbit-food eaters." I was a big fan of migas, but had never tasted the tofu version. One Sunday morning a woman up the hill made tofu migas for everyone and I was hooked. Now I make it myself and have added my own ingredients to make a fast, healthy, and delicious dish. They say that tofu takes on the taste of the ingredients you add, so fresh is the word. Tofu is a complete protein and has more chance to be used for protein synthesis of lean muscle and antibodies. It's good stuff and has zero cholesterol.

- 1½ pkg. extra firm organic tofu
- ⅓ c. onion, chopped
- 1 small clove garlic, chopped fine
- 1–2 green chilies or poblano chilies, chopped
- 2 T. canola oil
- ½ tsp. sea salt
- ½ tsp. crushed red pepper flakes
- 1 large tomato, chopped
- 2 c. Guiltless Gourmet Baked Unsalted Yellow Corn Chips (or you can fry up your own corn tortillas and put salt on 'em if you want to be authentic!)
- ½ c. grated sharp organic cheddar cheese
- 4–6 whole wheat tortillas to serve with dish
- ⅓ c. fresh cilantro, chopped
- 1 large avocado, sliced
- salsa to taste

Drain the tofu on a butcher block with paper towels and blot away any excess water then smash up in a mixing bowl.

Use a cast-iron skillet to sauté the onion, garlic, and chili in the oil. I like the onions to be a bit brown. Add the tofu and salt, turn up the heat to high and stir-fry until it's thoroughly cooked and some of the tofu is starting to brown.

BOB LIVINGSTON'S TOFU MIGAS (CONTINUED)

Turn down the heat to medium, add the crushed red pepper and tomatoes, stir and cook for another 2 minutes. Add the chips and stir and simmer for more 2 minutes. Turn off the burner. Grate the cheese on top and cover for 2 minutes.

While you do this, heat the tortillas. Serve hot, garnished with fresh cilantro, avocado slices, and salsa. Yield: 4 servings.

SHOW DATES: 1976, 1978

SERVING UP: Country

A FEW INGREDIENTS: Like a great stew, Lost Gonzo Band's ingredients evolved over the years, but the recipe has always been satisfying. It was 1973 when Bob Livingston, Gary P. Nunn, John Inmon, Kelly Dunn, Tomas Ramirez, and Donny Dolan formed the original Lost Gonzo Band. But over the years, many other colorful musicians have been stirred in to the lineup, including Jerry Jeff Walker, Michael Martin Murphey, Ray Wylie Hubbard, Bobby Smith, and Lloyd Maines. The Lost Gonzo Band has released six albums, and after several years of hiatus they reunited for a few concerts in 2007 and 2008.

MORE TASTY MORSELS: texasmusic.org/lost_gonzo_band

BOB'S CHARITY: SIMS Foundation, simsfoundation.org

DAVID MURRAY

Baked Texas Polenta

This is a dish that I enjoyed preparing and serving to countless hungry Texans at the East-West Center and Casa de Luz when I used to cook to stay out of trouble. It's very hearty and is sure to please. Carefully follow the steps below and you will make friends.

- 4 ears fresh corn
- 2 T. sea salt
- 2 c. cornmeal
- 2 c. coarse corn grits
- ½ c. corn oil
- 2 c. yellow or white onion, diced
- ¼ cup diced jalapeño peppers (optional)

Turn off cell phone! Turn on Freddie King CD. Preheat oven to 350°.

Shuck corn, remove kernels with sharp knife, and scrape cobs to get all of the sweet goodness. Boil water with corncobs and salt while completing the next step.

In large mixing bowl, add cornmeal, corn grits, and oil, and mix thoroughly.

Remove cobs from the boiling water, and pour over cornmeal mixture in bowl, stirring thoroughly. Careful, as it will be very hot. Now mix in fresh corn kernels, onions, and jalapeño peppers.

Grease large glass baking tray with, you guessed it, corn oil! Pour mix in to oiled glass tray, cover with foil, and bake at 350° for 1 hour (or longer, depending on depth of tray). It is hard to overcook, as I like a bit of a crust.

Let cool for 30 minutes. Cut into squares and serve. You can cover with pasta sauce, or this fine dish will stand on its own.

SHOW DATES: 1991, 1994

SERVING UP: Roots rock, blues, country rock

A FEW INGREDIENTS: David Murray is an Austin, Texas, musician, songwriter, producer, the owner of Murray Music, and a proud father. He has toured and/or recorded with Angela Strehli, Marcia Ball, Lou Ann Barton, Doyle Bramhall, Kelly Willis, Monte Warden, Jimmy LaFave, Jimmie Dale Gilmore, and many others.

Beyond writing and producing songs in his downtown studio, he works on documentaries and independent films, such as *Nobel-ity*, *The High-Line*, *Ya Bastas*, and *Springs Symphony*. OK, it's true, he also wrote, "Men Have Feelings Too" and "Touch a Mountain" for MTV's *Beavis and Butthead*.

DAVID'S CHARITY: Big Brothers Big Sisters of America, bbbsa.org

THE OAK RIDGE BOYS

Victoria Sterban's Lasagna

Submitted by Richard Sterban

My mother came to America from Italy via Ellis Island. Her homemade lasagna has always been a favorite of our family.

- 3 T. + 1 tsp. olive oil or salad oil, divided
- 1 small onion, chopped
- 1 clove garlic, minced
- 1½ lb. ground beef
- 1 (29-oz.) can tomato puree
- 2 (6-oz.) cans tomato paste
- 2 (6-oz.) cans + 6 qt. water, divided
- 2 tsp. salt, divided
- ½ tsp. oregano
- ½ tsp. black pepper
- ¼ tsp. sugar
- 1 lb. lasagna noodles
- 1 lb. ricotta cheese or cottage cheese
- 8 oz. mozzarella cheese, sliced thin
- 4 eggs, hard-boiled and sliced (optional)
- ½ c. grated Parmesan cheese

In a large saucepan over medium heat, cook onions and garlic in 3 T. of oil. When vegetables are golden brown, add ground beef. Cook until beef is brown and crumbly.

Stir in tomato puree, tomato paste, 2 cans of water, 1 tsp. salt, oregano, black pepper, and sugar. Cover and simmer for about 1½ hours.

Add 1 tsp. each of salt and oil to six quarts of boiling water. Cook lasagna noodles in water for approximately 15 minutes. Drain and run under cold water.

Spread a thin layer of the tomato sauce you have already prepared in the bottom of a 9 × 3–inch baking pan. Add one layer of noodles, ricotta, mozzarella, and hard-boiled eggs. Repeat until noodles are gone, about three layers. The top layer should be the remaining tomato sauce and Parmesan cheese.

Cover and bake at 350° for about 45 minutes.

GUSTER

Potato and Cabbage Peasant Pasta

Submitted by Joe Pisapia

I had something similar to this when I was in Italy at the home of a friend. It seemed like she could go in her kitchen and make culinary magic happen with whatever she had lying around. I tried to remember what was in it and improvised when I got home to make my own version.

In our current low-carb obsessed culture this dish isn't for everyone. But if you want some simple delicious comfort food, look no further.

- 1 large (softball-size) or 2 small (baseball-size) potatoes
- 3–4 c. water
- olive oil
- salt and pepper to taste
- 4 cloves garlic
- ½ jalapeño or serrano pepper
- 1 stalk celery
- 1 medium yellow onion
- ½ head green cabbage
- pinch of oregano
- ⅓ box pasta (I recommend De Cecco Tubetti pasta)
- 2 (12-oz.) cans chicken stock (or equivalent of home-made, if ambitious)
- fresh grated Romano cheese to taste
- a few sprigs fresh mint

Peel potatoes and dice into ½-inch cubes and boil them in 3–4 c. of water with 1 tsp. of olive oil and a pinch of salt and pepper. When potatoes are cooked al dente after 5–8 minutes of boiling, set them aside by straining them into another saucepan and saving the water. It is important to remember to save the potato water.

Mince garlic, jalapeño, and celery rib. Cut onion and cabbage into small strips or bite-sized slices. In a large pot combine a few T. of olive oil, onions, and cabbage with a pinch of oregano, salt, and pepper, and simmer over medium heat. Let onions get somewhat translucent and then add minced garlic, jalapeno, celery, and a couple of ladles of potato water to thicken the mixture.

In a separate pot cook pasta al dente in chicken stock. Toss pasta with potato and cabbage mixture. Top with grated Romano cheese and fresh mint.

JOE GRACEY

Joe's Texas Enchiladas

Submitted by Kimmie Rhodes

The enchilada is the king of the tortilla dish family. They are a part of all Mexican regional cooking, but each area's enchiladas are different, with different peppers, sauces, and fillings determined by local custom, climate, and produce. The Texas enchilada is a corn tortilla wrapped around a cheese or meat filling, cooked in a red chili sauce. It is time-consuming, multi-step, special occasion cooking, but one of its advantages is that it an excellent way to use leftovers in a new and appealing incarnation. Plan on about two hours from start to finish once you have mastered all of the steps below.

The first step in making enchiladas is to create the sauce. Along the Texas border the pepper of choice for a chili dish has always been the ancho, which is the dried red poblano.

1½ c. broth or water
3 large dried chile anchos or 3 T. red chili powder (6 if you like it hot)
1 yellow onion, chopped (save a handful for the topping)
2 cloves garlic, minced
2 T. unbleached white flour
corn oil
1 T. cumin powder
1 tsp. dried oregano
freshly ground pepper and sea salt
1 dozen corn tortillas
enchilada filling (either ¾ lb. of grated white cheese [Monterey Jack, cheddar, or Queso Blanco], or 3 cups shredded chicken meat, or shredded pork, or scrambled eggs, etc.)
¼ lb. white cheese, grated

Simmer broth or water in a saucepan. Tear the tops of the chiles off and take out as many of the seeds as possible. Rinse the the chilies and add to the simmering liquid.

After 10 minutes, the peppers should be rehydrated and soft. With a slotted spoon, remove the peppers to a blender and add only enough of the pepper liquid from the pot to cover them.

In another pan sauté the chopped onion in 1 T. oil until soft and translucent. Add the sautéed onions and the garlic to the blender.

JOE'S TEXAS ENCHILADAS (CONTINUED)

Blend to a purée. (Start on low speed or you'll spew boiling hot-pepper napalm all over the kitchen.) In a 12" skillet, sauté 2 T. of flour in 2 T. of oil until the flour is just cooked.

Pour the pepper purée into the skillet. Use the rest of the pepper liquid to rinse out the blender, and add this to the skillet. Add the cumin, oregano, salt, and pepper. Simmer for at least ½ hour or more, until the flavors marry.

Keep the sauce warm. If it gets too thick, add more broth or water. (At this point, if I am making chicken or meat filling, I like to add the shredded or chopped meat to the sauce. I think it makes a better, less dry filling, especially with white chicken meat.)

Heat ¼ inch of oil in an iron skillet until almost smoking. With tongs, dip a tortilla into the hot oil for 5 seconds, turn it over for 5 more, lift it and let the oil drip back into the pan.

Dip the tortilla into the warm sauce until coated. Put two tablespoons of prepared filling on the tortilla, roll it up, and place it seam-side down in a greased baking dish.

Repeat this sequence 11 more times. Now pour the remaining sauce over the enchiladas, top with grated cheese and finely chopped raw onion, and heat in a 400° oven for 10 minutes, or until the top is melted and the dish is bubbling.

Don't leave it in too long or the enchiladas will turn to mush or dry out. Serve immediately, two per plate (or three, but they are filling), with pinto beans and rice. Yield: 12 enchiladas, or 4 to 6 servings.

SHOW DATE: 1997

SERVING UP: Country

A FEW INGREDIENTS: Joe Gracey is a self-taught cook and a lover of good food and wine. He has, at various times, been a radio program director, a music journalist, a talent coordinator for *Austin City Limits*, a producer-engineer for artists like Willie Nelson and Stevie Ray Vaughan, and a musician. He now manages a record label and various other cottage industries with wife Kimmie Rhodes, as well as playing bass guitar in her band.

JOE'S CHARITY: American Cancer Society, cancer.org

GLENDA FACEMIRE

Belgian Holiday Dressing

Angele Felique, my dear and sweet grandmother, showed me how to prepare her favorite Flemish recipe from her homeland. She made it every holiday season and I think it is absolutely the best dressing I have ever, ever tasted. It has a very unique and spicy taste, and goes great with wild game, turkey, or ham, but this recipe alone could be a meal in itself. Bon appetit!

2 (10- or 12-oz.) pkg. herb dressing
1 lb. mild or hot sausage meat
  (or meatless mild sausage)
safflower oil
4 c. celery, chopped
3 c. onion, chopped
¾ c. parsley, chopped
½ lb. fresh livers, chopped
½ c. fresh cranberries, chopped (optional)
1½ tsp. savory seasoning
1½ tsp. sage
1½ tsp. thyme
1 tsp. nutmeg
1 T. salt
¾ tsp. pepper
dash red pepper
2 (10.5-oz.) cans consommé soup
¼ c. butter

Make herb dressing as package label directs. Cool.

In large skillet, sauté sausage meat, stirring until lightly browned.

In another skillet, heat safflower oil and sauté celery, onion, and parsley until tender, about 8–10 minutes. Add chopped livers and stir until they are fully cooked.

Combine cooked vegetables and liver with sausage meat, cranberries (optional), savory seasoning, sage, thyme, nutmeg, salt, black pepper, and red pepper in a separate bowl.

Transfer contents of bowl to herb dressing bowl and mix together. Add the two cans of consommé soup. Mix until lightly moist. Add a little water if needed.

Transfer to two greased loaf pans. Brush some melted butter over the loaves. Cover with tin foil and bake in oven at 250° for 20 minutes. Serve warm. Yield: about 15 cups.

MORE TASTY MORSELS: glendafacemire.com
GLENDA'S CHARITIES: American Humane Association, americanhumane.org, Lance Armstrong Foundation, livestrong.org, and Emancipet, empancipet.org

THE OAK RIDGE BOYS

Duane Allen's Strawberry Christmas Treat

Submitted by Duane Allen

This is a special tradition during the holiday meal at the Allen house each year.

1 large bag frozen strawberries, chopped
1 large can whole cranberry sauce
1 small can crushed pineapple, drained
1 c. chopped pecans
1 box strawberry JELL-O® (optional)

Mix the first four ingredients and serve chilled. If desired, stir mixture into a large package of strawberry JELL-O® and prepare as directed. Optional: Top with homemade, sweetened whipped cream.

B. B. KING

B. B.'s German Chocolate Double Delight

The following is the original recipe, but since B. B. King is a diabetic, it was converted to the diabetic version. His original recipe follows.

4 oz. German sweet chocolate
½ c. water
1 c. butter
2 c. sugar
4 egg yolks, unbeaten
1 tsp. vanilla
2½ c. cake flour
½ tsp. salt
1 tsp. baking soda
1 c. buttermilk
4 egg whites, stiffly beaten
Coconut-Pecan Frosting (recipe follows)

Melt the chocolate in boiling water and let cool. Cream the butter and sugar until fluffy. Add egg yolks, one at a time, and beat well after each addition. Add the melted chocolate and vanilla, and mix well. Sift flour, salt, and baking soda and add alternately with buttermilk to chocolate mixture, beating until smooth after each addition. Fold in the beaten egg whites. Pour into 3 round 8- or 9-inch layer pans lined with paper and bake at 350° for 30 to 40 minutes. Cool and frost middle and top only with Coconut-Pecan Frosting.

COCONUT-PECAN FROSTING

1 c. evaporated milk
1 c. sugar
3 egg yolks
½ c. butter or margarine
1 tsp. vanilla
1⅓ c. coconut, shredded
1 c. pecans, chopped

In saucepan, combine milk, sugar, egg yolks, butter, and vanilla. Cook over medium heat stirring constantly until thickened. Add coconut and pecans, and beat until thick enough to spread.

Montezuma's Oatmeal Cookies

Submitted by Jeremy Bruch

This recipe is easy! There is no baking! And the chocolate and chili do wonderful things to the brain . . .

½ c. almonds
1 stick unsalted butter
2 c. sugar
4 T. cocoa
½ c. whole milk
1 tsp. salt
1 tsp chile powder (I prefer ancho)
1 tsp. vanilla
4 c. oatmeal

Toast almonds in a 350° oven on a cookie sheet until you can smell them, about 10 minutes. Grind in a processor or wrap in a clean towel and bang on the counter.

Bring all ingredients (except oatmeal and almonds) to a boil, thoroughly dissolving sugar. Remove from heat and stir in oats and almonds. Spoon onto wax paper, or straight into mouth with a cold glass of milk. Yield: 30 cookies.

THE SUBDUDES

Intensely subdued Red Cake with White Frosting

Submitted by Donna Cunningham

- 1 subdudes CD
- 1 stereo
- ½ c. shortening
- 2 eggs
- 1 tsp. vanilla
- 1½ c. sugar
- 4 T. red food coloring
- 2 T. cocoa
- 1 tsp. salt
- 2 c. flour
- 1 c. buttermilk
- 1 tsp. vinegar
- 1 tsp. baking soda
- White Frosting (recipe follows)

Insert CD into stereo, increase volume so that it can be heard over mixer. Enjoy music!

Preheat oven to 350°. Mix and beat until fluffy first 5 cake ingredients. Sift and mix next 3 ingredients in small bowl, and add to first mixture, alternating with buttermilk. Slowly add vinegar and baking soda, alternating between the two ingredients. Pour into 2 8-inch greased square pans. Bake in a 350° oven for approximately 30 minutes. Cool on wire racks when finished baking.

WHITE FROSTING

- 1½ c. milk
- ¼ c. + 2 T. flour, divided
- dash of salt
- 1½ c. sugar
- ¾ c. shortening
- 1½ sticks of margarine
- 1 tsp. vanilla

Cook the first 3 ingredients on stovetop until thick, stirring constantly. Set aside to let cool. Beat sugar, shortening, and margarine until fluffy, then add first mixture and vanilla. Beat until similar to whipped cream.

Put icing on the top of the first layer of cake, add second layer and continue frosting until covered. Enjoy!

GLENDA FACEMIRE

My Favorite Key Lime Pie

I always loved preparing a Florida Key lime pie for any occasion, even for the holidays. This is one of the recipes I learned while living in Miami Beach, Florida. It's so simple to prepare and so delicious to eat. I promise you, you will receive many compliments.

4 free-range eggs, separated
1 can fat-free sweetened condensed milk
½ c. lime juice
dash of salt
1 store-bought graham-cracker pie crust
1 small carton of heavy whipping cream
½ lime, thinly sliced
crushed almonds (optional)

Preheat oven to 250°.

Beat egg yolks in a medium bowl until light and fluffy. Gradually add condensed milk, lime juice, and dash of salt to egg yolks. Mix until blended. Set aside.

In a separate bowl, beat egg whites with an electric beater until they form soft peaks. Fold egg whites into egg yolk mixture and stir until smooth. Pour mixture into pie shell and even out.

Place pie in oven for 15 minutes to set pie. Cool on rack. Refrigerate for a few hours.

With an electric beater, whip your heavy whipping cream until it thickens and forms peaks.

Top pie with whipped cream and arrange a few lime slices on top for decoration—be an artist! And a very light sprinkling of crushed toasted almonds does no harm. Serve cold.

And I'll be right over.

DAVID KUIPERS

Crawfish Bisque

After every *Austin City Limits* taping, David Kuipers removes his engineering hat and dons his chef's hat. He typically provides a couple of made-from-scratch soups for the crew, staff, artists, musicians, and volunteers to enjoy while watching the playback of the evening's director's cut and maybe drinking a beer or two. He sometimes provides other fare, including the staff favorite—Hot Dog Night. He has special Koegl Vienna-cased hot dogs shipped from Michigan and serves them with his award-winning Tex-Mich(igan) Chili. This after-show ritual brings the staff together and helps us all relax after a tough day of production.

I asked David to include one of his delicious recipes for the cookbook. Enjoy! From all of us, thank you David!

1 T. olive oil
1 medium yellow onion, diced
1 green bell pepper, diced
2 (16-oz.) cans Cajun stewed tomatoes
½ c. brandy
1 tsp. paprika
2 T. tomato paste
1 qt. shrimp stock
1 fish bouillon cube
12 oz. crawfish tail meat
1½ c. heavy cream

Sauté onion and bell pepper in olive oil until softened. Add tomatoes and brandy. Cook until liquid is reduced to almost nothing. Add paprika, tomato paste, shrimp stock, and fish bouillon. Simmer 30–40 minutes.

Purée this mixture in batches. Strain and return to soup pan. In a separate pan sauté crawfish meat in hot oil for 1–2 minutes. Add crawfish meat to the purée. Stir in heavy cream and heat through, but do not boil! Serve.

Capo II

Guitar Solo

Words and Music by Michelle Shocked

Rhythm Gtr. Lead Gtr.

1. C — D7
Saturday morning found me itching
G7 — C
To get on over to my grandma's kitchen
D7
Where the sweetest little berries was cooking up right
G7 — C
And then we'd put them in a canning jar and seal them up tight

Chorus

D7
We were making jam
G7 D7 G7
Strawberry jam
D7
If you want the best jam
G7 — C B C
You've gotta make your own

2. C — D7
We have Smucker's, Welches, Knotts Berry Farm
G7 — C
But a little homemade jam never did a body no harm
D7
A little local motion is all that we need
G7 — C
To close down these corporate jam factories

Repeat Chorus

2. C — D7
We have a little revolution sweeping the land
G7 — C
Once more everybody's making homemade jam
D7
So call your friends up on the telephone
G7 — C
Invite 'em over, make some jam of your own

Repeat Chorus

LIST OF CHARITIES

ALS Association (DC/MD/VA Chapter)	alsinfo.org	BRUCE HORNSBY
ALS Association (Greater Los Angeles Chapter)	webgla.alsa.org	LITTLE FEAT
ALS Therapy Development Institute	als.net	GUSTER
American Cancer Society	cancer.org	C. J. CHENIER, JOE GRACEY, RIDERS IN THE SKY, AND ROBBIE FULKS
American Diabetes Association	diabetes.org	LORETTA LYNN
The American Humane Association	americanhumane.org	TONI PRICE, THE CRICKETS, AND GLENDA FACEMIRE
The American Indian College Fund	collegefund.org	JIMMY LaFAVE
American Red Cross	redcross.org	THE OAK RIDGE BOYS, PAM TILLIS, AND PAT GREEN
American Society for the Prevention of Cruelty to Animals	aspca.org	JERRY LEE LEWIS
American Youthworks, Austin, Texas	americanyouthworks.org	JOE ELY
Amigos Charity	amigos.org.uk	JOSS STONE
Amnesty International	amnesty.org	ROY ROGERS
Angel's House: Newnan Coweta Children's Shelter	theangelshouse.org	ALAN JACKSON
The Angelus	theangelus.com	THE CHARLIE DANIELS BAND
Armstrong Community Music School, Austin, Texas	austinlyricopera.org	DARDEN SMITH
Art for Autism Awareness in Lancaster		JANIE FRICKE
ArtDocs	artdocs.com	WIDESPREAD PANIC
Artists for Media Diversity	a4md.org	BARBARA KOOYMAN

Attachment Parenting International	attachmentparenting.com	DELBERT McCLINTON
Austin Animal Trustees	animaltrustees.org	CINDY CASHDOLLAR
Austin Food Bank	austinfoodbank.org	BOB SCHNEIDER
Austin Humane Society	austinhumanesociety.org	DOUBLE TROUBLE
Autism Society of America	autism-society.org	THE SUBDUDES
Band Against MS	bandagainstms.org	CLAY WALKER
Big Brothers and Big Sisters of America	bbbs.org	DAVID MURRAY
Big Brothers and Big Sisters of Middle Tennessee	bbbsmt.org	DIAMOND RIO
Big House Foundation	bighousemuseum.org	THE ALLMAN BROTHERS
Brady Center to Prevent Gun Violence	bradycenter.org	THE COWBOY JUNKIES
Bread & Roses	breadandroses.org	JOAN BAEZ, DAN HICKS AND THE HOT LICKS
Buddy Walk for Down Syndrome	buddywalk.org	MONTE WARDEN
Cal Farley's Boys Ranch® and GirlsTown, U.S.A.®	calfarley.org	GARY P. NUNN
The Camp Lisa Foundation	lisaloeb.com	LISA LOEB
The Carter Center	cartercenter.org	JOHN GORKA
Child Help	childhelp.org	PAM TILLIS
Children International	children.org	JIMMIE VAUGHAN
Cocker Kids' Foundation	cocker.com	JOE COCKER
Common Ground Relief	commongroundrelief.org	OLD CROW MEDICINE SHOW
Conscious Alliance	consciousalliance.org	THE STRING CHEESE INCIDENT
Critical Resistance	criticalresistance.org	OZOMATLI

Daily Bread Food Bank	dailybread.ca	BLUE RODEO
Dell Children's Medical Center of Central Texas	dellchildrens.net	CORY MORROW
Dolly's Imagination Library	imaginationlibrary.com	DOLLY PARTON
Eager to Learn, Austin, Texas	ci.austin.tx.us/library/ recentgrants.htm	WHAT MADE MILWAUKEE FAMOUS
Emancipet	emancipet.org	GLENDA FACEMIRE
Epidermolysis Bullosa (EB) Foundation	ebkids.org	THE OAK RIDGE BOYS
Farm Aid	farmaid.org	WILLIE NELSON
Feed the Children	feedthechildren.org	THE OAK RIDGE BOYS
Feeding America	feedingamerica.org	SUZY BOGGUSS
The Field Band Foundation	fieldband.org.za	MANHATTAN TRANSFER
First Candle	firstcandle.org	LOS LONELY BOYS
The Friends Foundation, Dripping Springs, Texas	thefriendsfoundation.org	JOHNNY GIMBLE
Garth House	garthhouse.net	MARK CHESNUTT
Ghetto Youths' Foundation	ghettoyouths.com/foundation.html	DAMIAN MARLEY
Gilda's Club Worldwide	gildasclub.org	RIDERS IN THE SKY
Greyhound Adoption League of Tucson, Arizona	galgreys.com	NEKO CASE
Health Alliance for Austin Musicians (HAAM)	healthalliancefor austinmusicians.org	ASLEEP AT THE WHEEL, LLOYD MAINES, AND OMAR AND THE HOWLERS
Hill Country Conservancy	hillcountryconservancy.org	JAMES MCMURTRY
Hill Country Youth Orchestras	hillcountryyouthorchestras.com	ROBERT EARL KEEN
The Hope Food Pantry at Trinity United Methodist, Austin, Texas	tumc.org/hope	KELLY WILLIS

Horses for Healing	horsesforhealing.org	BR549
Hospice Austin	hospiceaustin.org	KIMMIE RHODES
The Humane Society of East Texas	hsoet.org	MIRANDA LAMBERT
The Humane Society of Sumner County, Tennessee	sumnerhumane.org	LORRIE MORGAN
Joe Niekro Foundation	joeniekrofoundation.com	THE OAK RIDGE BOYS
Juvenile Diabetes Research Foundation	jdrf.org	B. B. KING AND MY MORNING JACKET
Lambi Fund of Haiti	lambifund.org	BLOC PARTY
Lance Armstrong Foundation	livestrong.org	GLENDA FACEMIRE
The Land Institute	thelandinstitute.org	ELIZA GILKYSON
Loaves and Fishes	loavesandfishesmn.org	CHUCK PROPHET
M. D. Anderson Cancer Center	mdanderson.org	BILLY JOE SHAVER
Magnolia Baptist Church and Fairview Baptist Church, Baton Rouge, Louisiana		BUDDY GUY
Make-a-Wish Foundation of America	wish.org	JASON MRAZ
Marathon Kids	marathonkids.org	SHAWN COLVIN
The Miracle Foundation	miraclefoundation.org	SARA HICKMAN
MusiCares	grammy.com/musicares	KATHY MATTEA AND MARTY STUART
National Trust For Historic Preservation	nationaltrust.org	MARY CUTRUFELLO
Neuse River Foundation	neuseriver.org	TIFT MERRITT
New Orleans Artists Against Hunger and Homelessness	noaahh.org	THE NEVILLE BROTHERS
New Orleans Musicians' Clinic	neworleansmusiciansclinic.org	DR. JOHN, THE NEW ORLEANS SOCIAL CLUB, AND ROY ROGERS

Nuci's Space, Athens, Georgia	nuci.org	DRIVE-BY TRUCKERS
The Opry Trust Fund	opry.com/MeetTheOpry/ OpryTrustFund.aspx	PATTY LOVELESS
The Organization for Tropical Studies	otis.duke.edu	RICHARD THOMPSON
Osteogenesis Imperfecta Foundation	oif.org	MICHAEL MARTIN MURPHEY
Pathways to Spirit, Volunteering for the Future of Native America	pathwaystospirit.org	B. J. THOMAS
PAX Real Solutions to Gun Violence	paxusa.org	ROSANNE CASH
People Organized in Defense of Earth and Her Resources (PODER)	poder-texas.org	GRUPO FANTASMA
Project See Inc.		VINCE GILL
SafePlace	safeplace.org	ERIC TAYLOR
Salvation Army	salvationarmyusa.org	BELLAMY BROTHERS AND THE OAK RIDGE BOYS
Santa Fe Animal Shelter and Humane Society	sfhumanesociety.org	CARLENE CARTER
Sarah McLachlan Foundation	sarahmclachlanmusicoutreach .com/smf/content.html	SARAH McLACHLAN
Save Africa's Children	saveafricaschildren.com	MICHELLE SHOCKED
Save Darfur Coalition	savedarfur.org	THE POLYPHONIC SPREE
Second Harvest Food Bank	secondharvestnashville.org	HOLLY DUNN
The Seton Fund	setonfund.org	BETO AND THE FAIRLANES
Shriners Hospitals for Children	shrinershq.org	RALPH STANLEY
SIMS Foundation	simsfoundation.org	LOST GONZO BAND, THE GOURDS
Society for the Prevention of Cruelty to Animals (SPCA)	spca.com	SARAH McLACHLAN

Special Olympics	specialolympics.org	TAJ MAHAL
St. John's Riverkeeper	stjohnsriverkeeper.org	SUSAN TEDESCHI
St. Jude Children's Research Hospital	stjude.org	KEVIN WELCH, HAL KETCHUM, AND T. G. SHEPPARD
Street Child Africa	streetchildafrica.org.uk	FEMI KUTI
Surfrider Foundation	surfrider.org	RYAN BINGHAM
Swan Songs	swansongs.org	CHRISTINE ALBERT
T.J. Martell Foundation	tjmartellfoundation.org	SUZY BOGGUSS
The United Negro College Fund	uncf.org	BETTYE LaVETTE
Thoughtful House Center for Children	thoughtfulhouse.org	DIXIE CHICKS
Town Lake Animal Shelter, Austin, Texas	ci.austin.tx.us/tlac/adopt.htm	RUTHIE FOSTER
Tracy Lawrence Fund	tracylawrence .musiccitynetworks.com	TRACY LAWRENCE
The Uncle John Turner Foundation	ujtfoundation.org	CAROLYN WONDERLAND
United Nations World Food Programme	wfp.org	THIEVERY CORPORATION
The United Negro College Fund	uncf.org	BETTYE LaVETTE
United Way	unitedwayint.org	THE OAK RIDGE BOYS
University Kidney Disease Research Association, Los Angeles, California	universitykidneyresearch.org	DEANA CARTER
Women In Need, Inc.	women-in-need.org	ALLISON MOORER
World Hunger Year	whyhunger.org	CARRIE RODRIGUEZ
World Vision	worldvision.org	HAL KETCHUM